HYPNOTIC MARKETING

By Dr. Joe Vitale

Author of the #1 Bestseller, *The Attractor Factor*,
and way too many other books to list here.

Executive Editor: Suzanne Burns
Assistant Editor: Maureen Tompkins

Table of Contents

Step 2: Hypnotic Websites

Step 4: Hypnotic Social Media

Bonus Section

Appendix

EPILOGUE

INTRODUCTION

By Joe Sugarman

I've been a big fan of Joe Vitale ever since I started reading his books and following his career.

In a relatively short period, Joe has catapulted to success unimaginable by even himself a few years earlier. But what has really impressed me about Joe is how he has used his skills of observation and common sense to communicate wisdom that took me years and millions of dollars to discover. How does he do it?

I have a theory. Joe loves to read. He reads more books than anybody I know. His library must contain every book on sales, public relations, and marketing than you'll find in the biggest public library or any library for that matter.

And Joe loves to write. His copy is recognized as the most effective of any copywriter today. Combine his skill at writing with his skill at gleaning everything there is to know about his subjects, all combined with his personal experiences and you've got some idea of how much good information *Hypnotic Marketing* has in store for you and your business.

So it was truly a thrill to be asked by Joe to read *Hypnotic*

Marketing and if l was so moved, write an introduction for the book.

After about the first several chapters I called Joe and told him, "Joe, I don't think your readers are going to fully appreciate the powerful information you have in this book."

Hypnotic Marketing is a collection of some of the most effective and useful tips on sales, marketing and the Internet that I have read. And after reading it, I was so inspired by several of his concepts that I have made sweeping changes in my advertising and marketing campaigns.

Joe covers the gamut from how to mentally and hypnotically prepare yourself for success – something that is critical in any endeavor. He shows how to take an average news release and turn it into a powerful selling tool. He explains in a few chapters how to generate so much free advertising that often a business can be created overnight with practically no expense. And he relates all lessons with personal experiences and stories that are riveting and have real life payoffs.

His advice on how to profit from the Internet is priceless. The secrets he reveals work and he's living proof that they do. For Joe is a practitioner, a man who has walked the walk and talks the talk. This is not a book by some theoretician, but rather a book by a practical and pragmatic man who has experienced both failure and success, and learned from both.

If you're like me, once you start reading this book, you won't put it down. And like I did, you'll find dozens of ideas that will influence you for years to come.

Joe Sugarman
Author of *Triggers* and numerous other books.

FOREWORD

How You Just Saved Yourself $25,000

Are you ready to learn the most powerful marketing strategy in history? I've seen people take the four key steps to creating a Hypnotic Marketing campaign and transform their world. Here's proof. (You'll be meeting most of these people in the pages of this book).

One man became a millionaire.

One woman overseas got national attention for her product.

Another man created a wild idea that drove incredible new traffic to his website.

A Chiropractor nailed coverage on prime time national TV and was mentioned by Barbara Walters.

Still another man and his partner invented a new roll of toilet paper – and got their story picked up by the national news.

And I've managed to get national media coverage, sell out one of my books overnight, get people to pay me $2,500 each to "attend" e-mail only classes, make my e-books global bestsellers, see my Nightingale Conant audiotape program become a national bestseller, AND get people just like you to pay me $25,000 EACH for the secrets you're about to learn in this new e-book!

The list goes on.

I'll tell you about them, and me, and how we did it in the e-pages of this e-book. You'll learn the inside tricks and secrets for grabbing minds, getting people to send you money, including how to grab the mind of the MEDIA and getting IT to pay attention to you. All of this is powerful, even off the charts stuff.

And many people paid a staggering $25,000 each to have me show them this method and implement the secrets.

You, of course, just saved yourself a BUNDLE of money.

The thing is, none of this is that hard. Anyone can do it. Even a monkey.

One day I'll prove it by getting a monkey and sitting him here in front of my computer. For now, you can prove that this stuff works.

How? By reading this book, following the principles, and then implementing them. It's really that easy!

If I can create Hypnotic Marketing to make my clients rich – then you can do it, too. It all begins right here, right now, with a single click to get to the next chapter.

Make no mistake: This information is powerful, even potentially deadly.

What I mean is this: I am revealing the inside secrets to manipulating the media, and then people, to do YOUR bidding.

This is not some wild claim to get you to buy this book. After all, you've already bought it. What I'm suggesting is that you use the secrets in this book to help people, not to harm them, manipulate them, or con them.

As I've said repeatedly throughout my career: Be sincere. Have something people genuinely want or need; something that will make their lives easier, and them happier and the world a better place.

Enough said.

Are you ready for fame and fortune – to be ruler of your business and tsar of your own career?

If so…keep reading!

The Lazy Person's Way to Hypnotic Marketing

I've thought long and hard about how to begin this first chapter…

Well, that's not the truth.

Actually, I didn't think "all" that hard, really. What I did is what I want you to do right now.

What I did was plant a suggestion in my mind. I told myself, "I want to write a terrific book on

Hypnotic Marketing. I want it to come easily, and I want the chapters to be clear and practical I want my readers to love these ideas, get the message, and use what they learn to make money with my method."

That was step one.

Step two was to "let go."

What I did there was play. I went and did the laundry. All of it. (About seven loads). I went and read books, such as *Grow Rich While You Sleep* by Ben Sweedand. I watched a little television. I played with the cat.

At one point Nerissa, my then girlfriend (now wife), came downstairs and saw me lying on the couch.

"How's it going?" she asked.

"Going well," I said.

"What are you doing?"

"Writing my first chapter for my new book," I replied.

And that's what I — or at least another part of me — was actually doing as I lounged.

Here's the formula I used and the formula I want you to get:

Step One: I set an intention.

Step Two: I let go and occupied myself with other things.

Step Three: Is happening right now.

When I got the urge, the inner nudge to start writing this chapter, I turned on my computer and started writing.

And here I am.

So I didn't think long and hard at all. But I did take the time to think about my intention – or outcome – and I did occupy my mind with other things until I felt the inspiration to start writing.

It's the classic formula for creating anything you want. And that's what you can do right now, today, as your first assignment in this course on Hypnotic Marketing.

In short:

Step One: Declare your intention. What do you want to have happen as a result of reading this book? What is your desired outcome? State it so clearly the guy next door can understand it perfectly. In fact, go show it to him and see if he DOES understand it.

Step Two: Do other things. Read this lesson. Read whatever books I suggest you get. Take breaks. Watch TV. See a movie.

Step Three: Act on your impulses. As ideas come to you to help you achieve your outcome, act on them.

So chapter one begins with a mindset that business can be easy, that attracting what you want can be a breeze, and that wherever you are now will seem like dust in the wind once you put these lessons to use and warp speed your business to the next galaxy.

Fancy words?

I think not.

As I write this, it's nearing the end of September, 2001. The advanced edition of my best selling e-book has been selling and breaking records. (I'm referring to *Hypnotic Writing* and *Advanced Hypnotic Writing*).

My *Spiritual Marketing* book has been selling so amazingly well that Amazon keeps reordering it and there are 33 five-star reviews of it there (As of 2015, there are now 130 five-star reviews). It is listed number #22 on the lstBooks.com bestseller list.

And of course, I just found the love of my life, the home of my dreams, the car that makes my heart race, and my last sales letter raised $50,000 in only three days.

Life is good.

I'm not bragging. I'm using my life as an example of what is possible. And there are countless people far more successful than me. The point is, I started with nothing.

I was homeless in Dallas. I struggled for 15 years in

Houston. It wasn't until I learned about the easy path to success, the "Spiritual Marketing" approach, the Hypnotic Marketing method, that I knocked off my gravity boots and soared to the sky. You can have this kind of success – and far more.

So, this chapter is about having a *mindset* for success. It begins by realizing you CAN succeed, that there IS an easy way to greater wealth, and that this book WILL show you the formula to sell what you have to the public.

Now, let's get into the mindset of a Hypnotic Marketer ... and begin to explore the first step in the "Hypnotic Marketing Formula" ... a step that begins by stretching your mind with a "practically outrageous" idea or two...

STEP 1:
HYPNOTIC PUBLICITY

How to Hypnotize the Masses with "PO" Ideas

If there's any term I want you to grasp today, it's one I just made up: "Practically Outrageous." Call it "PO" for short.

What that means is this: You want to start coming up with ideas that are outrageous. Think of them as zany, or clever, or even crazy.

But add the word "practically" to remind yourself that you don't want "really" outrageous or crazy ideas, you want "practically" outrageous ideas.

And this means they are practical in a business sense, meaning the idea makes money in some way.

In other words, if you want to succeed in business today, you have to stand out from the crowd. Good publicity can do that, and that's the first part of the Hypnotic Marketing three-step process. But the publicity has to be practical. It has to get people to DO something: Call, fax, e-mail, visit you. SOMETHING.

You'll hear more about this new form of direct results publicity in a later chapter on EDR Publicity. For now, I want to tickle your imagination by stretching your mind to be creative, risky, bold, daring. And don't think you can't do any of this because you are a one person business or a small operation. That's precisely why you MUST think big!

In order to grab the masses with hypnotic publicity, you have to think bigger than you ever thought before and act bolder than you've ever acted before.

Relax. That doesn't mean you have to make a fool out of yourself or even appear on TV when you are shy. Again, this entire process can be easy and you can make it fit YOU.

Now stick with me on this. I'm trying to show you a new way of thinking. Just let my words, and the stories to follow, seep in…

Flying Midgets and the PR Folk Hero

I gain a lot of inspiration from ballyhoo artists from the past. One such giant is still considered a folk hero in the public relations business.

James Sterling Moran became a legend in the publicity business with such stunts as selling a refrigerator to an Alaska Eskimo. Moran pushed outrageousness to the outer limits to seize the attention of the buying public.

- He once searched for a needle in a haystack for 10 days to publicize a piece of real estate that was for sale.
- In 1946, he sat on an ostrich egg for 19 days, four hours, 32 minutes before hatching it, all to publicize *The Egg and I*, a bestselling book soon to become a film comedy starring Claudette Colbert.
- During the 1944 presidential campaign, he changed horses in midstream — literally — in a Nevada river after the ruling Democrats urged voters not to "change horses in midstream" by voting for Republicans in the middle of World War II.

In 1989, *Time* magazine called him "The supreme master of that most singular marketing device – the publicity stunt."

As you can see, Moran knew how to be outrageous.

But he also made his craziness practical. He tied what he did to a product.

One of Mr. Moran's cleverest schemes went nowhere in its time. An avid kite flier, he hit upon the notion of using kites to fly midgets over Central Park. The police refused to grant him a permit and nipped the scheme in the bud.

Morgan said, "It's a sad day for American capitalism when a man can't fly a midget on a kite over Central Park."

Well, that example proves that you need to be practical in order to succeed today. I'm not sure what Moran was trying to sell with the idea of flying midgets on kites, so I'm not surprised it never, well, flew.

But notice how clever Moran was. You and I want to begin to think like him. In order to succeed at marketing your product with Hypnotic Marketing, you will need a little "practically outrageous" thinking.

Let's take this thought even deeper ...

Eight Proven Rules for Getting Publicity

When Peter Shankman was downsized out of a job in 1998, he was nearly broke and not sure what to do next.

Of course, all problems contain new opportunities.

What his former employer couldn't take from him when they ripped away his access card was the inside knowledge of how media works. As a result, Peter's company, The Geek Factory, a public relations agency, expects to gross an incredible $1 million in its second year.

How did he do it? By using publicity to his advantage.

Here are some publicity stunts that worked for Shankman – and the underlying rules behind them.

RULE 1: Word of mouth is the best publicity, so give people something to talk about. When Shankman first launched his high tech consulting business, he donned a sandwich board and stood on the corner of 51st Street and Park Avenue in New York. He handed out resumes and fliers, which cost him under $30 to have printed. Two hours of effort – just two hours! – during a busy lunch hour netted him 189 phone calls, 74 interviews and 37 offers of work. He took on several opportunities, including the one that appealed most to him – helping the New Jersey Devils hockey team build their first website.

RULE 2: Reporters like stories that have a sense of immediacy, so look for ways to link your company's message to the big story of the day. Shankman didn't have enough money to buy the computer equipment he needed to get his new consulting business up and running. The hottest news and entertainment story of the day was the popularity of the hit movie *Titanic*. Shankman took his last $1,800 and bought 500 T-shirts on which he had imprinted a picture of the ship and the words "It Sank-Get Over It." He took the T-shirts to New York's Central Park and set up shop, selling them for $10 each. Two hours later, he'd sold all 500, making a tidy profit of $3,750.

RULE 3: Toot your own horn. If you don't tell the media what you've done, they'll never know. So prepare press releases and get on the phone to the people you most want to hear your story. Shankman, a regular reader of *USA Today*, suspected that the writer/editor of his favorite column might be interested in his story, so he gave her a call.

RULE 4: Timing is everything. Shankman called on a slow Sunday, the slowest day of the news week.

The *USA Today* editor was thrilled to hear from Shankman because it's hard to write a column when there's not much news. A bright, enterprising story like Shankman's made the reporter/editor's job easier.

RULE 5: Don't be old news. No media wants to report on events that have passed. Offering news about things while they are happening will not only get you valuable attention, but also sell more products. The first question the reporter/editor asked Shankman was whether he was going to continue selling the shirts because she didn't want to write about something that was no longer for sale. Shankman assured her he'd be selling the shirts. She asked where – on his website? Shankman didn't have a website, but he didn't let that stop him. "Yes," he said, "I'm selling them on my website." Then he went home and built a website.

RULE 6: Be prepared for the impact of your promotional efforts. Have the goods ready to sell and the systems in place to make it happen. The next morning, the Internet Service Provider hosting Shankman's site woke him up. The

35,000 responses to his site in three hours that resulted from the *USA Today* article had crashed four of the company's six servers, and they wanted to know if this was going to continue.

RULE 7: Don't stop now. Keep those press releases coming! While you can't always expect a published follow-up report, media outlets always like to know when they've had an impact, so share your success. In all, Shankman sold 8,000 T-shirts at $15 apiece and, after paying his upfront expenses, pocketed about $80,000 toward his business startup costs. The ink from *USA Today* got picked up and published in such far-flung publications as the *San Diego Union Tribune*, the *New York Daily News* and *U.S. News and World Report.*

RULE 8: Be nice. Say thank you. Media people are customers too. After Shankman got his business off the ground and grew it in less than a year to eight employees, he decided to hold a picnic and invite people who had helped him out along the way. It ballooned into a skydiving party to which 75 media people and clients were invited. Among the guests who ultimately wrote about their experience were reporters from *Forbes Magazine* and *Business Week.*

Shankman is modest about his successes and offers only one piece of advice. "Don't be afraid to do something stupid," he says. "The worst that can happen is that it doesn't work."

Wise words indeed.

Remember; just let these ideas sink in.

In a way, what you are reading are hypnotic inductions.

They are stories for your "inner mind" to absorb, to help stretch your mind – and later fatten your wallet. When you're ready, click here to find out how a former heavyweight boxing champion used media to sell sausage!

Pitching a Heavyweight Boxing Champion and His Sausage

Melody Campbell Goeken, Public Relations Account Manager, for the Center for the Persuasive Arts, in San Antonio, Texas, told me this story...

"I managed the George Foreman Sausage public relations account. I used the Internet to create a week long BUZZ campaign. I set up a bogus EVERYBODY LOVES GEORGE e-mail account on HotMail.com and sent out 1 message every day to a list of about 600. This list included all local and food trade media, local 'talkers' and politicos.

"Our first message of the week was: "It's a bird! It's a plane! It's the start of George's campaign!"

"We hired a plane to fly the message 'EVERYBODY LOVES GEORGE' on a huge banner over the city during peak drive times."

"Tuesday's e-mail was as follows: 'If you missed the message in the Monday sky, pay attention the rest of the week ... The word on the street says that GEORGE likes it hot, and for now, that is all we can leak.'

"The e-mail was great. I only had a dozen people who requested that they be removed from the list, but we got lots of fun responses!!"

"We knew we couldn't go up against the Eckrich sausages of the world in advertising dollars, so we decided to create BUZZ about George. Some thought we were publicizing then presidential candidate George W. Bush, others thought country music superstar George Strait was what's 'hot.' One of our sandwich boarders (word on the street phase), sporting a 'Everybody Loves George' sign, was stopped and questioned by the Secret Service during a unannounced visit by former President George Bush. This only added to the mystique of our campaign."

Clever! And the whole movement involves being "practically outrageous," which YOU can do, too. Ready for MORE amazing examples of hypnotic publicity?

Show Your Bra!

Something that always works to get hypnotic publicity is a contest – especially an outlandish one.

Gazebo, a full service lingerie store in Northampton, MA, gets truly hypnotic publicity from its annual "Show Us Your Bra" contest. The three-part project starts with the contest in which artists of any and all levels of talent create and name three dimensional replicas of bras. There's a bra made from matching red ketchup and yellow mustard squeeze containers.

There's another called "De fence" and made from barbed wire. Still another called "Eve's Bra" and made from two halves of an apple – complete with a serpent!

The entries are judged, hung in a show, and auctioned. Their third annual auction was covered by CNN.

The group then creates a calendar of the most notable entries and sells it for $20. With the assistance of sponsors, all proceeds from the auction and calendar sales go toward Gazebo's Breast Form Fund, which helps women obtain breast prostheses and post mastectomy bras.

As you can see, this is an outrageous event that is also practical: It gets media attention AND it sells bras.

Visit their website; check out details of the contest and

view more bras then you'll ever find anywhere else at: www.the-gazebo.com.

However, don't get TOO mesmerized at that site, as you have the next chapter to read!!!

21 Ways to Identify Story Ideas about You or Your Business

I'm not afraid to admit that I don't know everything. Just as you invested in this new book to learn more about Hypnotic Marketing, I'm always investing in books, tapes, and courses to learn more, too. The following is an excerpt from a great book by Joan Stewart and Tom Antion. It reveals 21 ways to identify story ideas about you and your business. I thought this excerpt (and their book) so good, that I asked their permission to use part of it here.

Here they are:

- Does this sound like you?
- You can't understand why the business reporter at your local newspaper has quoted your competitor in five separate stories but hasn't called you once.
- Your company sends out more than two dozen news releases every year about new employees and promotions, but they result in little more than a few lines of type.
- The 12-page speech your boss wrote when he spoke at the local Rotary Club luncheon would have made an excellent column for the local business magazine. But after you mailed it to the editor, you never heard a word.

If your attempts at media coverage have fallen flat, quit grumbling and start taking a proactive approach to free publicity by identifying interesting, compelling story ideas the media need.

Yes, NEED. Newspapers, magazines and trade publications have hundreds of thousands of column inches to fill; TV and radio stations have hundreds of hours of news and community interest programs they must broadcast. The number of media outlets is greater than ever, and competition is fierce for advertising dollars, viewers, and subscribers. The secret to savvy media relations is knowing exactly what they want, then giving it to them.

Here are tickler questions designed to help you identify the best story ideas within your company or organization:

- **What's different?** Is your company doing anything unique, or different than your competitors? Examples: A professional speaker who gives a quirky, memorable gift to every meeting planner who hires her. A website company that gives its customers discount coupons good for a website update for every referral a customer sends. An agency that buys creative toys for its employees to use during brainstorming sessions to get their own creative juices flowing.

- **The local angle.** Are you the local angle to a national or regional event? During the war in Kosovo, many local newspapers and TV stations ran stories about people in their own communities who kept in touch with their relatives in the war zone. During the Columbine shootings in Colorado, newspapers interviewed local child psychologists and counselors who offered tips on how parents can spot warning signs in their own children.

- **Piggyback on a news event.** After severe rains in Milwaukee a few years ago, a Minnesota company got several minutes of free advertising on a Milwaukee radio station by talking to the drive time radio host about a special pump that removes standing water and moisture in the air. The host interviewed a company representative and gave out the company's toll free number.

- **Piggyback on trends.** Do you sell a product or service that ties into a national trend? A credit counseling agency might offer themselves as a source for stories about the whopping credit card debt racked up by college students. A nonprofit agency that advocates safety for women can promote its community classes by offering the media tips on how business women can be less susceptible to theft of laptop computers in crowded places like airports.

- **Piggyback on a holiday.** Are you doing something different on a particular holiday? Are you a management consultant who can suggest ways that companies can keep their employees productive during the holidays? Have you determined that it's more efficient for your business to simply close down during the week between Christmas and New Year's? If you're of Irish descent and give all your employees a half day off on St. Patrick's Day, that story might interest the media. Remember that the week between Christmas and New Year's is the slowest news week of the year, and an excellent time to seek coverage. A Wisconsin company got a six minute story on the local TV station after it announced at the annual Christmas party that every employee was being treated to a trip to Disney World.

- **Tell the media about trends.** Have you spotted a new trend in your industry? Let the media know. Many accountants, for example, are becoming certified as investment counselors. If it's a trend a reporter is interested in, don't be surprised if they interview you for the story.

- **Offer free advice.** What advice can you offer that will help someone else solve their problems? Tell reporters they can call on you for advice when writing stories about your area of expertise. Give them specific examples of how you help people save time and money.

- **Write how-to articles.** Editors of many newspapers, magazines and trade publications want articles that tell their readers how to do something such as get out of debt, discipline their children, have a safer work environment, set up a home office, or acquire a business loan. Think of the number one problem your customers face, and then write a *how to* article about it. If it is printed, try to recycle the article for a different publication.

- **Take a stand on issues.** Is there a local, state or national industry or political issue that you lobby for, or that you feel strongly about? Find the reporters who cover that issue and share your thoughts with them. If, for example, your trade group is supporting local gun control legislation, call and offer to comment on the issue.

- **Publicize an upcoming event.** Are you sponsoring an event such as classes, an open house, a free demonstration, or a fun event? Don't just send a news release. Think of something visual that ties into the event. Then call your local TV station and ask if they are interested in doing a story a day or two before. Coverage before the event helps spark interest and boost attendance. THINK TECHNOLOGY. How are you using technology in interesting or unique ways? Have you found a way to draw lots of traffic to your website with resulting orders? Are you using the latest technology during your speaking engagements? Is your sales force using technology to stay in touch with existing customers and seek out new ones?

- **The labor shortage.** How are you attracting and keeping qualified employees? By letting them work from home? By recruiting in places like Fort Lauderdale during spring break? By setting up trust funds for children of employees who stay longer than a year? By offering casual day every day of the week? The labor shortage is a red-hot topic, and demographers predict that it will become even hotter.

- **Your lifestyle.** Does the type of clothing you wear, the home you live in, your hobbies, your relationships with your family, the food you eat, and where you travel on vacation say something unusual about you? These stories are ideal for lifestyle sections, food pages, travel pages and special interest magazines. Even though the articles are not necessarily business related, the reporter most likely will ask you what you do for a living, and that's a chance to plug your company or organization, particularly if it ties into the reason they are writing. (Example: You speak internationally and have an extensive collection of wine you have bought during your travels. This would be a GREAT story for food page editors, and it would publicize the fact that you are a professional speaker).

- **Alliances and partnerships.** Has your organization formed an interesting alliance or partnership with another business or nonprofit? Call the business reporter and share the information. Be willing to explain the results you expect to see from such an arrangement. And be sure your partner is also willing to speak with a reporter.

- **Talk about your problems.** What are the three biggest business problems you are facing? Find out the name of the reporters who cover your industry. Then share the information with them. Who knows? Someone might read your story and call you with a solution you might not otherwise have known about.

- **Talk about your mistakes.** What are the biggest you have made, and how would you advise other people from not making the same ones? Don't be embarrassed. Everyone makes mistakes. And if you're willing to discuss yours, there's a good chance the media will be willing to write about you.

- **Polls and surveys.** Are you taking a poll or survey, either among your customers or among the public? *Homewood Suites*, a Texas hotel chain, got great publicity from results of a survey that asked guests what they do in hotel rooms. Almost one in five respondents said they jump on the bed. IAMS Pet Food Company surveyed its customers about their relationship with their pets. An overwhelming 91 percent of the people polled, admitted saying "I love you" to their pets. In addition, 63 percent of respondents sleep with their pets at their sides. Results of the poll were released several weeks before Valentine's Day. (Brilliant)! How about taking a poll asking your customers about the most unusual way they use your product or service?

- **Clever contest.** Have you thought about sponsoring a clever contest? To celebrate its 100th anniversary, OshKosh B'Gosh launched a six-month nationwide search for the oldest pair of bib overalls. Thrifty Rent-a-Car sponsors an annual "Honeymoon Disasters Contest." Entries result in amusing feature stories printed in major newspapers and magazines throughout the country. For additional publicity mileage, the company announces results near Valentine's Day, giving the media a perfect story that piggybacks on a holiday.

- **The four seasons.** Think about story ideas that tie into the four seasons. Has your company found a way to keep cool or cut utility costs? Suggest it during the dog days of summer. Hospitals, clinics, and medical schools can offer the media a list of experts to pass along helpful tips on how to avoid getting colds and flu during the winter. Lawn care companies can share tips on how to prepare your lawn during the spring.

- **Celebrating an anniversary?** The fact that your company is celebrating an anniversary or birthday isn't news. But it would be more enticing to the media if you could tie it into a clever event. A button manufacturer published a lavish photo history of the button including its uses on shoes, clothing, furniture, and accessories. An accounting firm celebrated its centennial by publishing a giveaway book of commissioned original renditions of what select artists thought it meant to be 100. A national rental car company rented out its fleet of cars for free one day.

- **Create tip sheets.** Can you write a tip sheet that explains how to solve a particular problem, or how to do something? It includes helpful free advice. Topics sound like this: "11 Ways to Snag More Business from Your Website," "The 7 Secrets of Profitable Self Promotion," or "9 Ways to Save Money on Insurance Premiums."

Each tip sheet should have a short introduction of a sentence or two. At the end, print a paragraph that states the name of the author, the author's credentials, and contact information such as phone number, e-mail address, and website URL. Think of the Number One problem your customers are facing, and offer tips on how to solve it.

- **Changing your focus?** Is your company changing its focus, switching product lines, expanding services, entering new niche markets or making any major changes in the way it does business? If so, let the media know. Be willing, however, to talk about the reasons behind the change. If you're trying a new product line because the first one flopped, be willing to say so.

Excerpted from *How to Be a Kick Butt Publicity Hound* by Joan Stewart and Tom Antion. http://www.antion.com/publicityhound.htm. Used here with their kind permission.

Let's keep moving!

Running Water

Eric Villines, Director of PR for jobs.com, told me the following story...

"Formally I owned The Villines Company, a marketing firm out of Santa Monica specializing in Entertainment and Event Marketing. I've developed numerous large scale events to develop media attention, but I have to say, I'm generally most proud of media attention I've garnered from pulling off low cost and more grassroots oriented stunts.

"My most recent example of this: Shortly after coming to work for jobs.com (early 2000), I decided our sales reps in Boston, home base of our largest competitor (Monster.com), needed some local 'noise' to help them with their daily sales calls. The fly in the ointment here was that I had very little budget to work with, and I knew I'd be competing with Monster's $200 Million yearly marketing budget.

"I investigated events coming up in the area where we'd be guaranteed a large and demo- graphically mixed audience, and decided our stunt 'had' to take place at the Boston Marathon. But again I was working with little budget, and although I needed some sort of eye-catching concept, blimps with our logo and painted Humvees were out of the question.

"Ironically, with graduation coming up, and Boston being arguably the biggest college town in America, the answer was right in front of me. I checked with our trade show department to see what sort of promotional inventory we had in stock, and discovered we had a thousand water bottles with our Jobs.com logo.

"I immediately got on the phone with a local field agency I had used in the past, and hired them to hire six or so local college students. Additionally, I had the company purchase caps and gowns. During the Boston Marathon, we had the students cart around and hand out our water bottles, pens, printed copies of our logo, and anything else I could dig up.

"The day before the event I had put in a call to the *Boston Globe's* photo department, and gave them a 'tip' that college kids in caps and gowns would be running around the day of the event. In itself, I would have considered the day's efforts a success (final cost including expenses: $2,500), but getting our College Team's photo featured in the "Names & Faces" section of the Globe (April 7, 2000) with a caption plugging our company created an immediate morale boost for our sales department, as well as giving them another piece of fun collateral to bring on their sales calls."

Way cool! You see, getting appropriate attention can

be fun and very inexpensive.

Here's another story for you ...

Selling Bloody Games

Kirk Green of Green Communications in Rancho Santa Margarita, CA told me the following:

"Over the years I have been part of a number of stunts to promote and sell video and computer games...

1. When the LA Dodgers were up for sale, we announced that the company I worked for was going to buy the Dodgers ... all we needed was 10 million people to buy copies of our new Baseball game for the Sony PlayStation. No game had ever sold more than 2 million prior to this... it became a national story.

2. For the game *Carmageddon*, the object of which is to run over pedestrians and hit cars and is fairly bloody, our company staged a blood drive with the Red Cross and gave free copies of the game away to people who gave blood. We raised over 125 pints that day and the story made national news.

3. For the launch of the game *Wild 9's*, we staged a marathon video game contest at the Playboy mansion with Hef and the Playmates stopping by."

As you can see, being a little off the wall can help. But again, I want to temper your creativity with practicality.

Next, here's something simple and easy which virtually anyone can do...

One of the Easiest Ways in the World to Get Publicity

Sally Highducheck wrote the following revealing e-mail to me:

> "One of my clients is Leflein Associates, a New Jersey–based research firm that has been performing publicity surveys for both B2C and B2B businesses for some time. Currently, I am putting together a case study for Barbara Leflein, president of the company, and am amazed at the success that some of her clients have had by using surveys as marketing tools.

> "Clients get press coverage everywhere – local and national TV, newspapers (even *The Wall Street Journal* and *USA Today*), magazines, websites, wire services – all for a fraction of the cost of what even a simple advertising campaign would cost (and with more credibility and control of messaging, too). Even more importantly, the coverage turns into increased customers for her clients – ultimately THE objective of any marketing campaign."

As you can see, being "practically outrageous" can be as simple as a survey.

(Note: How do you create your own surveys? Easy! SurveyMonkey.com is focused entirely on allowing YOU to create surveys quickly and easily. No programming experience is required, no software must be downloaded. It's free, too. See www.surveymonkey.com).

But what if you used something obvious, yet overlooked – like toilet paper?

John Zappa and a friend were laid off from a computer company. They bought my Nightingale Conant audiotape program, *The Power of Outrageous Marketing* (available at www.Amazon.com), and then wrote a news release that is bringing them national headline attention. What they did was invent something called "Ticker Tape Toilet Paper," with printed readings of the fall of dot.com companies on the tissue paper. They then sent the release out. John wrote me saying,

> "It has only been six days since the release went out, and I've had more requests for inter- views than I could keep track of. Just last week, I was on a dozen separate radio shows and have been doing 20 to 30 other interviews *per* day. I am booked every day for more radio interviews for the next two weeks, including a couple nationally syndicated shows."

> "Even more bizarre is that *Dow Jones Newswires* has picked up the story and that should be released in the coming weeks. Not only that, but a reporter from *Bloomberg Financial* is actually coming to Austin to interview me in person and taking me to lunch.

Anyway, it looks like things are going to snowball from here. I may have inadvertently created the next fad."

Since the above e-mail from John, the *Associated Press* AND *The Wall Street Journal* picked up on his story. Home runs!

What can YOU do to grab media attention? All it may take is imagination – and some toilet paper.

Here's another wild example of original thinking to grab national publicity: Thinking creatively – and outrageously – can lead to a million dollars in global publicity. Just ask Jason Black and Frances Shroeder. They went online to sell their newborn baby's name – and for $500,000, no less.

They posted their "item" for sale on eBay. Shortly after that, *USA Today* and numerous other publications across the land picked up the story. While there haven't been any buyers (that I'm aware of) the very Barnum–like event has caused enormous publicity.

How did the parents create their bold idea? Apparently, Black and Shroeder wanted a new house. So they sat and thought about ways to raise the money quick. That brainstorming led to the idea of selling their newborn baby's name.

When I wanted to buy a BMW Z3 Roadster, and wanted to pay cash for the luxury sports car, I generated the idea to teach e-classes online. The result brought me $65,000 in five months. (And I LOVE my hot rod)!

Again, what do you want? A new car? New house?

Wanting something BIG can lead to a colossal money making idea – whether or not you have a child who needs a name.

So, how do you come up with ideas for yourself?

How to Install a "Success Wish" in Your Mind

This chapter is about expanding your mind.

It's about learning to think with a flair for the theatrical.

It's about allowing your mind the freedom to be crazy.

It's about considering there are no rules and that anything goes – even flying midgets on kites.

At this point, you may not know how to think like Moran, Shankman, or any other results driven publicist. That's perfectly okay.

Remember how I began this book? I said I set an intention for how these chapters would come to me, and they began to happen in exactly the way I intended. So your first step is to create an intention for yourself regarding learning how to think like a Hypnotic Marketing wizard.

That means looking for "practically outrageous" ideas to promote your business. That means declaring an outcome, an intention, a goal for yourself and your sales.

That means deciding that you CAN do it, by selecting your intention and turning it over to your subconscious/unconscious/higher mind.

Why is this so important? Let me explain:

If you're wondering why I'm not talking about the nuts and bolts of marketing in this chapter, it's because I'm talking about an inside-out approach to success, which, to me, is far easier and far more powerful. I've seen people implement direct mail campaigns, publicity blitzes, and online marketing – and get no results.

None.

Zip.

Zero.

The problem was usually with the person, not with their product or even their marketing.

If the person had a death-wish, no amount of marketing could save them.

If the person had a succeed-wish, it almost didn't matter what amount of marketing they did. They would succeed.

For example, I had one client who sold adjustable massage beds. I have one and love it. They relax you in minutes. I created a direct mail postcard for him. I also had another friend create a short infomercial for him. The results? It all bombed. Why? Because the CEO of the company didn't want to succeed! For whatever reasons, he sabotaged our efforts. He mailed the card to the wrong list. He never gave people the video.

The same thing happened with a client I met in Australia. He invented eyeglasses to reduce computer eye strain. I love the glasses and am using a pair right now, as I type these words to you. I arranged to find a U.S. distributor for the glasses. As it happens, I know one of the greatest infomercial kings in the world, a man who made a fortune selling sunglasses. So I introduced him to my Australian friend. The result? Nothing. Why? Because my Australian friend wouldn't act on anything my contact would offer! He had a death-wish. The result was failure.

My point is this: YOU are the most successful ingredient in your marketing campaign. If you don't believe in your product or service, it will fail.

It all begins right here, right now, and INSIDE YOU.

So spend a little time reflecting on yourself.

Ask yourself such questions as:

- Do I honestly want to succeed?
- Do I believe in my product or service?
- Do I believe my business serves people?
- Do I feel capable of telling the world what I do?

Once you answer those questions with a solid "YES!," you are ready to actually create Step One in the Three-Step **Hypnotic Marketing** strategy.

And what exactly is Step One? Create a PO — a Practically Outrageous publicity event!

And how do you come up with such an idea?

By first believing you CAN do it, and then by brainstorming wild, zany, crazy ideas that MIGHT work.

Want some more help on creating some PO events?

The Top Three Ways Guaranteed to Always Hypnotize the Media

Would you like to know the top three ways to always hypnotize the media? Here they are:

- Babies
- Pets
- Women

I could probably rattle off countless stories of how just those three topics could be and have been used to capture the attention of the media.

- P.T. Barnum held baby contests back in the 1800s to generate interest in his museum.
- Pets are often used to get attention in photographs in ads.
- Women are notoriously used – and maybe used is the wrong word – to get attention. Put a few bikini clad young women on motorcycles and send them around your new restaurant and you're sure to get media attention.

Without going one step further in this book, those three topics alone – used in some creative way could be your ticket to Step One in *Hypnotic Marketing*.

One woman complained that "using women" to get

publicity is sexist. Well, it might be.

But you'll notice that women, as well as babies and pets, are continuously magnets for publicity. It's not sexist as it is so much human nature. The world at large is simply interested in women, babies, and pets. Rather than complain about it, either use these facts to get hypnotic publicity for yourself, or just think of some other way to grab the media's attention. I'm just reporting what works – and works virtually every time. In fact, why not stop right here and make a list of some ways you can involve women, babies, or pets in YOUR business?

Just make a list right here:

_____

_____

_____

_____

But let's not stop now!

Ready for more proven ways to grab the ears and eyes of the media?

10 Tips on Becoming Newsworthy from a Media Tigress

I learned a long time ago that you can't do all your marketing yourself. Not if you want colossal success, anyway. All the greatest got advice from others and weren't afraid to delegate duties.

I'm the same. I went to media expert Marcia Yudkin and asked her for some tips on how to grab media attention. Here's what she said:

"Compared with advertising, media coverage costs you virtually nothing. With a phone call or simple press release, you can entice print or broadcast media to spread the word about what you do.

"However, unlike advertising, you have to earn publicity. You have to provide a compelling answer to the all-important question of an editor or producer:

"Why would our readers or listeners be interested in you now?

"There are as many successful ways to answer that question as there are stories in the media every day. Here are 10 of the possibilities cited in *132 Ways to Make You or Your Business Newsworthy*, available in full from www.yudkin.com/downloads.htm.

"Concoct an interesting characterization of yourself. (Rick Davis of Temple, NH, created The Institute of Totally Useless Skills).

"Piggyback on the news or current entertainment. (In the summer of 2001, anything about sharks appeared timely, while the summer that Jurassic Park came out, the media focus was dinosaurs).

"Agree or disagree with newspaper columnists by writing them. (Many use or mention their mail in their column).

"Send free samples of your product to the media. (And enjoy the cachet of being able to say Channel 6's Anchor wears your earrings).

"Prove a stereotype wrong. (The Beach Boy Engineers).

"Turn your liabilities into news. (More in-laws involved in your business than at any other establishment in town).

"Don't do something everyone else does. (One doctor refuses patients who smoke or have other unhealthful habits).

"Borrow Hollywood story lines. ('The Comeback,' 'The Big Break,' 'Hero Risks All').

"Run for office. (In 1988, entertainer Ron Bianco of Providence, RI, ran his singing dog, Bilbo, for President).

"Adopt a catchier business name. (The day 'Bundy Very Used Cars' changed its name to 'Rent-A-Wreck,'

CBS arrived to feature it).

Note: Marcia Yudkin is the author of eleven nonfiction books, including the classic *6 Steps to Free Publicity, Internet Marketing for Less than $500/Year* and *Freelance Writing for Magazines & Newspapers*. She publishes a free weekly e-mail newsletter called "The Marketing Minute," available from www.yudkin.com/marksynd.htm.

The above was used with her kind permission.

The Seven Laws of Baseball's Greatest Publicist

When I was a child, I wanted to be a baseball player. I think I saw a movie about Babe Ruth and got inspired to hit balls out of ballparks. But I was never that good and soon learned that I was better suited to hit typewriter keys. So here I am.

But baseball can teach you a lot about hypnotic publicity. Possibly the greatest baseball promoter of all time was Bill Veeck. In a recent book about his philosophy, titled *Marketing Your Dreams*, the author (Pat Williams), offers "Veeck's Immutable Laws of Promotion." I'll paraphrase each of them right here, right now, to help you further think of "practically outrageous" ideas to drive traffic to your website.

> Law 1: The power of illusion. Dress up your product or service and it becomes more appealing. Baseball becomes more than a game when you tie to people drinking milk. Bring in your milk bottle cap and you got in free.
>
> Law 2: The incongruity property. Give away something that makes no sense. Everyone gives away free TVs to get attention. Veeck once gave away 4,000 pickles. The oddness captures attention.

Law 3: Clean bathroom = happy fan. Treat your customers and clients like royalty and they'll continue to praise you and do business with you. Veeck paid extra money to have cloth towels in restrooms. He remodeled the women's bathrooms. This isn't far from something you can do. Sincerely help your clients and they can bring you media attention.

Law 4: Winning is an end, but not a means. One time Veeck hosted a "Grandstand Managers Night." He had a group of 4,000 fans vote on major managerial decisions during an actual game. While Veeck wanted his teams to win, he also wanted his fans to have a glorious time. This, of course, led to incredible publicity.

Law 5: Spend money (preferably someone else's) to make it. Veeck got sponsors to flip the bills for his wild stunts and giveaways. The person who donated 1,000 pickles of course benefited from the publicity Veeck generated. Same goes for anyone involved. Create win-wins and cross promotions to grab media attention.

Law 6: The promotion never ends. You can't ever stop publicity, marketing, or selling. One time, neighbors called the ballpark and complained of the noise. Veeck seized the moment to help them, as well as himself and held a "Good Neighbor Night."

Law 7: None of these laws are immutable. Anything goes. The intent is to draw Hypnotic Publicity to you or your business in order to drive traffic to your website, and then sell them what you offer. Veeck was willing to break rules. He once proposed a "Missing Tooth Night," where anyone with a missing tooth got in the game free.

Again, think on these laws. See how they stretch your mind to think of "practically outrageous" ideas YOU can implement.

Make some notes right now, if you want.

And when you're ready, jump to the next Chapter!

The Psychology of Hypnotic Publicity

I love old books. People often wonder why I collect so many of them. Truth is, they are packed with wisdom you can still use today.

For example, I am a fan of the writings of Kenneth Goode and Zenn Kaufman, business writers from the 1930s and 1940s. One of my favorite books by the duo was titled *Showmanship in Business*. It is an absolute delight to read. Packed with stories of how average business people can add "show biz" to their enterprise to grab attention, it's as valid today as it was when it came out after The Great Depression.

The authors said there are four proven ways to grab attention:

- Make them laugh.
- Make them cry.
- Thrill them.
- Talk of love – with words and music.

They went on to explain some of the psychological elements of those four ways of getting attention for your business. Because these are so thought provoking, I want to share some of them with you.

- **Conflict**

"People like action," they wrote. "Action in competition, whenever possible."

- **Firsts**

"There's no news in seconds – even when better than most firsts," wrote the authors.

- **Humor**

"You can't laugh people into buying your goods – that's been said often enough," they wrote. "But you can laugh them into wanting you, which is a long step toward making a sale."

- **Mystery**

"Mystery books sell big ... Mystery pictures pack movie houses. Your public loves mystery."

- **Animals**

"One of our friends who has a knack for getting lots of free publicity attributes a great part of his success to his regular use of animals in his story," they explain.

- **Magic**

"Hyatt Bearing has scooped interest at industrial shows by using optical illusions as attention getters."

- **Symbolism**

"The word 'Prosperity' elected McKinley," they write, speaking of President William McKinley, the US President born in my home town, Niles, Ohio. "People like labels better than ideas."

Again, all of this is to fuel your mind with IDEAS.

And again, write down some ideas that come to you right now.

Do it now, and then jump to the next chapter to learn a forbidden way to get attention! And when you're ready, jump to the next chapter!

Edgy Top Secret Ways to Absolutely Nail Media Attention

I'm very hesitant to write this particular chapter.

You see, people can misuse what I am about to tell you. Many people – the few who already discovered this underground information – are already using it to manipulate the media, which means they are using it to manipulate you and me.

I'm sharing this information with you to first help you become aware of how the media works. And second, to help you break into the news with your own message.

Again, this is powerful stuff, and not to be taken lightly. Please don't share it with anyone else. Here it goes:

Activists know how to get into the news. Whether by staging a protest, doing something outlandish like jumping off a building, or actually cramming the culture by upsetting conservative events like animal shows, or even stopping fishing with bombs or threats of bombs.

Again, activists know how to get our attention.

I remember years ago helping a client, a well-known attorney, promote his book. He boldly told me, "I can get a hundred people to protest my book if it will get me on the news."

He was serious. I knew he could do it. He was so popular, and such a keen promoter, that he didn't have to stage a protest – and yet, created one of the biggest book release parties in the history of the city we lived in (one of the largest in America).

So what do activists know that most of us don't?

I suggest you grab a book called *Making the News* by Jason Salzman. It's an incredible work. It's written for non-profit organizations and activists. It explains how the media works, and details ways to get into the media. It is still in print, and well worth buying and memorizing.

Salzman says that the most successful media events are entertaining. They are theatrical. In one chapter in his book he lists and explains numerous ways for coming up with ways to create newsworthy stunts. Here are a few of them:

1. Cameras love costumes. Dress up your staff or you and call the media.
2. Dramatize a popular expression. "Waffling on the issues" led to a press conference outside a waffle house.
3. Grade people or organizations. The press loves winners and loser. "Report card for the Energy Secretary" got headline news.
4. Depict a symbol of your concerns. Forty thousand pairs of shoes were put on a lawn to depict the 40,000 people killed by guns.
5. Get your ad rejected. Create an ad you know won't run, get it rejected, and then host a press event to

complain.

6. Conflicts make news. You can always challenge your competition to a showdown, playfully or for real, and invite the media to witness it.

Well, I told you these ideas are edgy!

By now you might be wondering if you can do ANY of the wild, zany, outrageous or even bizarre ideas presented in this and the former chapters.

You must remind yourself that the world is packed with people and organizations scratching and clawing to get into the news. A simple news release by you won't likely get you the national media attention you want. You have to think bigger. Bolder. You have to think like P.T. Barnum. You have to act like a Donald Trump.

Even if you are a so-called "small potato," you must think and act like a HOT potato to get into the news.

Again, this is the first step in your Hypnotic Marketing strategy. Let's explore it even more...

How to Get Rich with P.T. Barnum's Secret

I'm fond of this quote by P.T. Barnum – which he wrote on his deathbed in 1891:

"I am indebted to the press of the United States for almost every dollar which I possess ..."

— P.T. Barnum, 1891

Barnum knew the power of the media. It made him one of America's wealthiest men, and one of the most famous worldwide. And it helped make many of Barnum's stars – from Tom Thumb to Jenny Lind – also rich and famous.

You can do this, too. I'll show you how in this chapter.

And maybe more importantly, I'll explain how I use news releases as direct response mechanisms.

In other words, I "embed" reasons to get people to your website *within* the body of my news releases. I call it E-DR Publicity, and I'll be explaining it in a later chapter.

First, let me say that I've written at length about how to write news releases in my other e-books, particularly *Advanced Hypnotic Writing*. If you've read that, you can skip this chapter, or just review this section again.

Ready?

The tool you'll use to get publicity for yourself is simply one sheet of paper: A news release. A news release is what it says: A release of news.

But few people writing them seem to understand that fact. Instead, they are sending out ads and calling them news. Editors get hundreds to thousands of news releases every day! If yours is a thinly disguised ad, yours will get trashed.

So, how do you stay out of the trashcan?

THE HEADLINE

As you might tell from the opening section of the last chapter, headlines can make or break your chances to get media attention. Re-read the headlines I came up with for Jeff, Barry, and myself. Aren't they all catchy? Don't they all signal news?

Want a tip on how to write headlines for YOUR news releases?

Listen to the commercials that try to get you to watch the TV news. You'll hear short teaser phrases such as,

"Can your eyes be healed in 45 seconds?" or

"Can this dog save your life?"

Another I heard was:

"Meet the man who committed the crime that shocked our nation!"

Those teases are headlines! And they are very hypnotic!

In other words, while you watch TV tonight, note how

the teasers during the commercials lure you into watching the news. What they are doing is hooking you with spoken headlines.

You can follow the same principle when writing news releases. This works for ALL the media and is used by everyone from Oprah to Larry King, to your local favorite television news station. Start to think like a reporter and generate headlines for news releases for your (let's say) e-book. Ask questions such as –

• What's the news in your e-book?
• What's the news about you?
• How does your book affect readers?
• The world?
• Your neighborhood?

Fish for the news and then turn that news into a one-page hard hitting news (and news only) release.

This will all make more sense as you can continue with this book and review the examples to follow. So let's not stop here!

THE STRUCTURE OF A HYPNOTIC NEWS RELEASE

Use your business letterhead. If you don't have letterhead, don't worry about it. What the editor cares about is your news, not you. A letterhead just adds some credibility.

Under it, on either the left or right, type the phrase

"NEWS RELEASE."

Under that, type the name of a contact person (which can be you) and your phone number.

On the top of the page, on the opposite side, write the words "FOR IMMEDIATE RELEASE."

In the center of the page, maybe one third down from the top, type a headline. Remember to make this sentence newsworthy.

A few lines below that, begin your release. Though it is okay to type the release single spaced, editors are used to seeing it typed double spaced. Keep in mind that a release is a NEWS source. Give your facts: who, what, when, where, how and why. And present them in order of importance.

Your following paragraphs should fill in details and complete the news story.

At the very end, give your name and address and say "For More Information Call (your number)."

HOW I WRITE NEWS RELEASES

Now let's make all of this even clearer:

When someone hands me a book to promote, or any other product, I look for the "story" that it fits into. In other words, I don't want to write a press release to promote "a book" as that usually isn't much news, but I probe to learn how the book fits into a larger picture. This is how I create hypnotic writing.

For example, let's talk about the fellow who got a call from a reporter eight minutes after he faxed out my release. His book is called *Fun Projects with Wooden Pallets*. If I were like most publishers, I might whip up a release saying the book was now out and say a little about it. But I don't think that's very powerful. I prefer a double whammy approach, which I achieve by combining the "new book" release with a "feature story" approach.

After some thought I came up with the following headline:

"New Ways to Make Furniture — and More— from Scrap"

Note how that headline has a more "news feel" to it? It doesn't even mention the book. That, to me, isn't as important as what the book helps you do. In advertising we talk about features and benefits. The book is a feature; what you can do as a result of having the book is the benefit. I focused on the benefit.

The next thing I looked for was a killer opening line. I believe that the first line in your feature news release should be a grabber. If you don't hook the editors there, they probably won't go on to the rest of your release.

It's worth mentioning right here that your editors will decide to read your release – or not – based on your headline. If it intrigues them, they'll read on. But the next potential stopping point for them is your first line. In the case of the above client, my first line was this:

"You know those wooden pallets stacked up in and behind

many businesses?"

That's an opening line that I still love. Why? It gets the reader nodding his or her head, saying "yes" internally, and puts them in a receptive mood. It also pulls the reader into the next paragraph. It makes you ask, "What about those pallets anyway?"

From there I created a story about how to use the pallets to create furniture – the news – and I quoted from the book and the authors, thereby plugging the book within the context of the feature story. Do you see the difference? Rather than focusing on the book, I focused on the story and mentioned the book within the story. Here's the entire release:

• • •

News Article from Awareness News Service
Contact: Joe VitaIe
Phone: 512-847-3414 For Immediate Release
New Ways to Make Furniture—and More—from Scrap
(Silsbee, Texas. September 1, 1995) — You know those wooden pallets stacked up in and behind many businesses?

According to "Fun Projects Using Wooden Pallets," ($14.95 postage paid from Applecart Press, PO Box 612, Silsbee, TX 77656) a 115-page, fully illustrated new book by Don and Peggy Crissey of Silsbee, Texas, you can pick up those pallets, usually for no charge, and turn them into over a hundred easy, practical, and fun home projects, such as beds, chairs, fences, planters, toys, steps, and tables, to name just a few of their uses.

"There are over 460 million pallets made each year in this country," says Don Crissey, an engineer with over 20 years of experience in recycling everything from government surplus paints to ocean cargo containers. Crissey adds that 53 percent of these pallets are used once and then discarded.

"What people don't realize is that half of the expensive hardwood cut down goes into making these pallets," explains Crissey. "That means there's some very fine and expensive wood in those pallets – wood you can use to make some beautiful furniture."

According to Don and his wife Peggy, a former retail shoe store display designer, a single pallet can fit in the trunk of most cars, and each pallet can be easily turned into any of over a hundred simple, fun, and practical do-it-yourself home projects.

"We spent three years picking up pallets and using the wood," said Don Crissey. ''I've made everything we describe in the book, from benches to beds to utility cabinets. Our front lawn has planters, steps, and chairs sitting on it, and no one ever realizes they were all made from pallets!"

"Besides the joy of making these projects," adds Peggy Crissey, "It feels good to know you are doing your part to be earth friendly."

For a free sample of directions on how to make one project from a wooden pallet, send a self-addressed, stamped envelope to Don and Peggy Crissey, Applecart Press, PO Box 612, Silsbee, TX 77656.

To order the new book, "Fun Projects Using Wooden

Pallets," by Don and Peggy Crissey, send a check or money order for $14.95 (postage paid) to Applecart Press, PO Box 612, Silsbee, TX 77656.

— end —

• • •

INSIGHT SECRET

Note that within the news release I requested that people send for free information. That's how I create direct response news releases.

What you will do is focus on getting people to go to your website. So you might plant within your news release a suggestion that more information is at your website. This is the equivalent of asking people to "Send for more information."

Another example:

Another time an author called me about a book she had written on lawyer abuse. I liked her and the book but had to search to find a way to create a feature release that I could plug the book into. After a few days I came up with the following headline:

"Wife, Mother, Business Woman
Hauls Her Lawyers to Court – and Wins!
Reveals How to Prevent 'Lawyer Abuse' in Surprising New Book"

I like this headline because it sums up the entire release in just a couple of lines. The "wife, mother, business woman" suggests an unusual bit of news; this woman isn't just a housewife, but is living out several roles. "Hauls her lawyers to court" is obviously attention-grabbing news. "And wins!" is the punch line. My subtitle, or headline under the headline, is my attempt to build even more enthusiasm for the feature release.

My next effort was to come up with a terrific opening line. I read through the pile of background material the author had sent me and came across a line that I turned into a lead I doubt few could read and forget.

I wrote:

"Janice Tucker Hedlund wonders why juries are locked up at night and lawyers get to go home."

I then went on and wrote a release that told her story and plugged her book in the process. Again, I didn't focus on her book. I focused on the news and used the book for my quotes. This was a less "advertising oriented" approach to getting the editors attention. Since a common complaint among editors is that releases too often tend to look like thinly disguised ads, I wanted my release to look – and actually be – news.

Now here's the entire release:

• • •

NEWS from Awareness News Service

Contact: Joe Vitale

Phone: 512-847-3414

For Immediate Release

Wife, Mother, Business Woman Hauls Her Lawyers to Court—and Wins!

Reveals How to Prevent "Lawyer Abuse" in Surprising New Book (Laguna Beach, CA, July 7, 1995). Janice Tucker Hedlund wonders why juries are locked up at night and lawyers get to go home.

"My husband and I spent eight years embroiled in lawsuits," Hedlund writes in her new book, "Help! I've Hired a Lawyer!" ($14.95 from EmptyPockets Ventures, 412 North Coast Highway #380, Laguna Beach, CA 92651). "The last three of those years were spent suing our own attorneys."

After losing millions of dollars in legal fees on a series of twenty lawyers who weren't doing their jobs, Hedlund decided to fight back. She took three lawyers to court for legal malpractice, and won.

"Stay out of the court room," warns Hedlund, a Laguna Beach wife, mother, and business woman. But she adds that it may be impossible for everyone these days.

"This country is run by lawyers. The government offices are filled with them. The major portion of the President's cabinet is made of attorneys. And almost every Congressman and Senator has a law degree."

Hedlund wrote her just published book, the first in a series of planned self-help titles, to help others from being abused in court. She calls her book "the first insider's guide on how to hire, deal with, fire and even sue a lawyer!"

Among her suggestions for checking out an attorney are:

1. Trust your gut. Hedlund says attorneys are taught

to wear symbols of success, such as having a Mercedes-Benz, dozens of legal assistants, and a high-rise office. "But when you ask for his client list and it can't be located, perhaps he's not as successful as you think or he's lost his clients to an over-enthusiasm for Ferraris."

2. Watch him perform. Hedlund suggests you attend a courtroom when your prospective attorney is about to appear. "Observe if the judge admonishes him for failure to show up last week, or for not presenting properly presented drafted motions or other problems."

3. Be cautious of retainers. "When the attorneys I hired saw me coming, it had to have been Champagne City for them," Hedlund writes in *Help! I've Hired a Lawyer!* "I handed over retainers that could keep a family of four eating for years." Be sure you completely understand what you are asked to pay, and what you can expect to receive.

4. Ask for file availability. Hedlund says you should always have the right to walk in at any time and request to see your file. She once found notes in her files from her attorney saying she was "A real pain in the ass!" and another inviting an opponent to an expensive club at Hedland's expense. These notes led to Hedlund suing her own lawyers.

"Help! I've Hired a Lawyer!" by Janice Tucker Hedlund, is available for $14.95 from EmptyPockets Ventures, 412

North Coast Highway #380, Laguna Beach, CA 92651. The 149-page paperback offers a wealth of information for readers from all walks of life, lawyers included. It offers strategies, tips, tactics, and inside information on how to work with attorneys in a wide variety of situations.

—end—

• • •

INSIGHT SECRET

What's missing in this release?

Now that I can look back at it after several years have passed, I think the release would have been more powerful by directing people to a website where more of the author's tips could be found.

The press wants helpful tips, but they don't mind telling people where to get more tips.

Next, let me show you the example of one more release for yet another author.

Mike Knox wrote a riveting book on kids in street gangs. While the book is excellent, I knew I couldn't write a release on just *it*. I needed a bigger story. And since Knox hired me to write one release per month for three months, I needed three terrific stories. What I did was read his book and look for the news. After an hour, I came up with the following headline:

"Ex-Cop Reveals the 'Big Lies' that Pull Kids into Street Gangs Tells How Parents and Schools Can Stop It in New Book"

There's a chapter in Knox's book where he talks about

the three lies that lead kids into gangs. I made that my focus, hence the headline. The sub-headline was my way of letting editors know a little more information about the book. As for my first line, here's what I wrote:

"After fifteen years on the Houston Police Department, Mike Knox had seen enough about kids in street gangs to write a book. And he did just that."

This sounds interesting. You have a cop with a lot of experience in a big city. It suggests he has a story to tell (as he "had seen enough"), and it has universal appeal, as it's about kids.

Here's the entire release:

• • •

NEWS from Awareness News Service

Contact: Joe VitaIe

Phone: 512-847-3414

Date: August 10, 1995 For September 1 Release Ex-Cop Reveals the 3 "Big Lies" that Pull Kids into Street Gangs Tells How Parents and Schools Can Stop It in New Book (Houston, September 1, 1995).

After fifteen years in the Houston Police Department, Mike Knox had seen enough about kids in street gangs to write a book.

And he did just that.

"The police officer is the last and weakest link in this ugly web of gangs and juvenile crime," explains Knox, now a popular speaker on the subject of gang prevention and a special trainer to the police. "Parents and school officials have to wake up and take action now, before it's too late."

Knox helped create the Houston Police Department's Westside Command Divisional Gang Unit in 1988. He has taught gang recognition and investigation at the Houston Police Academy, University of Houston, and the Houston Drug Enforcement Agency.

He says youths are being drawn into gangs in an almost natural process. He wrote his new book to help blow the whistle on this process.

"There are three big lies which pull kids into street gangs," says Knox in his eye-opening new book, "Gangster in the House" (now at book stores, or $12.95 from Momentum Books, 6964 Crooks Road, Troy, Ml 48098).

Lie #1: The gang will provide protection to the member. "Children are increasingly concerned about their safety in the community and in the school," writes Knox in "Gangsta in the House." He adds that many kids will choose to join the largest and toughest gangs simply because they are perceived as the safest.

Lie #2: Membership will garner the respect of the community. "Typically gang members will mistake fear for respect," writes Knox. He says that kids don't know the difference, but seek the recognition of being in a gang and being feared.

Lie #3: The gang will become a family. Knox says this is an illusion because gang members don't even trust their own friends. One of the reasons they use street names or monikers is so each remains anonymous.

What can adults do to help?

"Ultimately the parents' responsibility in this safety net is to reteach the child how to make good friends," writes Knox. "They must be willing to get back into their child's life and reteach him about respect, friendship, and responsibility."

Knox's book, "Gangsta in the House," takes readers directly into the world of gangs, and begins with a riveting and uncomfortable description of a fictional drive-by shooting. The book is written in a conversational style and reveals what gangs are all about, why boys as well as girls are drawn into them, and what parents, teachers, and the legal system can do about them.

—end—

• • •

You might note that in the above examples, I gave truly helpful information that came from the books I wanted to promote.

In other words, the first one offered a free plan to build something from a pallet, the second gave tips on working with lawyers, and the last revealed some myths about gangs. This is "giving to get." The press loves it.

INSIGHT SECRET

But again, it would be wise to give just a handful of tips, and then direct people to your website for more tips.

When I wrote a news release for my client to help promote his trilogy of videos on *The Las Vegas Showgirl's Diet and Workout*, we included the girls' dieting tips. That free information gave us national publicity when the GLOBE ran the story – and Barbara Walters mentioned it on national television!

The Amazing Breakthrough Formula Called E-DR Publicity

Master copywriter David Garfinkel and I were talking one day, when he declared that I was the only person on earth that could get a direct response from publicity.

"Huh?" I replied.

"You have invented a new way to get publicity," he explained. "Most people send out news releases to make themselves feel important. You send out news releases to get response."

I hadn't thought of it before that moment with David, but he's right. My news releases are designed to get people to DO something. I call them "direct response" news releases. And since I more often than not distribute my releases online, using a media service such as www.directcontactpr. com, my releases are all "electronic."

So I came up with this phrase to describe my releases: "E-DR Publicity." It stands for "Electronic Direct Response Publicity."

Here's how E-DR Publicity can work for you:

When you offer something free within your news release, do your best to mention that the free item is AT YOUR WEBSITE. This is E-DR Publicity.

In other words, I embed within the news release a reason for people to go to the website, where they will see the free information, AND see whatever it is I want them to buy.

Do you follow this?

You write a news release, embed it with a reason/news to get people to your website, and you send the release out via the web.

THIS is how you use "practically outrageous" publicity to send people to your website!

THIS is the first step in Hypnotic Marketing!
Example:

Read the following and see if you can determine how E-DR Publicity is used:

• • •

Contact: Melissa Heller

Phone: (941) 467-8771 FOR IMMEDIATE RELEASE

Who's going to crack next?

How to tell if you or someone you love is about to snap. Stress at work, home, and even at play is causing more people to crack, or mentally breakdown, than ever before. The problem is leading to a staggering increase of murder, suicide, road rage, family abuse, drug abuse, unhappiness, and much more.

But according to a mental health expert, there is now a way to detect if you or someone you love is about to crack. "If you can spot the person about to mentally snap, you can help them with treatment," says Dr. Leland Heller, a Florida family physician, mental health expert, and author of the new book, "Biological Unhappiness" (Dyslimbia Press,1999).

Dr. Heller says some obvious signs of latent snapping are when a person begins saying things like, "I don't want to live. There's no point to living. Life has no purpose, I'm worthless, There's no point in trying, or Everyone has it in for me."

He adds that anyone talking about suicide and/or homicide, who performs self-mutilation, who talks about violence, hate, or death, or who demonstrates road rage is also showing signs of snapping. "Snapping is part of a biologically based problem that is treatable," explains Dr. Heller. "The trick is to spot someone before they snap." Dr. Heller has a free screening test to find out if a person is about to snap located online at www.biologicalunhappiness.com.

The test helps determine if someone has any of a variety of disorders, from Attention Deficit Disorder or Bipolar Disorder, to Borderline Personality Disorder or Generalized Anxiety Disorder, all of which can lead to snapping, and all are treatable.

"If we catch the problems now, we can help stop more people from snapping," says Dr. Heller. "No one has to suffer. No one has to kill or be killed."

Editors: For a review copy of the book, "Biological Unhappiness," more information, or to interview the author, call (941) 467-8771.

—end—

• • •

Did you notice that the "free screening test" mentioned above isn't in the release itself, but is embedded there as a command to get people to GO to the website to see it?

THAT'S E-DR Publicity!

More Samples:

You can see samples of news releases online every day. Visit www.prweb.com and look around.

• Also take a peek at www.publicityforum.com, The New Publicity Forum and www.directmarketingnewswire. com the Direct Contact News Wire.

• Paul Krupin has a terrific new book on how to get publicity which includes about seventy (70) examples of news releases that got fantastic results. Learn about it at www.trashproofnewsreleases.com.

INSIGHT SECRET

As you look at other news releases, note how many of them don't ask anyone to do anything. In other words, they aren't direct response news releases or E-DR Publicity releases.

Far, far too many news releases that go out every day just say "new product" or "new book" or "new location" which has limited news value to the media.

Again, you want to give the media REAL NEWS, and within that news you want to embed a command to get people to go to your website.

As you read the news releases you find online, note how many lack what I want yours to have.

A New Way to Get 30 Times More Replies from the Media!

Here is a truly million dollar tip.

It's a new way to send out your news releases. I discovered it by accident, while helping an impatient client get in the news.

Simply stated, instead of sending out a news release, you send out the same message but as a "pitch letter."

In other words, you take your news release, knock off the contact information at the top, and instead begin it with "Dear Editor."

It's the same message – it can even be the exact same news release – but you simply put it in letter form. When I did this for my antsy client, he got 30 times MORE replies from the letter, than from the news release.

Keep in mind that editors will always want to see traditional news releases. So don't stop sending them out. But if you notice a lull in replies, you might want to send out the same writing as a letter to editors.

Here's an example of what I mean.

First, here's the news release in the traditional format:

• • •

Contact: Phone:

E-mail:

FOR IMMEDIATE RELEASE

Proven Tips to Morph from Chief Cook to CEO

Executive Coach Reveals Stall-Stoppers

Why do most growing companies stall at the $3-10million dollar range? Why do most upcoming executives get stuck at one level in the company? Why do most entrepreneurs stop growing at a certain point?

Paul Lemberg, executive coach, strategic consultant, and author of the new book, "Faster Than the Speed of Change," (http://www.paullemberg.com/articles.php) offers 19 tips for moving through stalls in a company or an individual. "Most entrepreneurs running companies today were at one time in sales, marketing, finance, engineering, research –whatever," explains Lemberg. "They were never trained to be CEOs."

Lemberg says these entrepreneurs and executives need a push to get past the stage they're in. But they aren't the only ones who stall.

"Companies almost always stall somewhere in the $3-10 million range," adds Lemberg. "One of the key reasons for this is the CEO holds on to one or more critical areas – thinking he/she can do it better, or there's no time to train anyone anyway. That's plain wrong."

Lemberg's 19 tips for moving out of a stall are located online at http://www.paullemberg.com/articles.php. Here are some of his points:

*Ask of each new task before you: "Who is the best

person to be doing this task?"

*Ask specifically for what you want, including conditions of satisfaction, and time frames. Don't expect people to read your mind.

*Skip the morning news on TV It's primarily negative.

Skip the late night news on TV. It's even more negative than the morning news. Go to sleep earlier, read, or write a journal.

*Start each day with 30-60 minutes of reading – business, educational or inspirational.

*Whatever you are currently complaining about – stop it.

* Figure out what you are very good at doing – delegate or outsource the rest.

*Ask yourself, "Is what I am doing the highest value contribution I can make now?" If not, don't do it.

EDITORS: To reach Paul Lemberg, author of "Habits of the Rich," call (858) 951-3055. His contact page is http://www.paullemberg.com/contact-us/. Website is http://www.paullemberg.com/articles.php. His complete tips are at http://www.paullemberg.com/articles.php.

—end—

• • •

And here's the same release turned into a pitch letter:

Dear Editor:

Why do most growing companies stall at the $3-10 million dollar range? Why do most upcoming executives get stuck at one level in the company? Why do most entrepreneurs stop growing at a certain point?

Paul Lemberg, executive coach, strategic consultant, and author of the new book, "Faster Than the Speed of Change," (http://www.paullemberg.com/articles.php), offers 19 tips for moving through stalls in a company or an individual.

"Most entrepreneurs running companies today were at one time in sales, marketing, finance, engineering, research – whatever," explains Lemberg. "They were never trained to be CEOs."

Lemberg says these entrepreneurs and executives need a push to get past the stage they're in. But they aren't the only ones who stall. "Companies almost always stall somewhere in the $3-10 million range," adds Lemberg. "One of the key reasons for this is the CEO holds on to one or more critical areas – thinking he/she can do it better, or there's no time to train anyone anyway. That's plain wrong."

Lemberg's 19 tips for moving out of a stall are located online at http://www.paullemberg.com/articles.php. Here are some of his points:

- Ask of each new task before you: "Who is the best person to be doing this task?"
- Ask specifically for what you want, including conditions of satisfaction, and time frames. Don't expect people to

read your mind.
- Skip the morning news on TV; It's primarily negative.
- Skip the late night news on TV; It's even more negative than the morning news. Go to sleep earlier, read, or write a journal.
- Start each day with 30 to 60 minutes of reading — business, educational or inspirational.
- Whatever you are currently complaining about – stop it.
- Figure out what you are very good at doing – delegate or outsource the rest.
- Ask yourself, "Is what I am doing the highest value contribution I can make now?" If not, don't do it.

To reach Paul Lemberg, author of "Faster Than The Speed of Change," call (858)951-3055. His contact form is http://lemberg.com/contact-paul/. Website is http://www.lemberg.com. His complete tips are at http://www.paullemberg.com/articles.php.

Pretty simple change, wasn't it?

And did you note that both versions were E-DR Publicity in action?

Both gave a few tips but said the entire list of tips was online, meaning you had to go there to get the entire list.

Try it!

14 Instant Ways to Send out Your News

I use Paul Krupin's service at http://www.directcontactpr. com. I've known Paul for years now. He is so honest that he won't send out any release if he feels it won't get any replies. You can e-mail him at Paul@DirectContactPR. com.

Other Press Release Resources:

• http://www.gebbieinc.com
• http://www.directcontactpr.com/
• http://www.srds.com

Press Release Distribution Services:

• http://www.prweb.com/
• http://www.internetnews.com
• http://www.urlwire.com
• http://www.businesswire.com/portal/site/home/

And here's a surprise bonus tip:

You can get the media to come to you by being alerted when the media is about to do a story in your area of expertise! I tested this service and was talking to a reporter from Business Week magazine the next day. See http:// www.PRLeads.com.

And now let me tell you how to get on virtually any radio or TV show you can think of !!!

Two Words That Can Get You on Virtually Any Radio or TV Show (and a Secret Way to Even Get on Oprah)

One day, a client of mine e-mailed me a copy of his recent news release. I looked it over. It was actually pretty good. But this is what I wrote back to him:

"Dear Scott. I like your news release. The thing is, I no longer believe that news releases are the best way to break into the news. For one thing, everyone and his brother (and his sister, cousin, and dogs and cats) are sending out news releases. Some stations and papers receive hundreds of news releases every day. That's tough competition, my friend.

"So what do I suggest you do today? Call them. Call the shows or the papers. Tell them you have a story idea. They will give you about 30 seconds to pitch your news. If it grabs them, you're in. If it doesn't, no news release would do the trick."

I still believe that news releases are a good way to get news to the media. But those news releases had better be pretty darn hypnotic.

Today, I believe that to really get the most bang for your efforts, calling the media will almost always be a better choice. Here's why:

- You make instant personal contact. You'll either talk to someone who can make a snap decision, or you will get to leave a voice recording offering your news. You never know who, if anyone, will see a news release. Calling makes instant contact.

- You will be forced to think of news, and not selling. If you call a show and say you are the world's greatest whatever, they will snub you. You will be instantly pegged as a salesperson. But if you call the shows and offer them a story, you'll be seen as a person helping them with their job.

Again, if you want to get on a radio or television show, call them. Here's how:

- Get a copy of the Media Directory for the city where you live. These are usually sold by the Chamber of Commerce for that city. Media Directories list every radio, TV, newspaper, magazine, etc., in that city. You might also do a search at http://www.directcontactpr.com/ for the contact information for the show or newspaper you are trying to reach.

- Think through your news story. You want to offer a story idea. Pretend you are a reporter. What would he or she consider to be genuine news? Remember, you can't pass advertising off as news. You want to hide your selling within a news story. Think NEWS.

- Call the station or news desk. Ask for the story editor or assignment editor. Do your best to have a name to ask for. Once on the phone, quickly pitch your idea. Say something like: "I'm calling with a story idea. In a nutshell, here it is –" And then tell them what would normally be your news release's headline. Get that person's attention.

That's all there is to it.

I understand that you may be shy about making the call. I can relate because I've always basically been shy. I would much sooner write an e-mail than make a call.

The thing is, calls are immediate and get results. There's no way around it. If you truly want to use *Hypnotic Marketing* to get rich in your own business, then you need to be willing to make calls.

And keep in mind that if for some reason making calls is keeping you awake at night, then hire someone to do it for you. Just be sure this person has good phone manners so they don't inadvertently cause you damage.

In short, the two words that can get you on any radio or television show are these:

Call them!

And when you have a reporter on the phone, always remember the other five words that they love to hear but rarely hear:

"How can I help you?"

In other words, once you have a media person on the line, ask how you might help them. See what THEY need. The more you can help them, the better they will want to help you.

When FOX TV News in Houston called me one day (as a result of a news release I sent locally), I treated the reporter like a queen. She came out, interviewed me, and we had a great time. But before she left, I asked her, "How can I help you?" She looked at me. I went on to ask, "What stories are you looking for? I might be able to help you with them."

That one question made me look wonderful in her eyes. Whenever I called her after that day, she always treated me well, and was always glad to hear from me.

One more thing…

If you're trying to get on Oprah, forget calling her.

She doesn't work that way. Instead, get the following book:

The Ultimate Guide to Getting Booked on Oprah: 10 Steps to Becoming a Guest on the World's Top Talk Show is a book packed with inspiring tips to help you become an irresistible Oprah guest.

My colleague Susan Harrow, a media coach, publicist, and marketing expert, explains how you can use the secrets of top publicists to get yourself invited on the most influential talk show in America. Get it at: http://www. PRSecrets.com.

Enough!

Now that you've learned the first step in the *Hypnotic Marketing* strategy — that is, create Hypnotic Publicity — it's time for you to jump into the next step — which is, create hypnotic websites!

I'm excited! Are you?
Let's keep rocking!

STEP 2:
HYPNOTIC WEBSITES

Your Keys to Hypnotic Websites

Now you're ready to hear about the second step in your three step marketing strategy for becoming tsar of your own business online.

To recap:

- Step One is to create a media event – something Practically Outrageous – to drive people to your site.
- Step Two is to have a hypnotic website – something people will love to see, love to tell others about, and will cause them to return repeatedly for more of whatever you got, or buy instantly once they visit your site.

What is a hypnotic website? I think there are two kinds:

- The first kind are deeply information oriented. They are resources. They are knowledge-based sites where people return repeatedly for more information. Over time, people make sales.
- The second kind are instant sales closers. These are sites with such strong, hypnotic copy that sales are made instantly.

For example, www.amazon.com is a hypnotic website of the first kind. I go to it nearly every day. And I buy something from it virtually every week.

Why is it hypnotic? Because I am a bookaholic and I

can get any book I want with a simple click. So, for me, that site is riveting. It is the ultimate resource for books. For me, that's hypnotic.

An example of the second category is the site Mark Joyner, my friend and CEO of Aesop Marketing Corporation, put online to sell my video *How to Create Advertising That Sells*. The site was not originally designed for repeated visits, but for a direct sale. It would accomplish that by seeing a quiz when visitors would go there. The quiz was very interactive.

And that's another clue to a hypnotic website: They are interactive. Browsers get to DO something.

Again, part of the secret is in how it interacts with you. We made the quiz fun and engaging.

Still another website put together by the brilliant Mark Joyner is for Paul Krupin's great book on how to write news releases. Go to www.trashproofnewsreleases.com and you'll see your own name in the headline.

Now THAT is hypnotic! Why? Because the site personalizes itself for you.

And there's another hint for making hypnotic websites: Make them personal.

Again, let me show you what I mean. When I went to www.trashproofnewsreleases.com, the site asked for my first and last name. It then loaded with the following:

Click here to view the page: www.trashproofnewsreleases. com.

Seeing your own name on the web page is very hypnotic, isn't it?

Again, go there and see for yourself. When you see your name in the headline, it's hard to ignore the rest of the web copy!

Ok. I said there are two kinds of Hypnotic Websites: Information rich and direct sales.

But — Which is best?

When I attended Mark Joyner's seminar in Las Vegas in October of 2001, he said the most effective websites are those that have one purpose only. His websites are all examples of that philosophy.

If you want my *Hypnotic Writing* book, you go to www.hypnoticwriting.com. If you want my *Advanced Hypnotic Writing* book, you go to http://www.hypnoticmarketing.com/ His sites are focused, filled with strong copy designed to go for and get the sale. As a result, those sites are hypnotic.

I could go on and on talking about websites that I think are hypnotic and noting what makes them so.

For example, the site for my first e-book, *Hypnotic Writing*, is a hypnotic site from the second category. Every time I read the sales letter at that site, (at www.hypnoticwriting.com) I want to order the book being sold – and I wrote the book!

Click here to view the page: www.hypnoticwriting.com.

My own website at www.mrfire.com is more of a site from the first category. It is an information site. It is not totally information based, as it is "Joe Vitale's" site. That means it is still ego driven. So, you see, my own site doesn't qualify as a fully hypnotic website. It has elements of a good site because there is loads of information there. But because nearly everything is by or about me, it's not a hypnotic website as I define it.

What you are going to learn over the next few chapters is how to create a website or improve the one you have – so it can be declared a truly Hypnotic website.

To accomplish that, I'm going to go to the experts – peers of mine – and ask them for some help. You're in for a treat!

A Master Copywriter Reveals His Inner Secrets

Master copywriter David Garfinkel sent the following e-mail to me:

Hi Joe,

I'd certainly recommend my site as an example – http://www.davidgarfinkel.com

It gets me prospects out of the blue and gives a lot of confidence to people who were already thinking of working with me.

One of my clients, Internet Dental Alliance, puts together sites that I would definitely call hypnotic. Take a look at this one as an example: http://www.internetdentalalliance.com/

I know from research that this site gets the dentist 23 new patients a month.

I would say a site that is hypnotic is a site that, when viewed by a qualified prospect, renders the prospect incapable of not acting and makes it very hard for that prospect to say "no!"

What makes it hypnotic?

The writing starts "in the prospect's world," as opposed to most Websites, which start in the world of the business that owns the site.

Each page starts with a compelling headline.

The language and content of the site is inviting and interesting, and moves the reader into a state of trust and subsequently into taking action.

Hope that helps.

Cheers,

David

David's site is focused on you – the prospect – and what you can get from his services.

Here's his front page:

Click here to view the page: http://www.davidgarfinkel. com.

His site is packed with information to help you make a decision to hire him.

As for the dental site that brings in 3-5 new patients, it looks like this ...

Click here to view the page: http://www. internetdentalalliance.com/.

Did that site grab you?

I bet it didn't – unless you're looking for a dentist!

And that's the point: A hypnotic website is targeted. It knows who it wants, and it is written to their interests.

When you create your website, always, always, always, think of the prospects you want to reach. Focus on them. Speak to them. Address them.

Remember my motto: "Get out of your ego and into their ego."

Do that and you're well on the way to having a hypnotic

website that those people cannot resist – even if you're a dentist!

A Forbidden Persuasion Master Reveals His Secrets

Blair Warren is a producer for a nationally syndicated TV show. He's also the author of an amazing underground book titled *The Forbidden Keys to Persuasion*. I asked him for his vote and insights about hypnotic websites. Here's his reply:

Hi Joe,

The only website that really grips me is http://www.drudgereport.com.

I'm not alone in this opinion. Virtually everyone I work with and see every day makes multiple visits to this site daily.

It is a stark, black and white, very basic site that is really nothing more than a collection of great links to other news stories.

What makes me visit it multiple times a day is that he revises it minute to minute. He often breaks new stories and always has the biggest headlines available within minutes of them occurring. Drudge usually has a counter on his front page that shows him getting about 2 million hits a month. Pretty impressive.

What do I think makes a website hypnotic? Great copy.

Period. Except for generating a thematic feel, graphics don't mean a thing to me. I want engaging copy ...especially copy that I don't have to click all over the place to read. Every time I have to click to continue reading is another moment I have to pull my head out of the trance and think about what I'm doing. Suck me in and pull me to the close. Don't make me hunt and peck to go through your message.

Not very flashy, but that's what I think makes a website hypnotic. Website designers may not appreciate the simplicity, but I think web visitors do.

I'm sure I can come up with more ideas if this isn't enough for you. I saw your new photo gallery and articles. Looks great...as always!

Hope all is well. Say hi to Nerissa.
Blair

This is a site from the first category of hypnotic websites: It's an information one.

People love it. In fact, 3,594,082 people visited that site in one 24 hour period! As far as I can tell, there is no selling going on there.

But note: The opening headline about the news traitor who wrote a book makes me want that book! So it may lead to sales, after all.

Before I leave this chapter, let me introduce you to a place to get good news.

It's at www.newsforthesoul.com and it's a breath of fresh air in a chaotic time. It, too, is focused on giving information – but of a positive kind.

Click here to view the site now: www.newsforthesoul.
com.

The point here, however, is that a deeply information rich site that changes content often can be magnetic to browsers.

Keep that in mind as we explore a few more fantastic websites ...

A Practical Mystic Reveals His Website Secrets

John Harricharan is the award winning author of *When You Can Walk on Water, Take the Boat*. (Get a free download of it at www.waterbook.com). I asked John for his votes on hypnotic websites, too. Here's his reply:

Hi Joe:

Thanks for your note about "Hypnotic Marketing." And thank you for asking about hypnotic websites for review. Two of my websites that have been drawing lots of traffic are:

http://www.insight2000.com
http://www.powerpause.com

I also find http://www.askalana.com intriguing. It was first mentioned to me by Jonathan Mizel and then later by Declan Dunn.

Then there's Rick Beneteau's site: http://www.interniche.net

I'll see if I could find some others.

I have completed (at least for now) a special website to help those who've been severely affected by our national tragedy.

The URL is http://www.twintowerssupport.com (2015 Update: this website is no longer available).

>   *At this site, my small contribution to the crisis is the gift of electronic versions of two of my books.*
>
>   *Chapter 16 in "When You Can Walk on Water, Take the Boat" will bring a feeling of tolerance and hope to those who read it. "Morning Has Been All Night Coming" will assist many to deal with despair, grief, mourning, and loss. (I think you've read the first one, Joe, so you know what I'm talking about). I think we can change the world, one person at a time. Talk to you soon, my friend.*
>   *John*
>
>   *John is the award winning author of "When You Can Walk on Water, Take the Boat." FREE download at http://www.waterbook.com. Also visit http://www.insight2000.com and http://www.powerpause.com*

Rather than look at all of John's above mentioned sites, let's just take a peek at the opening page to his famous http://www.powerpause.com site. I think you'll notice something fascinating about it.

Click here to view the site: http://www.powerpause.com.

What did you notice?

Besides the strong testimonials which help convince you to read all the web copy, John does something I love. It's one of my favorite ways to write hypnotic copy anywhere. Do you know what I'm referring to? Story.

John tells a story.

I've written about "story selling" in most of my books, and mention it on most of my tapes. Stories are a hypnotic way to grab attention, hold it, and deliver a message. John's website above is hypnotic, largely because of the story it begins to tell.

I'll show you how to write a story no one can resist a little later on in this book. For now, let's keep examining hypnotic websites to see what else we can learn.

Ready?

Declan Dunn Shocks Me with His Website Secrets

Declan Dunn is one of the original Internet marketers. His name is well known and his successes are case stories for all of us to study. Here's his reply to my e-mail requesting his favorite hypnotic websites:

Hi Joe,

What an interesting e-mail. Let me share my feedback.

I'm going to take a chance outside just marketing sites …let me share a few…

1. remember.org; it's the subject matter. The word, Holocaust, is not only the 600th most searched for keyword on the Net, it's also the code concept that comes up whenever a tragedy happens. People come to this site and the sheer imagery, the word, and the impact of the event is beyond hypnotic.

2. fuckedcompany.com; the swear word is a trigger in the URL, and the color and writing style, watching all the crashed dot coms, is mesmerizing. (2015 Update: this website is no longer available).

Like the Holocaust, it is an overwhelming event that is almost unbelievable in a different context …surreal. That's very hypnotic, the combination of colors and language, especially the focused single keyword that sums up the site.

3. http://www.simpleology.com/; as a marketing site, Mark Joyner continually is hypnotic in his copy, and addressing the user directly.

On this page, he asks you to check boxes about yourself, and uses a blue box to emphasize his primary message. In this case, the language is what is hypnotic, orienting you on his message and making you act, so you are part of the sales letter.

What makes a site hypnotic:

Engaging copy that focuses you on nothing else but the message in front of you. Colors that allow you to dive into the copy, rather than distracting you with pictures. Trigger words like Fucked, Holocaust, and in ROibot's case a question like:

Be honest – which of the following phrases have you said to yourself? What this does is take you out of the passive watcher to an involved user.

In the Remember.org case, it is the trigger word 'Remember' and 'holocaust stories,' in FuckedCompany, it is the trigger word and the stories; in Simpleology, it's the copy, the engagement, and once again, the stories.

Trigger words, color, and stories ...that's hypnotic. Hope this helps.

Peace,

Declan

I had never seen the remember.org site before. I had

heard Declan talk about the site once in Atlanta, at a conference he and I both spoke at. I just now looked at the site and was blown away.

Click here to view the site: http://remember.org/.

You can probably guess that this is a hypnotic website from the first category: Information rich.

You may also note that this site does sell some things, such as books. The information on this site attracts people by the herds. Once here, part of being a complete service to them is offering related products they can buy. This does it beautifully.

Hats off to Declann.

As for his other favorite site, I admire Declan but have a problem with a website focused on negativity.

Fortunately, Larry Chase, another man I admire, posted this in one of his Fall, 2001 newsletters: www.luckedcompany.com (2015 Update: this website is no longer available).

Lucked Company was the companion site to its dark twin, F****d Company. Where FC is filled with uncensored business failure rumors riddled with profanity, LC offered, ah, good news and positive rumors.

Next, let's look at some of the most hard hitting direct selling sites you'll ever find online!

What Are the Hardest-Hitting Direct-Selling Websites Online?

And my dear friend and co-author Jim Edwards wrote the following:

Joe,

Hmmmm.... well here are some websites I have always thought just made me want to take action.

www.amazingformula.com

www.fsbohelp.com

www.instantsalesletters.com

www.mortgageloantips.com

www.gimmesecrets.com

and of course ... www.7dayebook.com which is a damn good site with almost 5% conversion!

I think a hypnotic website:

1. *Moves you emotionally rather than intellectually.*
2. *It gets you thinking not about whether you want the product or not ... but how you can get whatever it is selling and put it to work for yourself.*
3. *It appeals to your gut ... rather than your brain.*
4. *It is subtle in how it moves you ... but it builds incredible emotional momentum as you move through it.*

5. *It gets you talking inside your head ... visualizing the positive results you can get.*
6. *It is believable, inspiring and motivating all at the same time.*
7. *It gets you to paint a clear, vivid and bright picture inside your head about the end result.*

   That's what I think on this Monday night about that ... hope it helps.

Jim

While it may seem self-serving (hey, I am a marketer!), let's look at the 7-Day E-book website: Click here to view the site: http://7dayebook.com.

Which category of website is this?

It's not the end-all and be-all of information on e-books, so it's not from category one.

But this site goes for the sale – directly and relentlessly. So it's a hypnotic website from category number two.

Just a few things to notice about this website:

1. Hard-hitting headline
2. Powerful endorsements
3. Strong benefits
4. Irresistible guarantee
5. Free bonuses for added value
6. Compelling PS's
7. A warning that actually encourages sales

What else did you notice about that website?

Make some notes for yourself and then zip over to the

next chapter and learn about hypnotic websites –from one of the world's greatest hypnotists!

Some Sexy Advice from the World's Greatest Hypnotist

And master persuader, hypnotist, and author Kevin Hogan wrote me the following:

Hi Joe,

Nice to hear from you. Sure you can review kevinhogan. com

I like my friend's website wendi.com for similar reasons as you will read below:

I think what makes a website profitable (at least ours) is the new articles we post every 7-10 days. People can gather information on everything related to mind, body, persuasion, NLP, hypnosis. In each article, we give enough information away, free of charge, that people KNOW they will always win with my products and services. I don't know if this is "hypnotic" in the terms of waving pocket watches, but it sure works in lining the pockets that hold the watches...

Kevin Hogan

Well, let's look at Kevin's site. You'll see that Kevin found a way to make sex help him sell his products and himself. Here's part of the first page of it:

Click here to view the site: http://kevinhogan.com.

Kevin knows what he is doing. His site is an informative one which also leads to sales.

What else can you do to transform a so-so site into a hypnotic one?

Keep reading and see!

How to Transform a So-So Website into a Truly Hypnotic Website

You can learn a lot by studying before and after websites.

In other words, the following is the copy one website was using – which wasn't working. Read it and then look at what I wrote for them later. (2015 Update: the Gold Mine. net website is no longer available).

—The Gold Mine.net is a multi-faceted, multi-dimensional online recruiting tool. It was specifically designed with the serious Network Marketer in mind.

At The Gold Mine.net, we are dedicated to helping you explode your business by providing the best tools available. Our goal is to assist you in uncovering "the gold" you desire!

With The Gold Mine.net you will have a professional web presence with our simple, attractive websites. There are several templates to choose from. A fully automated system allows you to update your picture, story and contact info 24 hours a day, 7 days a week without having to know any programming at all!

The Gold Mine.net will allow you to "strike the gold" in your business by giving you the ability to generate/ pre-qualify your own leads with our striking flash presentation. In addition, turn those prospects into hungry business partners with John Kalench's bestselling book, "The Greatest Opportunity in the History of the World" by giving away this book to your website visitors/prospects for FREE! Also, motivate your prospects from "offline" to "online" by offering them this inspiring book and let it ... "Sell the Dream."

The Gold Mine.net will supply you with the highest quality leads in the industry, too! (*Plans with leads). Our "Gold Mine of Leads," are home-based business opportunity seekers, waiting for you to contact them about your opportunity.

Utilize our leads and get access to our state of the art lead management system, "The Virtual Mining Machine." Let "The Virtual Mining Machine" bridge the gap from high tech to high touch by automatically developing rapport with your prospects via e-mail. Whether you like to build your business face to face, by phone, or on the Internet, "The Virtual Mining Machine" will "mine the gold" by finding, tracking, sorting, and motivating your prospects! It also gives you the flexibility to enter your own generated leads into the system.

The Gold Mine.net is not just another web based program for you to try. We support your vision. We want to become your business partner and assist you in achieving the results you so richly deserve.

Our mission is to be the most successful company of our kind at delivering the ultimate experience for Network Marketers, worldwide!

We will meet the customer's expectations with:
- *Highest quality*
- *Competitive pricing*
- *Simplicity*
- *Leading technology*
- *Superior service*

We look forward to partnering with you and taking your business to the next level.

Now look at what I wrote for them below:

- Are you looking for *qualified* hot leads delivered right TO YOU?
- Are you looking for a *guaranteed* system for turning leads into cash?
- Are you serious about making *A LOT* of money in network marketing?

If you answered "YES!," then you've found GOLD! (Read on to see how you can have all of this for FREE).

Dear Network Marketer,

You may not realize it yet, but you've just discovered the most fantastic, proven, time-tested, simple, and even guaranteed way to turn your networking marketing business into a raging river of residual income!

MILLIONS of dollars have been made with our high quality leads and proven system!

How? You'll soon see that we've created a literal

gold mine for recruiting leads. Our system works and we can prove it to you.

For example, our leads come from websites that get more than 6,000,000 unique visitors every month! Think of it! Over SIX MILLION people go to our sites! And from those six million people, we handpick the golden leads for YOU.

As you probably know, you don't want just "any" lead. You want a *qualified* lead. And that's exactly what we find for you.

You won't get fool's gold from us. Instead, you get the mother lode.

<u>When you join now</u>, you'll get all of the following:

Qualified leads will be fed right to you (as many as you choose)!

• You'll get our time-tested, proven system for turning these leads into profits!

• You'll receive a vault full of free tools, books and materials to give to your leads!

• You'll get your own recruiting flash website to get online fast!

• You'll get a simple, step-by-step system to generate your own gold mine of leads!

The list goes on and on!

As you can see, <u>when you join now</u>, you sign-on to make money! You'll have access to such money-making services as these:

The Virtual Mining Machine™ our patent pending

lead management system is designed for effective recruitment of new, motivated business partners. With our simple at-a-glance technology, you can master The Virtual Mining Machine system in a matter of minutes. With its unique paper less organizer, you'll never lose a hot follow-up again. Point and click for follow-up alerts; point, click and view notes for a lead; point, click and view your lead's detail; point, click and MAKE MONEY!

Also, leverage your valuable time by only spending time with the serious prospects. The Virtual Mining Machine's special "Internet Mining Technology™" will track your prospect's moves and alert you to any actions your leads take to any correspondence.

Prospector's Pipeline™ is our copywriter & e-mail management system. Leverage your time and let our e-mail system funnel your leads through our Prospecting Pipeline for you; point and click and build rapport with thousands of prospects via e-mail. Choose from professionally written letters by world renown copywriter, Joe Vitale, or get trained by the greatest copywriters in the world with our unique copywriter training system and write your very own custom e-mails to close your prospects.

The Virtual Vault™ - You'll have your very own virtual vault full of treasures to unlock vast resources of priceless knowledge and power at "The Virtual Vault. net." *(2015 Update: this website is no longer available).*

These free items you'll receive are all handpicked to keep you motivated, educated, inspired and successful! Plus, you get to give away these items to your prospects for FREE. You'll have all the right tools to make you a master prospector. Imagine having hundreds of miners mining gold 24 hours a day, 7 days a week sharing the dream of network marketing to your leads, which will lead you to a gold mine.

And you'll get an amazing amount of FREE products to keep you and your new leads motivated, trained, and focused on the gold!

AND you can even have all of the above for FREE.

How? Simple. Once you join now, any time you refer 3 people to us, YOU will get your leads and system for FREE. We call it our "3 and it's FREE" policy.

And would you like to know the best news of all?

It's our guarantee.

It's totally unconditional.

If you're not happy within 30 days, let us know and you owe nothing.

Look. Other "systems" out there promise you the moon but deliver nothing but fool's gold. Try them and you'll find out the hard way. The truth is, fool's gold is worthless!

What you want are HIGHLY QUALIFIED leads and a proven, simple system.

You want to hear from and deal with people who are hot to make money and want to work for it.

Right?

Then you've come to the right place. We GUARANTEE your complete satisfaction – or you get your money back. Period!

You'll be given leads of people who declare they want to learn about your product or service. And these leads are usually college educated, make about $50,000 a year on average, and state they WANT to know more!

Can you imagine how easy life will be for you when you can stop cold calling and start milking hot leads?

And just think of how you can make money when you use our proven system to help your leads get out there and build their own business IN YOUR GROUP!

It's all simple, fast, proven, and guaranteed! Are you ready to strike gold?

<u>Join now</u> and start singing "Eureka! I've found GOLD!"

Can you see the differences?

What I do with any copy is *translate* it.

I take what is handed to me – such as the first copy I showed you in this chapter -and I translate it into features and benefits, using active writing and clear benefits – such as the second example above.

That's what you want to do with all your writing.

Look at each sentence and meditate on how you can translate it into something your reader wants to see.

For example, in the first example, there are a lot of "we" sentences. That means the copywriter was focused on his company, not on you, the reader. The thing is, you are the person expected to shell out your money! The copy has to be written to appeal to your interests!

So the second example has a lot of "you" statements in it. That's because I translated the first copy into language you would relate to.

Are you with me?

In order to write hypnotic copy anywhere, you have to focus entirely on your readers, not you.

I admit that this is a tall order. But that's why good copywriters are paid top dollar. When they manage to write copy that brings in sales, that copy can be worth millions of dollars.

Again, your hypnotic publicity should focus on the public, not you; your hypnotic websites should focus on your visitors, not you; and your hypnotic writing should focus on your readers, not you.

But let's take a breath and then look a little deeper at what it takes to create a hypnotic website. Go get yourself a snack.

You deserve it!

How an "Inspirational Folk Musician" Can Create a Hypnotic Website

Todd Silva is a dear friend of mine from my old days in Houston. He's a delightful guitarist. He's performed at several of my book signing parties in the Houston area. He now has his first CD out. And he just put up a website. He asked me to look at it.

I did and I saw that it was nice. It had a nice picture. A nice lay out. Nice words.

But nice isn't enough. Nice isn't hypnotic.

So I made a few suggestions:

- I told Todd that the only people who will find his website are the ones looking for him, personally. While Todd is a wonderful man, he's not going to get a stampede from his name alone. So I suggested Todd arrange to sell other CDs on his site besides his own. This way he could have more profit, too. And the other artists would be interested in helping promote his site.

- But that's not enough. Todd calls himself an "Inspirational Folk" musician. I've never heard that phrase before. So I suggested Todd make his site THE clearinghouse for "Inspirational Folk" music. This could give him lots of reasons to get publicity, and could even lead to musicians begging to be placed on Todd's site.

• Finally, I suggested Todd give away samples of the music. Let people download and listen to anything they wanted. This idea isn't new, and Todd was already going to do it, but I wanted to remind him the when you give, sooner or later you get.

Click here to view the site now: http://sagetone.com/index.html.

In short, Todd's site became much more hypnotic once it wasn't "Todd's" site. Maybe the same can be said for your site. Is your site information-driven or ego-driven?

What You Can Learn from This Really Stupid Website

Today I let the dog in while I sat in my easy chair and caught up on my reading. Within minutes I saw *Hypnotic Marketing* come alive and go to work. Here's what happened:

I was reading *Blink*, a great printed magazine for EarthLink Internet users. I love the magazine because it's packed with great information, cool links, and other useful or just plain interesting material.

As I was browsing this issue, with one eye on my dog to be sure she didn't eat the curtains, I saw a mention for a website called www.stupid.com. It was said to be the best place in the world to buy, well, stupid stuff.

Now note what just happened.

Step One in our "Hypnotic Marketing Formula" kicked in.

In other words, publicity made me aware of the website. And because the mention in the magazine was enticing, it made me want to visit that website.

Are you with me?

Step One is getting publicity to make people aware of and want to visit your site. That's what just happened to me, through the pages of *Blink* magazine.

Later, after I put the dog outside and went upstairs to my office and my computer, I visited the website. And that's where I ran into Step Two in Hypnotic Marketing: I visited a truly hypnotic website.

You're going to have to visit www.stupid.com to see what I mean. You'll find colorful graphics, humorous copy, fascinating products, and much more. I found myself spending a lot more time browsing the site than I ever imagined I would ever spend.

Click here to view the site: www.stupid.com

More than that, I started to order things!

And that's Step Three in the "Hypnotic Marketing Formula." The sales copy on the site is so compelling, I almost couldn't help myself. I wanted to buy, buy, buy!

I wanted several massage pens. That's right: Pens that massage you with a vibrating end. Hey, Christmas is coming up (as I write this) and I wanted to impress a few close friends with a strange but useful new invention.

To give you an idea of how hypnotic their sales copy is, here's the description for their massage pens: (I'm using it here under Fair Use considerations for educational purposes only. The copy of course belongs to the proud owners of www.stupid.com).

Actually, that's not such a stupid device, is it?

I bet you want one, too!

Well, I sure did. I ordered five of them.

But the ordering process at www.stupid.com had a

glitch in it. My order was lost before I got to finalize it. And because most of what I was doing was impulse buying, I didn't feel any real need to stick around and go through the questionable process again.

So, in the end, www.stupid.com lost my sale, which, I guess, was pretty stupid of them.

But please note that they (unknowingly) practiced Hypnotic Marketing!

STEP 1: Their mention in *Blink* magazine got me to know of them and want to visit them.

STEP 2: Their website is fun, engaging, and fast, making it easy for me to get involved and enjoy myself.

STEP 3: Their sales copy was to the point and focused on ME, the consumer, making me WANT to buy.

If you want an example of Hypnotic Marketing alive and well on the net right now, dash over to www.stupid.com and see what I mean!

And to prove to you just how hypnotic www.stupid.com's web copy really is, compare it to this copy from another site selling the same pen:

Product Description:

The unique metal ballpoint pen with built-in massage

Rugged metal construction

Attractive design

Patented massage function

Replaceable ink refills
Batteries included

Is that boring or what?

Obviously www.stupid.com knows the power of a website with vivid writing.

And now let's move into the last step in creating a Hypnotic Marketing campaign.

STEP 3:
HYPNOTIC E-MAIL

The Secret Nobody Wants You to Know about Making Money Online

Jay Abraham and I were talking one day over the phone when he said something revealing:

"The real secret to making money online isn't in websites," Jay said. "It's in e-mail."

He went on to tell me that he thought I was the best user of e-mail marketing he had ever seen. He also said he looked forward to my e-mails and read them with interest. "They're fun," he added.

And my e-mails make money. Jay knows it, too. He went on to say, "I bet you make two million dollars a year from your e-mail campaigns."

I don't. Not yet, anyway. But Jay is absolutely right: E-mail marketing is the most overlooked tool in making money online.

For the purposes of Hypnotic Marketing, having a powerful, fun, interactive, and informative website is just one step of the four steps to success.

(As a gentle reminder, the first step is getting attention with practically outrageous publicity, the second is having a hypnotic website, and the third is using hypnotic e-mail to close sales).

The thing is, e-mail IS the easier and least expensive way I know of to help fuel your Hypnotic Marketing campaign.

How do you make it work?

- First, you need a regular newsletter. This is something you put on your website and have a place for people to subscribe. See my own site at http://mrfire.com for an example of this.

- Second, you need to keep every e-mail address you get in a separate file and protect their privacy. Never sell or give away their trust

- Third, you need to send out e-mails to that list on a regular basis. And right there — in step three — is where you can make yourself rich.

A friend of mine once said, "If you have a list of 10,000 names, you'll never have to work again." Think about that! Just a list of 10,000 names and you can send them e-mail offers – all relevant to their interests, of course – and you can get rich from that alone!

In short, e-mail marketing is the overlooked aspect of Hypnotic Marketing. I'm including it in this book, as the third step for creating a website that works, because this step alone can make you financially free.

Jay Abraham was right.

But how do you use e-mail to your benefit?

How a Famous Street Magician Can Help You Create Hypnotic E-Mail

Today, I watched a video of a magic lecture by famous street magician Jim Cellini. I found the 80 minutes of instruction to be, well, hypnotic.

While I'm not going to tell you any magic secrets in this chapter (or even in this book), I am going to share something that Cellini shared with me – something that can help you create absolutely hypnotic e-mail.

As I said, Cellini is a street magician. That means he performs magic tricks on streets in order to delight people enough into throwing some money into his hat at the end of his show. Street performers can make a lot of money. Some of them can become stars. Harry Anderson, famed actor of the popular television series Night Court, began his career as a street magician.

Making a living this way has to be tough work. You can imagine how challenging it must be to get on a comer and start talking, moving, singing, yelling or whatever it takes to get people's attention. You have to move fast and keep the action going – else you won't create, let alone keep an audience.

Street performers are pitchmen. They are doing

whatever they can to grab you, hold you, and get some money out of you.

I've only known a handful of pitchmen in my life (so far). One of the most famous is Marshall Brodien, a magician considered to be one of the top 100 most influential magicians of the last 100 years.

A year or so ago, Marshall picked me up at my hotel in Chicago and took me to his home, where he and his wonderful wife, Mary, entertained me with stories of pitchmen, early infomercials, and showmen of magic.

Marshall, now a product advisor to famed magician Lance Burton, even performed magic tricks for me. I still can't believe it. Here was one of the most legendary magicians in history, performing magic for me.

When Marshall took me back to my hotel, he talked about being a pitchman. He even remembered his old spiel to round people up. He started to deliver it right there in his car. It was amazing – and fun. I could see that being a pitchman took a lot of energy, courage, and talent.

But back to Cellini ...

During the video of Cellini that I watched today, Cellini summed up a street performer's job. I think it's the same job of your e-mail. It was certainly the same job of Marshall Brodien in his early days. Since it's so wise, so short, and so relevant, I want to share it with you here:

- Stop people.
- Hold people.
- Get money out of people.

That's it!

Again, that's also the job of your e-mail. Let's look at each step:

- **Your e-mail has to stop people**. I get hundreds of messages each day. If I'm not intrigued by the subject line of the e-mail, more often than not, it's trashed. So there's a hint for you: Make your subject line hypnotic.

- **Your e-mail has to hold people**. While you may have gotten me to open your e-mail with a good subject line, I won't keep reading unless your main benefits are right up front. So there's another hint for you: Make your opening paragraphs grabbers – packed with curiosity and/or direct benefits to ME, the reader.

- **Your e-mail has to make money**. You may not need every e-mail you send out to be a direct money-maker. Sometimes your e-mails will be to build rapport and relationships. So that's another hint: Never forget that your e-mail is intended to make money, either now, or soon.

Ever since the September 11, 2001 terrorist attacks, when the threat of biological warfare hit the country, more businesses are turning to e-mail to get their message and their offers to their prospects.

What does this mean?

Your e-mail box is gonna be stuffed!

You better focus on sending e-mails that are hypnotic – that do what Harry Anderson and Marshall Brodien had to do, and what Jim Cellini said all good street performers

must do:
- Stop people.
- Hold people.
- Get money out of people.

The next few chapters will help you do just that — like magic!

How to Create E-Mails That Secretly Seduce Your Readers

I was sitting in a doctor's office reading the book I had brought along when I had a major insight.

I was reading Vernon Howard's famous self-help classic, *Psycho-Pictography: The New Way to Use the Miracle Power of Your Mind*. The book is famous, still in print, and well worth your time to read it.

As I was reading, it suddenly dawned on me that the little stories Howard used throughout the book were in fact hypnotic inductions. He called them "Mental Pictures" and tied them to the title of his book. In essence, they were very brief stories that created a scene in your mind. These little scenes would then enter your unconscious and silently work to alter your thinking. They were subtle hypnotic commands.

Here's an example from Howard's book:

"A war drama on television showed a corporal captured by a pair of soldiers in enemy uniforms. The soldier tried to escape several times but was recaptured. It turned out to be a happy capture for the corporal, for his 'enemies' turned out to be members of his own army in disguise. A new truth is sometimes like that. We resist it, only to find later

that it is our friend."

That is a very short story from Howard. Some of his other "mental pictures" are longer, even several paragraphs very long. But the point is this: They are designed to deliver a message to you without being heavy handed about it.

When I read his book, I suddenly realized that just as Howard's "mental pictures" were entering my mind below my overly conscious awareness, "Hypnotic E-mail" containing sales messages could enter the minds of my readers.

Are you with me here?

A "hypnotic letter" doesn't have to look like whatever you think a hypnotic letter should look like. It can in fact be nothing more than a brief story, structured in such a way as to deliver the message you want your reader to get – and act on.

Now how can you use this insight to write your own hypnotic sales copy?

By remembering to tell relevant stories whenever you want to deliver your sales message. Here's an example of a "hypnotic story":

What makes this e-mailed sales letter hypnotic?
by Joe Vitale

I sent the following short sales letter by e-mail to my own list of some 800 names. There was an immediate boost in sales. Amazon.com had to back-order the book I was selling in the letter. My publisher's online server went down due to all the orders they got at once.

But something even more shocking happened.

Many people wrote to me and actually asked how I was able to *make* them read the letter. They said they couldn't stop reading it! Others said they felt compelled by some unseen force to read every word of it. Still, others just mindlessly read the letter but then automatically – as if obeying a subliminal command – went to Amazon.com and ordered the book I was selling. Afterwards, they wrote me and confessed they felt they had been "hypnotized."

What in the world makes this letter so hypnotic? Read it and see what you think:

• • •

I was nearly in tears...

Dear Friend:

I was just in the bathroom, reading a letter from my sister, when I got to the line...

"I got your book and I read it and I thought it was great. And after I read it, I went out and got myself a new car."

I thought she was kidding. My sister has been on welfare, struggled to raise three kids, been wrestling with health problems, and has fought toe to toe with poverty for years. I wrote my latest book, "Spiritual Marketing," for her, in an attempt to help her.

But it wasn't until moments ago that I discovered that my book had such a profound impact on her that she not only read it, and liked it, but she went out and made a dream of hers come true.

Later in the same letter she wrote, "Dad read your book before I did and he knew I wanted a new car and he told me that once I read your book, he would guarantee that I would buy a new car."

That's even more unbelievable. My father has never even acknowledged receiving any of my books, let alone taken the time to read them. But he read "Spiritual Marketing," and it apparently had an impact on him, too.

I'm sharing all of this with you today because you are someone on my personal e-mail list, and this is personal news which I think can inspire others to go for, and get, their dreams. Whether it's a new car, a new house, more money, real love, or happiness in this moment, it's all possible.

Just ask my sister.

Joe Vitale

PS — Amazon.com now carries "Spiritual Marketing." (2015 Update – *Spritual Marketing* is still available, however, the book has since gone through two revisions and is now titled: *The Attractor Factor: 5 Easy Steps for Creating Wealth (or Anything Else) from the inside out*).

• • •

Well, what do you think? Why does this letter hypnotize people?

Here's what I think:

The headline, "I was nearly in tears ... ", which was the subject line on the e-mail I sent out, is riveting. People want to know why I'm nearly in tears. Did something bad happen? Or something good? Was I crying? Or laughing so hard I cried? Your headline has to be a gun in a prospect's face. While most headlines have to be benefit-oriented, curiosity-invoking headlines are proven to grab readers, too.

The opening sentence, "I was just in the bathroom, reading a letter from my sister, when I got to the line...," not only compels you to read the second sentence, it is actually impossible to complete the first sentence – because it doesn't end! Those dashes are grabbing your nose and pulling you into the next sentence, which happens to be the next paragraph.

The letter weaves a story. Stories sell. Stories compel. Stories pull people into the drama unfolding and make them a part of the action. As this letter reveals its story, it also conveys selling messages to you hypnotically – messages that urge you to get this book now.

The letter reeks of sincerity. I learned that sincerity sells. Sincerity is hypnotic. Don't lie or mislead or gyp people. Tell your story in the most hypnotic way possible and the people most interested in it will respond.

The ending PS, "Amazon.com now carries 'Spiritual Marketing,'" is a subliminal call to action. While I'm still known for writing fiery PS's that warn you of dangers if you don't act now, my PS above works in a soft-sell way. The story in the letter says "Buy my new book." The PS simply tells you where.

You can take my tried and tested e-mailed sales letter above and use it as a model to write your own hypnotic letter. Here's how:

Just think of a story – a true one, remember – of someone who benefited from your product or service in a record-breaking way, and write the event up, following my formula and my letter. It may help you to remember these key questions:

1. How can you make your headline so curious that people can't help but read your letter?
2. How can you begin your next letter in such a way that it actually forces people to keep reading?
3. How can you tell a story about your product or service that compels people to want it?
4. Are you telling the whole truth in your letter?
5. How can you more softly let people know how to buy your product or service?

Finally, I think the greatest secret to making any sales letter or e-mail message truly hypnotic is in being genuinely excited. My sales letter above is based on what actually happened to me. My sister DID write me. She DID buy a new car. It WAS a result of reading my new book. I was so moved by her news that I conveyed my joy in my sales letter – and that joy became hypnotic to my readers.

As you can see, stories are powerful – and persuasive.

Next, let's look at how to literally grab your readers – hold them tight!

The Five Best Ways to Create Hypnotic E-mail Openers

At the Mark Joyner seminar in Las Vegas in October, Alex Mandossian told me something surprising.

He said that people think of me as the man able to create the most powerful "Hypnotic Openers." When I asked him to explain, he said people always told him how impressed they are at my ability to write compelling openings to e-mail, sales letters, articles, books, and news releases.

I never realized people recognized my openings as hypnotic. I work relentlessly on openings to make them engaging. With that in mind, I thought I would teach you how to write hypnotic openers. Here are my five favorite ways:

1. Curiosity
2. Questions
3. Stories
4. News
5. Human interest

Now here are examples of each:

1. Curiosity: "I was nearly in tears."
2. Question: "What are the 5 best ways to a Hypnotic

Opening?"

3. Story: "I found money under my bed when I woke up this morning."

4. News: "Something shocking happened on October 6, 2001 in Las Vegas."

5. Human Interest: "Kathy didn't realize the power of her pinkie until she poked her assailant."

And here are some insights into each approach:

Curiosity not only killed the cat, but can lead to many sales. I love to intrigue people with openings that force you to read more to understand them. The way to use curiosity is to think like a magician. Tell people what they will get but not how they will get it. An example might be, "Seaweed made me lose weight even when I drank beer and ate pizza." That's curious. Trivia can be curiosity provoking, too. "Why did Joe Vitale put the phrase 'Ask me about the monkey' on his business cards?" Curiosity openers can also be odd. For example: "Marketing man channels P.T. Barnum."

Questions can wrap someone's mind around your sales pitch. "What are the 5 best ways to create hypnotic openers?" transforms a statement into high intrigue. I LOVE this method for creating hypnotic openers. Take any statement you want to make and turn it into a question. An example might be, "I can teach you how to drive traffic to your website" is weak but as a question, "How can I teach you to drive traffic to your website?" is strong.

Stories are magical! They are one of the lost secrets to success. Simply tell a story that conveys your message. Instead of telling me your new product is great, tell me a story about someone who used it and discovered it to be great. A secret tip here is to use lots of dialogue. People LOVE dialogue in stories.

News is what virtually everyone wants. That's why we read the newspapers, and watch TV. State your opening as a news story, in the way a reporter might write it. Example might be: "Today at noon a new software appeared that is making many people's lives easier."

Human interest tap into all of our hearts. This can be considered a combination of story, curiosity and news. Tell us about someone who uses your service. "Bonnie was on welfare until she read my latest book. Yesterday she bought a new car as a result."

Go ahead and take a few moments dabbling with some e-mail openers before going on to the next chapter.

How Can the Right Question Bring in 317% More Orders?

What's a proven way to get people to read your e-mail?

One of the best ways to get people to read your sales letters, ads, e-mail or other sales copy is to open with a question.

But there's a catch:

The *type* of question you use can increase your sales – or kill them dead.

Most people use a yes/no question for their headline. They may ask, "Do you want to save money on your taxes?"

What's wrong with that headline? The nature of the question leaves people with the ability to answer yes or no – and not read anything more! The more hypnotic headline is a question that people *cannot* answer *without* reading the entire body of your sales letter, ad or e-mail.

Here's an example of how you can use this method:

Instead of "Do you want to save money on your taxes?" change it to the more open ended, "Which of these ways will help you save money on your taxes?"

The word "which" is the key in that example. Obviously, you can't answer the question without reading the entire sales copy below it!

I once increased sales in an ad by a documented 317% with this method. The ad the job placement service ran for their new software asked, "Will this new software help you find more recruits?" You can answer that question with yes or no and forget the ad. That's not hypnotic.

I changed the ad to the much more engaging, "How will this new software help you find more recruits?" Here, the word "how" is the key. It is now a question that no one can answer without reading the entire ad. As a result, sales exploded 317 times over the previous ad.

Want more proof?

Note the title of this very chapter: "How can the right question bring in 317% more orders?" You can't answer it without reading this chapter! And note how I began this chapter. I used the question, "What's a proven way to get people to read your e-mail?"

Again, you have to keep reading to find out!

And now that you have read this chapter, you can go on and create hypnotic headlines of your own.

Hmm ... which e-mail will you try this hypnotic technique on first?

E-Mail Sales Letter Samples That Are Making Me Rich

Late in 1999, I decided to teach an e-class. There's a whole fascinating story behind that decision, which is explained in an article at my website called *How I Made $68,000 Teaching E-classes.*

What I want to share with you here are the e-mail letters I used to fill that first e-class – a class which was taught entirely by e-mail and which brought me more than $21,000 in less than a week.

(That's right: $21,000 in less than one week!)

Here is the first letter I sent to my list, which at that time was barely 800 names:

• • •

Subject line: Announcing Spiritual Marketing class online

You are invited to join a new online private e-class led by me revealing Spiritual Marketing: How to Increase Your Wealth from the Inside Out.

The following e-newsletter will explain the details. But first... You are receiving this because you either asked to be on The Copy Writing Profit Center's exclusive announcements list at http://www.mrfire.com, or you are a personal friend of mine. If you don't want to receive these monthly messages, just send a polite note to me at remove@mrfire.com, and I'll take your name off my list. BTW, your e-mail address will never be sold or given to anyone by me. Finally, feel free to forward the following to your friends. Thanks! Joe

* I've decided to offer a five-week, private, online intensive workshop to a select group of 15 people on the subject of "Spiritual Marketing." I'm not sure how to convey just how powerful this event can be for you. Not only will you learn the proven 5-step method for creating anything you can imagine in your life, but you'll also get my unpublished book on the subject, AND you will get 5 weeks of personal e-coaching from me so you know how to apply these steps to YOUR life and YOUR business.

What are the principles? And what can you do with them?

In short, I'm talking about learning to influence your world by what you do INSIDE yourself. In 1906, Elizabeth Towne wrote, "Man is a magnet, and every line and dot and detail of his experiences come by his own attraction."

Change the vibratory quality of your inner magnet, and you'll change the results you get in your life. The 5 principles you'll learn in Spiritual Marketing will tell you exactly how to alter the experiences you are getting (including the amount of money you make) by working from the inside out.

As for what you can achieve with these steps.... Anything you can imagine! I mean that literally. Most of my successes have come from this mental-spiritual way of walking through life. In this course, you'll hear of people who healed relationship problems, cured such "incurables" as cancer, increased their income, and much more. The truth is, there are no limits – other than the ones in your own mind. This e-course WILL expand your mind.

Here's how the e-class will work:

I'll allow 15 people, tops, to join. I have to limit this program to only 15 people so I can be sure to give each the personal attention they may want.

Each week I will e-mail out an article by me on that week's lesson. You can then reply to the article, by e-mail, and give me questions unique to you and your business. I will then answer them, giving you specific ways you can apply the lesson to your business. In this way you will not only get the lessons, but you'll get my personal e-coaching, as well. We'll do all of this by e-mail, simplifying the process for both of us.

Obviously, some of your questions may be more marketing-oriented than spiritually-oriented. No problem. I'm also willing to review any sales letters, ads, or news releases you may write during this five week e-class.

How much will this cost? If you paid my hourly rate for personal instruction over a five week period, you would have to pay several thousand dollars and maybe refinance your home.

But for this exclusive, limited new e-class, the fee is only $1,500. You can pay by credit card or check. It would of course make a great investment for your future (for the new year and the new century!), a great gift to yourself (a Christmas gift to you!) and it's probably tax deductible (check with your CPA). All in all, it's a small investment for such a life-changing, money-making new experience that will help you create whatever you can imagine.

Is the course guaranteed? You bet. Sign up now. If you're not happy after the first lesson, tell me and you can have ALL of your money back.

Will the principles work for you? It's up to you. I'm giving you the tools – hammer, nails, etc.. Whether you build a dog house or a castle is your choice. I say THINK BIG.

Isn't it time? Aren't your dreams worth it? Aren't YOU?

If you have questions, e-mail me at `joe@mrfire.com`. Again, only 15 people can attend. I urge you to register right now. And keep in mind that there are several people who will automatically register for this class as soon as they get this e-mail, so if you want in, tell me NOW.

Note: Course will begin Tuesday, January 11, 2000. You MUST register by January 5, 2000 to be included in this e-class. Remember, this is all done by e-mail, so you can receive and reply to the lessons at your convenience. I don't plan to offer this program again, so I urge you to sign up right NOW.

Merry Christmas – and Happy New Century!

Joe Vitale

****

`www.miraclescoaching.com`

Joe "Mr. Fire!" Vitale – Author of way too many books to list here so go see my truly amazing giant website at http://www.mrfire.com

• • •

Frankly, I was disappointed at the response. Only a handful of people replied. Of course, that meant about $7,000 – from one e-mailed letter!

But I wanted more.

So then I did something you should do in all your marketing...

Here's my follow-up e-mailed letter to my own list to encourage people to register for my first e-class:

• • •

Subject line: The Truth About Spiritual Marketing

Still wondering if you should sign up for my online class, "Spiritual Marketing: How to Increase Your Wealth from the inside out"?

Maybe the following will help ...

Quite a few people are wondering what kind of "spiritual" marketing program I am offering, or even qualified to teach. They've asked some excellent questions.

In the interest of helping everyone sort out spiritual matters the way I've experienced them here on the earthly plane – and to help people who might want this class decide how it fits in with their beliefs and their goals – I want to tell you a short bit about myself and my experience with spiritual marketing, and why I'm offering this class.

Then for those of you who want more depth, I'm

including a reprint from the unpublished book that is part of this course.

"Spirit" as I have experienced it, is not only a religious or metaphysical subject. It is an alternative, and I think, a much more natural way of living all of your life, including, quite appropriately, the business portion of your life.

It's certainly more peaceful and rewarding than the conventional alternative – both in the inner peace it delivers, and also in the tangible accomplishments it makes almost effortless. I sometimes call "Spiritual Marketing" the "lazy way to success," as most of the time it works as if by magic.

For example, I have done the following …

Written nine books on sales, marketing, advertising and publicity.

Recorded a bestselling audiotape program for Nightingale-Conant.

Recorded a bestselling audio program overseas on marketing.

Made several people millionaires through one-shot publicity.

Helped promote one of the most successful infomercials of the 90s.

Saw my most recent book become an overnight bestseller.

…and virtually all of the above occurred without my "trying" but by relying more on a spiritually based approach to accomplishments.

Some of my colleagues – indeed, some of the highly successful authors and entrepreneurs I have consulted to – confide to me that their lives are shipwrecks of stress and anxiety. I have noticed, and many have admitted without my asking, that they feel a constant insecurity about what they have accomplished and they are driven by a relentless competitiveness that only causes them conflict, not greater success. Fulfillment is an unfulfilled promise for them. I would say that they have chosen a non-spiritual path to their money, fame and accomplishment.

But that's the way many people choose to succeed. It works, but at what cost? Would you rather have your life be difficult – or easy?

What I'm offering you is an alternative that really works and leads to peace of mind as well. Using information you'd have to dig long and hard to find on your own. Presented in an easy format to use and succeed with.

Read the following excerpt from my book and see what I mean:

****

"What do you do?" I asked. I was standing in a line of 700 people in a hotel in Seattle, waiting to spend a day listening to an author and spiritual teacher.

"I do energy work," the woman beside me replied. "It's hard to explain. It's different for each person."

"Do you have a business card?"

"No," she said, slightly embarrassed.

I was shocked. "Let me ask you a question," I began.

"There are over 700 potential clients here for you. Why don't you at least have business cards?"

A woman beside her smiled and told her, "You were just hit by an angel."

I'm not an angel. But I was curious why this business woman was missing a huge marketing opportunity. As I talked to a few more of the 700 people at this event, I realized all of these people were in business for themselves. And they all needed help in marketing themselves.

That's when it dawned on me that I could write a concise handbook on spiritually based marketing.

No one else seemed better qualified. I'm the author of "The AMA Complete Guide to Small Business Advertising" for The American Marketing Association, I've written nine other books, and I have over fifteen years of experience in spirituality.

I've interviewed many New Age spokespeople and have had some of them as my clients. Before I became a marketing specialist and author, I was an inner world journalist for over ten years, writing for several leading edge magazines. As a result, I've seen miracles with my own eyes. For example:

* I interviewed Meir Schneider, a man who was diagnosed as blind. He was given a certificate saying he was incurably blind, and yet today he sees, he reads, he writes, he drives a car – and he has helped hundreds of people regain their vision, as well.

*I spent time with the Barry and Suzi Kaufman at their

Option Institute and saw and heard of miracles there. Their own child was born autistic. They were told to give up on him. But they didn't. They worked with their son, loved him, nurtured him, accepted him – and healed him. Today he lives as an above average, happy, successful adult.

*I've sat in dozens of workshops where I saw people heal their relationships with their lovers, their parents, their kids. I've interviewed gurus and mentors, talked to people who have had "incurable" problems dissolved, and I've experienced miracles first-hand in my own life. I've come to believe that nothing – nothing – is impossible.

Recently I've been working with Jonathan Jacobs, a man called "the healer's healer" because his track record for helping heal people is so stunning that doctors are referring their own patients to him. I've seen Jonathan take people with everything from money problems to back injuries to cancer, and help heal them, often in a single session.

Besides, I had already created and tested a secret five-step process for manifesting anything you wanted.

I seemed like the best voice for a book and course on marketing with spirit.

I also knew that those 700 people at the seminar represented a still larger group of people who need help with their businesses. I further knew that they were all doing something *inside* themselves that was creating their outer results. In other words, their inner state of being was creating their business, or lack of it.

Said more simply, the woman who didn't have a

business card had an inner insecurity about her business that showed up in her life by her not having business cards.

And taking this logic a step further in the direction I want to take you later in this book, if that woman were truly clear about her business, she wouldn't even need business cards. Business would just come to her.

Her inner spirit would do her marketing.

As one successful person said, "Angels now hand out my business cards."

Confused? That's okay. Therapist, author and my dear friend Mandy Evans says confusion is that wonderful state of mind right before clarity.

Maybe the following story will give you a glimpse of what I'm talking about and set the stage for what is to follow:

I once read a delightful old book from 1920 titled "Fundamentals of Prosperity" by Roger Babson. He ended his book by asking the President of the Argentine Republic why South America, with all of its natural resources and wonders, was so far behind North America in terms of progress and prosperity. The President replied:

"I have come to this conclusion. South America was settled by the Spanish who came to South America in search of gold, but North America was settled by the Pilgrim Fathers who went there in search of God."

Where is YOUR focus? On money or on spirit?

In this book I intend to offer a new way for you to easily and effortlessly increase your business. It's based on proven marketing techniques and timeless spiritual principles. It will reveal how your inner state of being attracts and creates your outer results – and what to do about it so you can have, do, or be whatever your heart desires.

Do the techniques work? The proof will be in the pudding.

Try them and see. I can tell you about the successes I've had – and I do in this book – but nothing will be quite as convincing to you as using these simple ideas and seeing your own amazing results.

I could tell you that this method will help you manifest anything you want. You'll read about people who created cars and homes, healed themselves of cancer, and created new relationships. But I'm focusing on business because there appears to be a serious lack of spirituality in business. And I'm going to let you discover the magic of marketing with spirit because nothing will be more powerful as your own first-hand experiences.

Even right now, as you read these words, you can begin to play with new possibilities: What do you want to be, do, or have? Win the lotto? Why not? Increase your business? Why not? Heal something? Why not?

A friend of mine asked, "How do you know what is impossible?" I replied, "How do you know what isn't?"

****

Sign up for my online class on "Spiritual Marketing" and watch your life take wings. You'll get all of the above, the unpublished book, five weeks of lessons with me, online e-coaching, reviews of your marketing pieces, and you'll learn the 5-step process for creating whatever you can imagine.

The entire class is only $1,500. Send me e-mail if you have questions, or to get me to hold a seat for you. Class is restricted to 15 people so I can give each personal attention. Deadline is January 5, 2000.

Seize the day!

Joe Vitale

****

Joe "Mr. Fire!" Vitale – Author of way too many books to list here So go see my truly amazing giant website at http://www.mrfire.com

****

As a result of that follow-up letter, I filled my e-class!

I made $22,500!

Follow-up letters are worth gold!

A Little Known Secret for Doubling Responses to Your E-Offers

A secret of success in direct mail anywhere is to follow-up with different letters with the same offer to the same audience.

This principle also works online.

A follow-up sales e-letter can bring you 50% more sales. In other words, if you e-mail out your sales letter and 10 people bought from you, sending out a follow-up sales letter to the same list ought to bring you five more sales.

Is that cool or what?

This is why so many times you get repeated offers in your snail mail! Those follow-ups are sent out for one reason:

They bring more sales!

There's a company called The Franklin Mint who mails their customer list over 50 times a year.

Fifty times a year!

At least once a week a Franklin Mint customer will get a mailer about some new item being offered that week. Why does Franklin Mint do that?

Because it increases their sales!!!

I sometimes sit and watch television at night as a way

to relax. Nearly every night I see a commercial for an exercise machine called the Bow Flex. I think I've seen that commercial about 33 times now.

Well, last night I almost ordered it! And if they keep airing that commercial, sooner or later I'm going to break down and buy the darn thing!

How to Make Even More Money with This Unusual E-Mail Secret

In the last chapter I revealed that sending out follow-up sales letters can bring you another 50% in orders. In this chapter I want to reveal my favorite type of follow-up sales letter.

In short, it's the kind of letter where you don't say a thing. Instead, your satisfied customers do all the talking.

Here's an example of what I mean:

Somewhere in mid-2001, I sent out a sales letter offering an e-book that I found and brought back to life. The book is called *Attaining Your Desires*. I didn't write the book. I wrote the sales letter for the book. I sent it to my e-mail list of maybe 3,000 names at the time. Within 24 hours I made about $3,500.

And that was for a book I didn't write! Here's the letter I sent out to my list:

• • •

Subject: An Exciting Message from Joe Vitale:

"I finally decided to release the amazing book that changed my life – one of the 3 most powerful books of all time – and give you a magical FREE gift, too!"

Say YES, and in a few minutes you'll know how to

Attain Your Desires – and eliminate worry, stress, and strain – with the help of this woman's wisdom!

Dear Friend,

I just released Genevieve Behrend's long lost 1929 book – called "Attaining Your Desires: By Letting Your Subconscious Mind Work For You" – as an e-book. Here are the details:

When I moved from Houston to my current Hill Country estate, I only packed three books with me – out of my collection of 5,000 – for the trip. One of them was Behrend's incredible little book, "Attaining." I found a copy of this amazing book many years ago. It profoundly influenced my life. It taught me how to focus on the essence of something I wanted – rather than on the appearance of something – in order to magnetize myself to receive what I truly desired.

As a result of using Behrend's methods – simple as they may seem – I've manifested new cars, new homes, a new relationship, improved health, book sales, passive income, and a whole lot more.

My friend David Garfinkel, master copywriter, said this about Behrend's book:

"I would say this is the clearest, most comprehensive, most practical and indeed most do-able explanation of how the Creative Process works in real life that I've ever read."

The person who typed the book for me (so I could turn it into an e-book) wrote this:

''I've never seen a book like this before! It's inspiring me to pick what I want and showing me how to get it! Thank you for letting me type this book! THANK YOU!"

And my webmaster read over the book before putting it online and wrote me saying: "This is an amazing little book!"

What's the story on this almost miraculous old book?

Behrend wrote her book as a complete seven-lesson course. The writing is in dialogue form, between a "Sage" and a "Pupil." The Sage is a famous author and teacher; the Pupil is you. It is very easy reading, very tightly written, and very enlightening. Here are a few of the lesson/chapter titles:

Lesson 2: How to Get What You Want

Lesson 3. How to Overcome Adverse conditions

Lesson 5. Making Your Subjective Mind Work for you

Lesson 7. Putting Your Lessons Into Practice

Within these lessons is pure compressed dynamite. I mean it. Here are a few sub-headings to give you a sense of the staggering power of this rare material:

"The Secret of Controlling Your Life Forces"

"Don't Look for Coincidences In Your Life"

"How to Drive Anxiety Out of Your Mind"

"How You Can Control Circumstances"

"How Your Mind Is Related to The Universal Mind"

"How to Develop Health and Harmony"

The list of incredible topics, answers, and mind-expanding concepts goes on and on. The book even includes special sections on handling anger, disease, disappointment and much more.

You can now learn from this amazing author, too. I've taken Behrend's magical book, hired a typist to input the entire book, and just now put it online for sale as an e-book. You can download it right now by going to my MrFire article archive here: (http://mrfire. com/hypnotic-articles.html).

You may have read books on manifestation before – maybe even my own "Spiritual Marketing" book but I GUARANTEE you've never read a book like THIS one before.

When Bob Proctor (who wrote the Foreword to my "Spiritual Marketing" book) and I were talking one day about the books that influenced us, he asked me if I ever heard of the little known second book by Behrend. Bob had never seen the book, but had heard rumors of it. I told him I not only heard of it, I OWN it. I later gave Bob a photocopy of the book as a gift.

You can now own a copy of the book, too, as an e-book. It's only $19.95 and you can have it to read on your computer (or print out and read wherever you like) in just a few minutes.

What if it really can help you get more of what you want? Wouldn't that be worth only $19.95??

Order right now and you can also have a book that deeply influenced Behrend in writing her own book. It was written by the man she calls "Sage" in her book. It's truly awesome, and it's yours, FREE, when you order "Attaining Your Desires" right now.

Magically,

Joe Vitale

joe@mrfire.com

PS – Most people know of Behrend's first book, "Your Invisible Power," which is still in print, but almost no one knows of her second, much more rare and powerful book. With it you can manifest just about anything you can imagine. And to think it's yours for only $19.95! (And YES, your satisfaction is guaranteed or your money back). Remember, order now and you'll also get a FREE e-book by the "Sage" that influenced the author! (You'll love it)!

PPS – What were the other two books I took with me when I left Houston? The first was the now legendary "Robert Collier Letter Book." The second was Christian Godefroy's book "How to Write Letters That Sell." And the third, of course, was the one I am offering you today. Consider: If Behrend's book is so good that it is one of only three books I pulled from my collection of 5,000, shouldn't you at least take a look at it?

• • •

A week or so later I followed up by sending a second letter to my e-mail list. This letter simply restated the key benefits of the book and gave a few testimonials from the people who bought the book from the first sales letter. I had also found a book in the public domain and added it to the bonus gifts people got when they ordered. The result: I made about $1,300 from this letter.

Here's the follow-up sales letter I sent to my list:

• • •

Subject: PS —

I just found another book by "Sage"!

It's fantastic! But, instead of just telling you about this amazing 1909 book, I'll tell you how you can have a copy of it for FREE.

Here's the deal:

When you buy Genevieve Behrend's long lost 1929 book – "Attaining Your Desires: By Letting Your Subconscious Mind Work For You" – you'll now get access to TWO additional e-books by "Sage," the mystical author who influenced Behrend to write HER book!

If you want to see my sales letter again for her incredible book, go here: (http://mrfire.com/article-archives/copywriting-samples/attain-your-desires.html).

If you're ready to buy her book and get access to the two free bonus books by "Sage" right now, just go here: (http://mrfire.com/article-archives/copywriting-samples/attain-your-desires.html).

Do it now – and attain your desires!

Magically,

Joe Vitale

joe@mrfire.com

PS – If you already bought Behrend's amazing e-book, just go back to the link with the download instructions and you'll now see an added link for the second book by "Sage."

• • •

I then got busy with other projects and forgot all about the e-book. After a few months went by – which is actually too long in the world of marketing – I decided to send out yet another follow-up sales letter. This one would be very different than the other letters before it. Read it and see if you can see what I mean.

Here's the third letter I sent out to my list:

• • •

Subject line: Did you see this?

I LOVE getting e-mail like this –

"I am close to speechless after reading most of the Behrend and Troward materials. It seems so grossly insufficient to merely say thank you for providing these materials, but I don't know what else to say. These materials contain everything that I have ever known (although I realize every day that I know less and less as I learn more and more) and everything that I have always wanted to know. Thank you so much for following your heart to make these materials once again available to a broader audience. I am truly so grateful."

– Carolita Oliveros

"Joe, I would like to add my name to the list of people saying 'Thank You' for bringing the lost book of 'Attaining Your Desires' back to life for the rest of the world to read. After reading it, I now see why it was one of the three books you brought with you when you moved. It is having such an impact on my life, I am now reading from it at least four times a week because each time I read I get new insights. But it goes beyond that, within two weeks after reading the book I obtained a contract that will put thousands of dollars in my pocket. As it says in the book from the chapter on 'Putting Your Lessons into Practice,' 'The greatest magnet for acquiring money is ideas.' And it doesn't stop there.

Because of the book I have come up with an idea that should make even more money and it will be donated to the Red Cross efforts in New York. I wish everyone knew about the powerful information contained in the book. Joe, take a bow for bringing this treasure to the world."

– John Beaton, Calgary, Canada

"I printed the book out last evening and started reading – I can't put it down – it is superb and simply reinforces much of what I have already believed. The crystal clarity with which it is written helps me take the beliefs deeper than I ever have before. Can't wait to see how I actually apply what I am learning."

– Mary Heidkamp

"Recently I obtained the e-book 'Attaining Your Desires' on your recommendation, and I must tell you, it is nothing like I've ever read before! I've read books on Manifesting before and even have tapes on How to Visualize. And I have been practicing their methods for months now but never really 'got it' to achieve the level of spiritual advancement I desired. This book is what I needed to truly understand the workings of our Universe and to bring me to another level of personal growth. I feel so blessed for now I know how to connect with the true spirit of what I want to have in life. Just had to write to thank you for sharing it with us, as I'm sure like myself, so many others were inspired by it."

– *Malika Krish*

Obviously, the 1929 book I'm offering explaining "How to Attain Your Desires" is changing lives. If you haven't ordered it yet, here's your friendly reminder:

When you order this amazing book, you'll also get access to 2 other free e-books by the mysterious "Sage" who inspired the author. Just go here: (http://mrfire.com/article-archives/copywriting-samples/attain-your-desires.html).

Isn't it time you Attained Your Desires?

Magically,

Joe Vitale

joe@mrfire.com

PS – And here's yet another e-mail I love:

"Thank you for putting 'Attaining Your Desires' into an e-book. I downloaded the book and just had to keep reading. Thank you."

– Jane Foster

Here's the point:

Sending out a third follow-up sales letter to the same list can bring even more sales for you.

The rule of thumb is that you can get 50% more sales than the last letter. So if your second letter brought you 50 sales, a third letter might bring you 25 more sales.

And this is all from the same list!

Furthermore, your sales letter can be nothing more than testimonials. In short, you don't even have to write the letter!

That's the secret key I want you to get from this chapter. Sometimes all you have to do is relay what others are saying and you have a sales letter. That's what I did with the third letter above. I simply compiled the best endorsements – after getting permission to use them, of course – and then weaved them into one strong letter.

You can do this, too!

Just start asking for testimonials from satisfied clients and customers. It's that easy!

What Are Five Ways to Get People to Open Your E-Mail?

How do you get people to even open your e-mail? There are two ways:

1. **Your name is recognized by the receiver.**
2. **Your subject line is irresistible**.

Obviously, your whole focus has to be on number two. While the people receiving your e-mail may look at who it's from and maybe recognize your name, there's no guarantee they will open your e-mail and read it. After all, they aren't really interested in you, they are instead interested in what you can do for them. Big difference.

As with ads and news releases, your subject line is the "headline" that will get people to read your message or delete it without opening it.

The thing is, you can't use traditional headline writing tricks in your subject lines. Oh, you might get away with it, but it's not worth the risk.

For example, "Free" is considered the most powerful word in advertising. But don't use it in your subject line.

Why? Because more and more people are using filters to organize their e-mail! I'm doing this now, too. Since I receive hundreds of messages a day, I had to do something to cut through the clutter. What I did was set a filter on my e-mail! Whenever the word "free" shows up in the subject line – no doubt signaling an ad – that e-mail gets deleted automatically. I never see it.

Do you see what I mean? If you try to send an ad by e-mail, it may get deleted without ever being opened.

So what can you do?

Here are some of my favorite ways to guarantee my e-mail gets read:

- **Make it personal.** If at all possible, use the recipient's name in the subject line. "Joe, did you see this?" will get my attention.

- **Make it seem personal.** A simple "PS" can get your e-mail read. Or a "Did you see this?" One time I used "Re-send" as the subject and everyone opened the e-mail! Why? Because it seemed personal.

- **Make it newsworthy.** I often send out e-mails with the subject line "News from Joe Vitale" or "A Special Announcement."

- **Make it benefit-oriented.** When all else fails, simply state your offer. "Solve tax problems with this new software."

- **Make it curious.** Curiosity still grabs attention. "UFOs found where?" can be interesting. "Cats can sing" can get people to open e-mail. This is my least favorite approach, but it often works.

In short, spend time on your subject lines. They are as important as any headline. When they work, they can make you rich.

In the next chapter, I'll prove it to you ..

A Truly Killer Hypnotic Sales Letter Used Online and off

You better hold on to your chair or your knees because the following letter goes for your throat!

I mean it. Just wait till you read this amazing letter. You better stand guard over your wallet or purse, as this letter pulls out all punches in order to get you to part with your money!

John La Tourrette is a powerhouse writer as well as a powerhouse martial arts instructor. I'm constantly amazed at what he creates and how persuasive he is in selling what he develops. He's sincere, and he's a force to reckon with.

This letter is a good, recent example of his style. I urge you to read it and pay attention to how it makes you feel. It's certainly a muscular letter. But also notice his use of emotion, and how he lays on the benefits while backing you into a corner, forcing you to buy or get out of his face.

Also notice that he ties this letter to the very strong existing emotions around the September 11, 2001 horrors in New York City and Washington, D.C., when America was attacked by terrorists. While people are traumatized by the news of 911 in 2001, and feeling anger and fear as a result, along comes John with an offer to help keep you and your loved ones alive.

I don't think this is a misuse of his power. After all, as I write this, it is the end of October, barely one month after the attacks. America is at war. People are afraid to travel, and they're wondering what's next. John isn't taking advantage of people, he's helping them. Not only can his material help people stay alive, it can help people keep other people alive.

The only objection I have with this letter is that John says the people on the other three planes that were hijacked didn't take action. The fact is, those people didn't know they were going to die. And we don't really know what they did in their final moments.

John's letter is hypnotic. I'm including it here, with John's permission, for you to study.

And yes, in case you're wondering, I ordered his package after reading this letter.

Here it is:

"I fought hard to get this released, but it is adult martial arts material and comes with a FREE course called *"**Killing Time: How to take out a Terrorist in 2 Seconds or Less!**"* a $257 value...and is only given to Inner Circle members over the age of 18, and is definitely not for the faint hearted, and ***will NOT*** be sold ***nor offered*** to non-members. We are sickened by what happened on Sept. 11, and hope it never happens again, but if it does, because of these training materials, you will at least be able to fight back. That is the reason you received this report. Please do NOT share this information with anyone outside of your family. Thank you."

"The Astonishing ***IRON FIST*** Secrets

Of The SledgeHammer Blow Masters, the
Most Knowledgeable & Most Lethal
<u>Close-in</u> Fighters on the Planet!"

"Learn how to enjoy the *<u>tremendous power</u>* of SledgeHammer blows, <u>at any age</u>, in *<u>any physical shape</u>*, blended with the Blinding Speed and the Magic Insider's knowledge of 6,000 year old Strategies and Tactics of the Masters of Close Combat. This "just released" IRON FIST, IRON PALM crash course, for Inner Circle Members only, is dramatically changing the self-confidence level and street performance Survival levels of Black Belts literally overnight."

By Jack Williams

Dear Friend,

It's shocking to even have to think about killing people. We abhor the subject. **But** the terrorist attack did happen. Those sick fanatics did commandeer four of our airplanes, and only on one plane did our civilians have the courage and the knowledge to "*take them out,*" to do what must be done, to subdue those terrorists before they dive bombed that aircraft into another Trade Center.

We salute Jeremy Glick, an ex-wrestler and Judo

black belt, who became a hero, charging the fanatics who commandeered the cockpit of United Airlines Flight 93, ending his life the way he lived it: fearlessly, and for everyone else. Thank you Jeremy for taking out those wackos.

This report is worth your attention as an intelligent, caring, wise and wonderful person.

It is about power. It is about courage. It is about wisdom. And it is about "real workable" one-stop "take our shots."

We are talking about people like Sam, a martial arts trained cop in San Diego, that **bare handedly** attacked 8 creeps <u>raping a young girl</u>. Five of those creeps ended up in the hospital. Sam couldn't catch the other three.

We are talking about the tiny, but big knuckled Chow, who defended himself in a bar brawl, sending all <u>three of his attackers</u> to the hospital, one to die of massive internal injuries and brain damage. (more on next page – CONFIDENTIAL)!

We are talking about Oyama, when attacked by a thug with a knife, ***<u>killed him with one blow.</u>***

These people knew **<u>where</u>** to hit. They knew how-to-hit **REAL HARD**. They knew how to hit **real fast**. And when eye-ball-to-eye-ball against a man wanting to kill them, they knew how to fight back, and **had the guts** to fight back and do what was necessary.

We are NOT talking about the type of martial artist that make me sick. Their claim to fame is "they can break a coconut, 3 times out of 10 times."

I still remember this Korean master getting his <u>face caved in</u> at a local college bonfire. This skinny oriental fellow Pak claimed a 5th degree black belt and because of his "**hands-of-death,**" was appointed captain of the team guarding our bonfire against the athletes from OTI.

During the fight, Pak leaped up into the air and kicked the opposition full power in the chest...and bounced off like a handball. Then Pak punched the guy in the mouth...and that punch didn't even dent the big guy's smile.

The big guy just absorbed those <u>"baby slaps,"</u> grabbed Pak out of the air, held him up with his left hand and smashed Pak's face with his right...all the time muttering, "**don't you know that karate crap don't work?**" They succeed in burning our bonfire.

And it's real hard to tell the difference between the frauds and wannabes from the ones who can really **do** and **TEACH** what they say they can do.

Max found this out the hard way. We'll let Max tell his own story.

"My martial arts background comes from the Kyokushin Kai Karate, the ultimate <u>hardstyle</u> of karate under the 'Iron Fist' Master, Mas Oyama. I'd fought full-contact on and off for years, and when I first saw the Doc's techniques, I thought they were fluff."

"I got toe to toe with him at a seminar. I was

watching him hit people and saw them <u>dropping like flies</u>, totally unconscious. He was hitting them across the room with what looked like no effort so of course I thought either he or his students was fakes."

"I asked him to do it to me. I got in a <u>good attack stance</u> and I stood toe to toe with him because I was going to show him 'what was what.' Well, when I woke up on the ground a minute later I asked 'what the hell happened?' and the whole class was laughing."

"I asked a guy sitting next to me what had happened and he said 'Well when you threw your punch, he sucked it to the side then lightly 'tapped' you on the neck in different places, and you fell to the ground.' I'd never been knocked out in a fight before, especially by a 60-year old man that was about 19 pounds overweight. I was dumbfounded <u>but I sure learned a lot</u> once I started paying attention to what he was really teaching." (more on next page)…

"Now I know that when Dr. La Tourrette, the Speedman teaches, it is NOT a '<u>my daddy can beat up your daddy situation</u>'. The Doc really does care, and he shows how much he cares in the strictness and 'instant' street effectiveness of his teaching methods."

Not to be bragging, but to inform, the Speedman is Dr. John M. La Tourrette, Sports Psychologist, Huna Energy/Healing Trainer, 10th degree black belt and author of 18 different books in the peak performance fields. And over the past several decades he has trained

Mercenaries, Special Forces, Hell's Angels, cops, prison guards, police officers, and more than 32,721 civilians. His other two earned nicknames are "Jack Quick Kill," and "Dr. Death." Why? Because his martial arts technologies are so lethal! They really work when they need to work.

Let me give you some of the <u>amazing secrets</u> and <u>lost teachings</u> that the Doc will be presenting in his ***"The REAL Science Behind Sledge Hammer Blows, The SECRET & Forgotten Martial Science of Iron Fist & Iron Palm, That Hooks Up Brick Smashing With Street Effective Martial Arts!"***

You Will Learn...

About the four most important **<u>fighting secrets</u>** in history.

Beyond the rules of martial arts are Power Accelerators that turn any strike into a successful attack.

About the **REAL** reason to learn **<u>brick breaking</u>**.

How Master Chin could break a river boulder and taught it to his students in less than 30 days.

What is there about some hitting styles, like Paul Vunak's, that make them so <u>much more effective</u> than others?

What is the Ultimate Purpose of every strike?

What is the correct way to <u>generate 300% more power</u> on a punch?

How to avoid attracting *the wrong kind of attention* when attacking.

11 different samples of how to develop the Iron Palm.

The unknown secret of *Speed Accelerators* and how it connects to *SledgeHammer blows*.

A sample of how to use the Iron Fist in a **Mass Attack situation**.

17 samples of how to combine multiple Sledge hammer blows with a speed attack in less than 1 second.

How to **arouse the Internal Energy** to develop Iron Fist.

What is the first thing to do in developing Sledge hammer blows?

Find out the **purpose of breath** control for power.

How large deformed hands *can be avoided*.

Find out the 5 different purposes of **breath control for speed**.

See how Max *tripled the pressure* behind his power hits in 30 minutes.

Typical fighting openings that **divert the opposition's attention** and lead logically to you **easy Power Hitting** them.

What is the *eternal question* that stands up and looks you and every sincere martial artist squarely in the eye when they *face the puke* that wants to hurt them? (go to next page)...

How to link up **Poison Hand Secret Technologies** with Sledge Hammer Blows.

One of the *most effective training methods* we have

seen to turn your fist into a battering ram, and still have it *'look normal.'*

A technique that **double hitting speed in under a minute**.

How does the *opposition's mind think*?

How to put multiple Power Hits into the opposition **without being seen**.

How to crush him as if you were a 1,000 lb. Boulder.

How to **install confidence in yourself** without getting into a fight.

How to make your medium speed punch *twice as fast as their fastest punch*, even if they start first.

How to **spin your energies** into his **Path of Aggression**.

Secrets of moving from one *Power Hit* to another.

The **invention of the home** training tool, the **Power Board**.

A small touch that can *increase your speed of reaction* 10, 15, or 20 percent.

An effective technique to **increase Situational Awareness**.

Don't accidentally do these 5 things or the *bottom drops out on your power*.

Why most karate books have **incorrect Iron Fist teachings**.

In every self-defense situation there is a *critical moment* when your oppositions is not *convinced to attack* ... so what to do to get him to *turn tail and run*.

How to turn your opponent into a <u>marshmallow</u>.

One simple mistake that <u>robs</u> you of your power instantly.

The six *home training tools* that turn you into a sledge hammer blow **expert overnight**.

How to put a *powerful surge* charge into a wimpy hit.

How to smash the opposition and stay out of jail.

What 4 things do you need to do to turn on your "*Stealth Mode*" and turn all your strikes into *invisible secret weapons*?

The above technologies are just a drop in the bucket to what you will be learning. The above course is 4 **guerrilla** videos and comes with one large training manual. The titles are:

- Video #1, "**The Real Secrets Behind Sledge Hammer Blows.**" This video covers the secrets of developing **Sledge Hammer blows, Iron Fist** punches, and open hand Iron Palm Strikes. The proper tools and the proper training methods. **This guerrilla video is brand new**! Value $70.

- Video #2, "**The Real Secrets on how to Combine Iron Fist Training, and Iron Palm Training with High Speed Hits, Critical Distance, Tactical Awareness and Dim Mak, or Poison Hand nerve cavity technologies.**" This video is **brand new**! Value $70.

- Video #3, "**The Lost Teachings of Ancient Energy Secrets of Chi Kung That Instantly Increase Your**

Kicking Power and Kicking Devastation." Most people don't know it but Doc is one of the <u>top 21 certified</u> and qualified <u>Energy Medicine Trainers</u> on the planet. He is the only trainer in the world that has taken those advanced <u>Energy Secrets</u> and applied them to kicking in a manner that allows even those over the age of 35 to still kick hard, <u>powerfully</u> and <u>easily</u> with flexibility. This video is **brand new**! Value, $70.

- Video #4, **"How to Apply Sledge Hammer Blow Technologies to Kicking for Power Based Kicking, for Multiple Assailants, and for Flow Kicking."** This video is brand new! Value $70.

- Large Training Manual, **"The REAL Science Behind Sledge Hammer Blows, the SECRET & Forgotten Martial Science of ...Iron Fist & Iron Palm...That Hooks up Brick Smashing with Street Effective Martial Arts. Brand New**!" Value, $50. (Confidential materials, turn the page)...

That should be enough detail to give you an idea of the importance of the <u>Sledge Hammer Blow Secrets</u> in Docs *brand new* and PRIVATE, behind closed doors, crash course. There is an awful lot more, which you'll find that out yourself when you watch, study and practice them. In fact, according to *former* kung-fu editor for "**BLACK BELT**" magazine, Mr. Steven Barnes...

"Dr. La Tourrette has brought the (ancient) martial arts training into the twentieth century. His materials contain a series of <u>interlocked, easily applied, devastatingly effective</u> technologies. Anyone unawares of these powerful technologies is functioning in the Dark Ages. <u>Wholeheartedly recommended</u>!"

SPECIAL OFFER! You can receive the **entire** above package, a value of $330, for the lnnerCircle discounted price of **$197 + $17.50 S&H**, if you place your order within the next 11 days. **Call 541- 535-3188 and talk to one of the girls right now**. A package is waiting for you.

And, just like I mentioned on page one, the Doc is giving **FREE** the "filmed behind locked doors with the drapes pulled" the *KILLING TIME* Crash Course. <u>This course is a $257 value</u>...and is <u>only</u> given to the **first 50** lnnerCircle members over the age of 18 who call in right away. We did NOT make this "crash course" for public use, so you must promise to keep them to yourself and NOT share with anyone who is NOT a family member, or a high-ranking black belt you trust.

The PRIVATELY produced and NOT for the public Killing Time crash course consists of...

1. Video one, "**Killing Time, Terminal Retaliation: How-to-Kill a Terrorist in 2 Seconds or Less, Even If Totally Unarmed.**" These technologies are deathblow technologies. They show how to make the terrorist think you are frightened to death, but you are only drawing them into your most effective range. They teach you technologies of "nothing is

as it seems." They show secret blood strikes. Some of the techniques are notorious. If it comes down to a suicide mission and you are going to get it, ways and means of getting them first. Manners of turning the attackers into the victims. How to turn on your thirst for battle. Extinction technologies that are almost instant. Not for the general public. **A brand new guerrilla video**. Value, $89. **NOT to be sold to anyone**!

2. Video two, "**Secrets of The Instant Street Terminator**!" Methods a 6-year-old skinny girl could easily use to defeat the hulk. Methods of using natural weapons. Technologies introduced by bodyguards of the rich, famous, and of the royal families where terrorist attacks are much more common. **Total value $89**.

3. Large Training manual, "**It's Killing Time.**" These are the <u>private notes</u> of the Grand Master. They have not been put to the computer, but are copies of his handwritten notes of "**how**" and "why" technologies must be done the way they are done to get the "fight and win" conditions you need. They are tough, and his claws are extended all the way through. This is NOT for the weak at heart. It's a roughhouse and it's your funeral if you don't do something if you get caught in these atrocities. <u>**Value $50**</u>. **NOT** to be sold to anyone.

4. Training manual, "**Street Wise, Hard-Core Speed**

Fighting Secrets for Instant Self-Defense Even If Fighting Dirty Harry!" Note. These technologies are for information purposes only. So please exercise common sense and the reasonableness of a sane man in the practice of these skills and in the acquisition of these technologies. **Value $29**. (turn)...

Only because American people have been slaughtered are we releasing these technologies. The terrorists are on the prowl, and they are looking for the extinction of our people. Hopefully the grim reaper is not plotting for our destruction. But without these technologies we are pathetic and powerless when facing them.

That is sickening.

Hopefully these materials will never be necessary. Hopefully neither you nor I will become one of their new victims. But if you do, you now have ammo for your gun.

The total package is worth $257 + $330 = $587. YOUR price right now is only $197 + $17.50 S&H. Our claws are out and we want to give you serious methods to wreak havoc on those bloodthirsty fanatics who are wantonly killing innocent people who can't fight back.

And, I want you to see this amazing "set" at my risk.

I am not going to ask you to trust me on this. I respect you too much for that. Instead I've arranged for a special copy of this "crash course" to be rushed to you today (it's already prepared for you and in my office). The Doc has PERSONALLY approved of this method: We want you to watch the tapes, at your leisure, and spend as much time with them as you like...for 90 days. At the end of those 90 days, you can either keep them, or send them back, in any condition, for any reason whatsoever. The choice is entirely yours.

In essence, if you are a thief you can rip us off. Even if you like the materials. Even if you study them, read the manuals and train from the videos. Even if you dupe off the videos and like them, you can still send them back. But you are an InnerCircle Member. We trust you. If you don't like them, send them back and we'll refund it all (minus S&H). We believe so strongly in this "**Sledge Hammer Blow, Crash Course,**" and its **FREE Bonus** product, "Killing Time" that we believe you'll feel the same way. So study these technologies. These give you the real edge.

Sincerely,

Jack Williams

PS – There is one small "catch" to this offer. It's small, but important. We went to great expense in making these tapes, and even more by putting aside a set just for you. Our tiny office isn't "geared" for the mess this has created...so I need to put a strict limit on the time we will hold this set of special videos aside for you. Therefore you must place your order within 11 days of receiving this letter. That's not a lot of time, I know – to be safe, you should call (or write) right now, while you still have the letter in your hands. The entire $587 package is only $197 + S&H.

Here's what you need to do immediately: Call my office, at 541-535-3188, and tell them you are an InnerCircle member and you want the "**SHB**" tapes, which stands for SledgeHammer Blows, plus the bonus tapes titled "**KTT**." You are in a unique situation, but you must act right now to take advantage of it. I hope you do. I also hope you never have to use what you learn. Peace.

Copyright 2001, Group L Inc. Warrior Publications, 6252 Dark Hollow Rd. Med. OR, 97501, 541-535-3188, fax 541-535-8038.

Are you still breathing?

Obviously that letter is packed with power.

A good exercise is to review it, even analyze it, and look for what makes it powerful. The more you understand about great sales letters, the more you will be armed to write great sales letters.

The World's Most Unusual Way to Strengthen Your Hypnotic Writing

Let me begin by asking you a question:

How can you improve your Hypnotic Writing – which means your hypnotic publicity, your hypnotic websites, and your hypnotic e-mail?

If you are like most people, you answered with one of the following:

1. Have others read your writing and given you feedback.
2. Just run your copy and see what happens.
3. Hire an editor.

All three methods are valid. I've used them all, too. My favorite is the first. Nothing compares to handing your writing to someone and having them read it out loud to you. Whatever section they have trouble reading, you need to rewrite.

But I've talked about that method in my earlier books, such as *Hypnotic Writing* and *Advanced Hypnotic Writing*. Today, I want to describe a new way to strength your writing.

Brace yourself. What I am about to tell you is going to shock you.

It's going to sound strange, controversial, and even ridiculous.

But since I'm sure you have an open mind, you will at least hear me out and give this new method a try.

This third approach to improving your hypnotic copy involves kinesiology, or muscle testing. There are numerous books about this field of study. Just today I was sitting in my easy chair, dog at my feet, reading Dr. David Hawkins' fascinating book, *Power vs. Force: The Hidden Determinants of Human Behavior*.

Sounds like a mouthful, doesn't it?

It is. It's a heady work about Dr. Hawkins' 20 years of research into the anatomy of human conscious- ness. His main tool throughout his intense study was simply this: A muscle test.

Yes, a muscle test.

The theory is that your body doesn't lie. If you can ask questions of your body, you can get accurate answers to anything you want to know about.

Yes, including your sales copy.

Maybe an example would be best here.

Go get a friend. Anyone will do. Now stand in front of your friend, so you are facing each other.

Have your friend stick out his or her arm, in the "pretend you're an airplane" position, but only using one "wing." Now place two fingers of your hand on that person's outstretched arm, about where their wrist is.

Tell the person to "resist" as you press down on his or

her arm.

Do that now.

The person should have been able to easily resist your two fingers of pressure.

Ok. Now tell that person to think of Hitler as they resist and you press down.

Do that now.

Notice the difference? Your friend's arm should have gone weak and dropped as you applied pressure. OK. Now tell that person to think of something or someone they love as they resist and you press down.

Do it now.

Notice what happened? That person should now test strong.

Thank your friend and let them go. The test is over.

What just happened?

You just sampled muscle testing. According to Dr. Hawkins, this is a valid way to test the correctness of anything you can articulate. In fact, the back cover of his books says, "What if you had access to a simple yes or no answer to any question you wished to ask?"

His theory is that all of life is interconnected – you, me, the neighbors, the other side of the planet, you name it – and that we can have access to ALL information through this doorway to knowledge: Muscle testing.

I am vastly over-simplifying the method and his book to get to my own point, which is:

You can test any aspect of your hypnotic writing with

muscle testing.

You can test each word, each sentence, each paragraph, and each page.

And every time a word or sentence tests weak, you can strengthen it.

Dr. Hawkins says he tested every sentence in his 311-page book.

Do you see where I'm going with this?

If he can test every sentence in a full-length book, you can test every sentence in your news releases, web copy, or e-mail!

Hawkins has an entire chapter on muscle testing and the marketplace in his book. In it he writes, "The use of the simple kinesiologic technique we have described can instantly reveal whether an advertising campaign or given commercial is weak or strong."

What I am doing is expanding on his work by suggesting that you can test your hypnotic publicity, hypnotic websites, and hypnotic e-mail — the three legs of your Hypnotic Marketing campaign – BEFORE you ever push the green button to start any of it rolling.

"An ad that makes people go strong will always produce a positive feeling about the product rather than an aversion," writes Hawkins. "Similarly, advertisers who buy time during TV programs that make people go weak will find their product unconsciously associated with these negative feelings."

In other words, you want all aspects of your Hypnotic

Marketing to test strong – so that people will be drawn to it and want what you are selling. And all aspects can be tested.

So let me now explain how this works:

First: I felt it was a hassle to try to find someone to do a muscle test with, even though that is Dr. Hawkins preferred and even prescribed method of getting answers. I went online, did some focused searching, and found a few ways to do a muscle test by yourself. Since I basically work alone, I need to do these tests alone. (I could bother my girlfriend, but she already thinks I'm strange).

The best one person testing method I discovered works like this:

Hold out your left hand, with your fingers spread apart, as if you were going to hold a softball or large grapefruit. Now take the thumb and index finger of your right hand and touch the thumb and pinkie of your left hand.

Are you with me? You should have your left hand wide open and your right thumb on your left thumb and your right index finger on your left pinkie. Got it?

Now all you do is try to squeeze the left thumb and left pinkie together as you try to resist. Go ahead and do that now.

You should have found it easy to resist.

Now think of something negative, (Hitler works every time) and try to resist as you also try to squeeze. Your thumb and pinkie should have weakened.

Now think of something loving (your favorite pet

should work) as you resist your own squeezing. Your thumb and pinkie should remain strong and apart.

See how this works? I know all of this must seem wild to you. But hey, no one is looking and I won't tell. So let's keep going.

In the simplest way I know how to say it, you want your hypnotic copy to test strong. When it does, you should expect great results from it. When it tests weak, you have to revise your ideas until they are strong.

Let's look closer at language for a minute. In Dr. Hawkins' book, he has a priceless chart where he lists strong words versus weak words. For example:

Abundant is strong while excessive is weak.
Beautiful is strong while glamorous is weak.
Giving is strong while taking is weak.
Inspired is strong while mundane is weak.
Kind is strong while cruel is weak.
Natural is strong while artificial is weak.
Optimistic is strong while pessimistic is weak.
Praising is strong while flattering is weak.
Responsible is strong while guilty is weak.
Serene is strong while dull is weak.
Timeless is strong while faddish is weak.
Truthful is strong while false is weak.

In short, you want to use words that test strong in all your sales copy. That means taking out all those weak words and replacing them with strong words. The more strong words you have, the more powerful your copy.

Follow?

Now you can test every aspect of your hypnotic writing using muscle testing. Here are some pointers on how to do it to arrive at accurate readings:

Ask permission. Always ask, "May I ask about –?" and test to see if you can. Sometimes you cannot, and you have to either skip the subject for the time being or try to locate the block with a thoughtful line of questioning.

Avoid distractions. Turn off the television, the radio, or anything that may influence your answers.

Get clear. Ask yourself, "Am I clear to receive accurate answers?" before you begin testing.

Stay focused. Ask about specific aspects of your writing.

Example: When you first begin, look at something as a whole, say a sales letter. Ask "This letter tests strong." If it in fact tests strong, you're done. If it doesn't, narrow your search. Ask "The first half of this letter tests strong." If it does, test the latter half. In this manner you can hone in on the areas that need strengthened.

I know this may seem like a crazy way to improve your sales, but most people of genius have done wild things to seduce their muse. Squeezing two fingers together seems pretty tame to me. But if it helps you get the results you want, why not go for it?

And now, before I wrap up this book with an ending statement, a poem, and a call to action, let me reward your efforts by giving you some really juicy bonus chapters.

STEP 4:
HYPNOTIC SOCIAL MEDIA

"How Can This Shy Genius Teach You to Use Social Media Marketing to Build Your Online Empire with Her Top Secret Information?"

"This is the most exciting Hypnotic Gold interview of 2008!"
– Dr. Joe Vitale

Joe Vitale:

Hello everybody, Dr. Joe Vitale of Hypnotic Gold and mrfire.com. I am so excited for today's interview that I am beside myself. I'm almost shaking in my chair. You're going to need pencil and paper. If you are driving, you're going to have to be very alert here because we have a lot of information. This is new. This is leading edge. This is breakthrough. We're going to be talking about social networks, social network marketing, and all aspects of it. Believe me, I have a front row seat here because I want to learn this and know this and use this more than maybe anybody listening right now. This is going to be powerful material, informative material, and the kind of material you can take to the bank.

I have found a leading genius when it comes to this social

network marketing, and doing things with Facebook and some of the other ones like Digg, StumbleUpon, Reddit, Mixx, and these that you may never have heard of. I admit that I don't know all of them. I'm even very skeptical about some of the uses of all of them. I have found somebody who is truly a genius at doing this. She's a quiet genius. You're not even going to be able to find her because she doesn't want to give out her website. Fortunately, I know where she is. I found her, and I have her on today's call. I want to make sure she's on the call. Are you still there?

Alicia Wright:

Yes, I'm here.

Joe:

Alright. I'm talking to Alicia Wright. Alicia has extensive IT and tech background experience. She's been with C&E certified novel engineer, an MCP, Microsoft Certified Professional, as well as a ten-year active data tester for MS, Adobe, and other leading software companies. Her background, her experience goes really deep into web 2.0, social media, and community projects. She's got an understanding and a vision about how this works on a very detailed level. In fact, if I let her, she'll confuse the hell out of me. But, I'm not going to let that happen, because I want to learn how to use this in an Internet marketing, street-smart way.

We're going to be talking about social networks, social

network marketing, how to get more traffic to your site, how to increase conversion, word of mouth, Facebook, Myspace, and I'm going to be picking her brains -- being skeptical from time to time, but always looking for the practical use of all of this, including things you may never have heard of like some of these things like StumbleUpon, Ustream.tv., etc. Of course, you know YouTube, I think, Squidoo.com. I can just keep on going.

Anyway, I found the source. I found the Holy Grail. I found the guru. It's Alicia Wright. Alicia, thank you for being on here.

Alicia:

Thank you for the kind introduction. I'm flattered.

Joe:

Well you deserve all of this. I want to make sure people know just how good you are, and I'm going to tell a story of how you helped me.

A while back, I started a blog. I started my blog very skeptically thinking who's going to read my blog? Who cares about blogs? They all seemed like they were self-indulgent diaries with nothing really happening. I started it, and I got interested in doing it. I caught the bug of sharing myself, sharing my products, sharing my life. I found that doing a blog was a relationship builder. I also knew I wanted to drive traffic to my site. I wasn't sure how to drive traffic to a blog. I can certainly get it to Mr. Fire, and my Mr. Fire site has been up for decades, so it gets a lot of traffic automatically from all the search engines that have found it. Of course, I keep adding content to the site, which makes it interesting. But the blog, what do I do with the blog?

Well, Alicia Wright contacts me because she had been helping Pat O'Bryan, and Pat raved about her, so we exchanged a few emails. She came up with this idea of me writing something about Valentine's Day. I ended up spontaneously coming up with an idea that was titled, "Desperate Valentines." It was something like 15, 16 things that you can do if you're all alone on Valentine's Day. So, while the rest of the world was talking about how to buy flowers and candy and go on a date and have a good time, I went contrary, and I said, "What if you're all alone? What if you're desperate? What do you do?" So I came up with this to-do list, this little idea list, little brainstorming list called, "Desperate Valentines." I told Alicia about it. She did her magic, which today, I still don't know exactly what she did. Hopefully, she'll explain it. Very quickly, that particular post probably had 300 or 400 Diggs. She'll have to explain what Diggs is in a minute. But, more importantly, overnight, my blog saw 20,000 new visitors -- 20,000! This is on top of what was already going to my blog. Because of what Alicia did, because of that Valentines post, because it got dug, 20,000 new people went to my blog. I don't know about the rest of you, but that's pretty darn exciting to me. So, Alicia, let's just start there. How did you do that?

Alicia:

Well, that particular effort was finding the right content, and then bookmarking it in the right places. The cool thing about this that makes it real simple for everybody, if you just look at it this way, is to remember that we've been bookmarking for years. We started out by using my favorites on our browsers, by just when we found a site we like, a lot of people will click my favorite so they can remember to go back to it. It's that type of concept that started social networking and social bookmarking. We've done the same thing, fast forward to 2008. We take a post that we like, and I bookmark it on a popular social networking or social site. What it does is, it puts it in front of a vast amount of people all at once. It's sharing data. Very simply, that effort, if you bookmark strategically for your niche, and at the right time and the right place, then it propels new visitors to your site instantly.

Joe:

Wow. Well there are so many levels of questions right there alone. I'm in kindergarten when it comes to social networking and all of what you just explained, so break it down for me.

Okay, I understand bookmarking. When I go to a website, I can bookmark it there. I know how that works with my Internet Explorer. But you're talking about bookmarking it some place in particular. Can you give me an example or tell me where you went?

Alicia:

Yes. Okay. For example, what I do, I take the top 30 sites at Alexa.com, which is a traffic-ranking site. For instance, Google is number one. Digg is number 30. StumbleUpon is 69. I make sure that I'm in the top 30, or at least the top 100 sites. For whatever niche or particular blog or website that I'm trying to help, I help them identify a site in that list that would be appropriate for sharing their data with. Then what I do, is I teach them the content to write, or recommended content that would work on the different sites, because they're all different. Obviously a video works on YouTube. A fun story or top ten list works great on Digg. Just your blog in general will work great on StumbleUpon. So, you identify the correct type of site for your niche, and then you make the data on your site appropriate for the bookmark you're trying to create. Then the rest is just people. That's the power of the people, word of mouth.

Joe:

Meaning the people pick it up and they start distributing it virally, word of mouth, that type of thing?

Alicia:

Exactly.

Joe:

Okay. Well let's back up here. I know when you encouraged me to write a blog post, you knew that a holiday was coming up. In this particular case, it was Valentines Day.

A week or two in advance, you suggested I write something tied to the holiday. So, first of all, is that a good rule of thumb? In other words, whatever…July 4th is coming up, Christmas is coming up, maybe it's an unusual holiday. Maybe it's St. Patrick's Day. Is that where we begin, by just kind of looking ahead to see what's going to be talked about in the news?

Alicia:

Yes. This applies across the board. I think anybody, in marketing, the first thing they should do is take out a calendar and circle all of the dates for the entire year that are important. There are two reasons for this. Naturally people are going to search for those search words more in the search engines, and it's going to be more appropriate to what is going on that particular week.

For instance, if the Olympics are coming up, it'd be a great idea to write a post about the Olympics. If Mother's Day is coming up, it'd be a great idea to write a post about appreciating your mother. Then you're going to get found in the search engines. You're going to rank very high, your blog post is, anyway, simply because your blog post is about something relevantly searched for in that particular time period. That helps your book- marking efforts, identifying on a calendar all the major days that you could use to write about. It's the same thing Hallmark does with their cards, and Wal-Mart does with their displays. It's just doing what they do, online.

Joe:

I love that. Well, that's traditional publicity, really. A good publicist is always thinking about *how do I tie what I do*, not necessarily even on the Internet, but *how do I tie what I do to an upcoming news event*, meaning a holiday, a special occasion, something we know people are going to be talking about. So, you're putting it online, and you're suggesting that I write something from my blog, I write something from my website, tying it to what I know is going to be talked about in the next weeks or months or something like that.

Alicia:

Exactly.

Joe:

Okay. So, that's a great first step there. But, how do I know, or how do I even find those sites? I mean, even if I go to Alexa, and I see that there are 30 different websites that are very top ranked, how do I get them to bookmark what I've just created? I'm missing something in my thought process here.

Alicia:

Okay. Well, it is a process. It's not something that you can just instantly do. I think that's the number one mistake that most marketers make. They go out, and they just try to instantly use the sites without doing some research. I think it's very important upfront for you to research the sites that you're interested in distributing your content on, or having your readers distribute your content on.

The key is to make it easy for your readers who are usually pretty savvy. I mean, as days go on, people are getting more and more savvy about what Digg is and what StumbleUpon is, and they enjoy sharing your information. How many times have you gotten an email or heard a story, and you call up Pat or someone, and you want to share it with them? A lot I bet. It's the same concept.

Let's say your blog readers read a post, and they're like, "Oh my gosh, I want to tell this to my friend." Well, a few years ago, the way to share it was to email it to a friend.

Now, the way to share it is to bookmark it. A lot of friends share bookmarks. It's the same concept except these sites, like Facebook and Digg and StumbleUpon have become aggregators for people's favorite topics. All you're basically doing is providing data that people can share.

Joe:

Let's break that down even more. You mentioned for example, Digg. I know there are going to be Hypnotic Gold members that don't know what that is. Can you define Digg and explain why it's even at all important? What is Digg?

Alicia:

Okay. Digg was started by Kevin Rose and Jay Adelson, (two geniuses), just a few years ago, believe it or not. They have become a leading news source online. What happens is, that every day, people submit stories to Digg that they find interesting. They're voted up or down by the community. If it's popular, it can drive an immense amount of traffic to your site. I've seen it drive as much as 400,000 hits in three hours. Unique hits.

Joe:

Wow. That's amazing. How does somebody Digg a story? First of all, do they just go to Digg.com to see what this is all about?

Alicia:

Yes. Then what I would recommend doing is, I would, if your niche is let's say, self-help, I would go to search on Digg, enter self-help, and see what kind of articles are doing well. Look at the ones that have the most Diggs. That gives you an insight as to what works on Digg. Then, I would read them and see what kind of content it is, see if your content is like that, and if it is you can tailor it, like a top ten list. I know they do very well on Digg. Just like your post on Valentines, it was a favorite because it was a different take on Valentines. There was so much mush and love that was on there that day, yours was one of the few posts that told people what do you do if you don't have that. People really liked it. It think it's just using your creativity.

Joe:

You mentioned top ten lists. I want to point out too, that that's a traditional publicity technique to use. I've talked about it just for getting traffic to a website, not necessarily a blog, even before Digg came around where I'd write a top ten list which could be like David Letterman's top ten jokes of some sort. It could be practical, like the top ten ways to save on your taxes. But, it's tied to whatever the person's expertise is.

For example, if I wanted to promote… I've rewritten *The Attractor Factor*. It will be coming out soon as a revised, expanded book. If I wanted to write about the law of attraction to help create some traffic and purchases for *The Attractor Factor*, I might write a top ten ways to engage the law of attraction, or the top ten funny ways the law of attraction has been used. Am I on the right track with that?

Alicia:

Exactly.

Joe:

Okay. Alright.

Alicia:

The key is that I really think helps you, is if you do a little bit of research beforehand, or have someone in your office do some research for you, and find out what has done well. Also find out what has already been posted because you don't want to post something that's a duplicate. Digg is one of the communities online that you really have to be pretty savvy to post on. For instance, you don't want to put a picture on there that was on there two days ago. The best thing to do before you do a post is just to make sure that you take a moment, and do some research. It's amazing…a video the other day was posted on Digg. This is a classic example. It had 9 million viewers in two days.

Joe:

What in the world was the video?

Alicia:

This particular video was a Matt Damon and Jimmy Kimmel video. It was not necessarily safe for work video, but it still had 9 million views posted. It's amazing what people sharing data, the power of it, how far, the reach of it can be. It's just amazing to me. That's why I do this. I love it.

Joe:

I can see why. I'm loving that you are talking to us about it, and breaking this down so we can do it. How do you get anybody to Digg your article? In other words, when I post things on my blog, there's a Digg button there where somebody can click on it, and they can go and Digg my article, meaning that they're going to endorse it, I guess, and get it listed on Digg. How do you get people to do that? Is there a way, a means, or a secret?

Alicia:

I think two things. I think it's very important to have a conversation with your readers and say, "I'd like to get the word out to even more people, and you can help me by doing that." Make them part of the process. Educate them in case they don't know. Say, "We're going to be adding some new buttons to our site. One of them is Digg.com."

Just tell them, "It's a site that I'd love for you to go and vote up my content there if you like this post." You know how a lot of people, and I noticed on your blog you say, "If you enjoyed this post, buy me a cup of coffee." It's kind of the same conversation. If you teach your readers to do what you want them to, they'll do it.

Joe:

So, I have to educate them.

Alicia:

Yes.

Joe:

It's just a blog post. It's not a big deal. I just tell them what I'm…like for example, I'm starting, you may not even know about this yet, Alicia, because I've started something to help end homelessness in this country. It's called Operation Yes. I have one little video that's on my blog. It's already had 70 some Diggs. People are liking it, without me encouraging them; they are Digg-ing it. Most of my people, that go to my blog, I don't think they know how to Digg. I think there's a Digg button there. I don't think they know what it is. You're suggesting I need to tell them, and tell them why it's there and how to use it, what it's for.

Alicia:

Exactly. Something as simple as saying, "If you liked this blog post, why don't you share it with a friend by Digg-ing it? There's a Digg button on the site now." Write them a short little paragraph about what Digg is and how you're using it. I think they'll appreciate it because a lot of people that read your blog in particular are interested in marketing ideas, and this will help them market their blogs as well.

Joe:

You know, we're talking about marketing here, but I know that somebody listening has probably got the thought. Even though 9 million people go look at a video, or even though I've got 20,000 new visitors to my Valentines post, does any of that convert to actual sales or money, or do we worry about that at all when we're just trying to drive traffic? Are we just trying to create a relationship? Are we just trying to get popular, just trying to get noticed? Is there a secret to maybe even embedding a product within whatever it is that we just got posted, we just got dug? What are your thoughts on that?

Alicia:

Okay. It goes back to, I think there's a new trend. I think the trend is web 2.0, social media, social marketing. I think people in general, don't like being sold to. They don't like the spammy calls. They don't like the spammy email. They would much rather participate in a conversation. Just like you or I, we're going to act on a friend's recommendation, or a referral from a friend, a lot more than we are by just something that's shown to us on TV.

If we participate in, if we talk to people, our fans, our volunteers, our customers, other bloggers, influences of our own, if we talk to them, and then we give them a reason to talk about ourselves, then we have the tools in which to spread that message, that's one big conversation. Then, the key is to track that conversation and find out how it's working or not working for you. It's the same thing that you do now. You find out what ads work or copy works, except this time, conversation is what you're tracking.

Joe:

So, with my Valentines post, I got 20,000 people coming to visit, I don't know that I looked at it beyond that to see if it actually meant anything, or if I tried to do anything to sell anything. For example, what should I have done differently, if anything, to make that more profitable for me? You know, 20,000 new visitors are wonderful, but they didn't all stay. I don't have 20,000 new ones that are there every day because of that post. Am I missing anything in here, or is that just part of the process of doing the social network marketing?

Alicia:

It's part of the process, but also one thing that I would recommend doing is everybody should be using Google analytics. What you should do is, you should see how many new RSS subscribers you got. You should see how many people came the next day, or if your visitors picked up at all. I mean, can you tell me if they've increased at all since then?

Joe:

I'm sure they did. I don't know anything about Google analytics. I've heard of it, but for those who don't know besides me, where do they get that, and what is it?

Alicia:

Okay. You go to Google.com, and you literally type in the word analytics. It will take you straight to it. There will be a link to Google analytics, and it will take you straight to it. There is a simple code that you can get either your web person, or there's instructions there for you to install it yourself on your blog or your website. There's also a

WordPress plug-in if you use WordPress, for instance. There's a WordPress plug-in that you can download, again at WordPress.org. It's free, and it's very, very simple to install. It takes two minutes. It will help you track your return on investment on your blog every day.

Joe:

Okay. I've got to do that.

Alicia:

Yes. It's great. It's something everyone should be using.

Joe:

Well, that's a major tip right there. Let's keep going here. What are the most popular social sites, and why and how should I use them for my business? Why should we even care? All these popular sites, I hear about things like Facebook, which I finally joined, MySpace and Twitter and there are so many of them, it's driving me crazy. How do I know, what are the most popular ones, why should I care, how do I use them?

Alicia:

Okay, great. I think it depends on the business. That again is where if you're like a doctors office, your social sites are going to be different than the ones if you're a business. Let's just say if you're a regular business, and you have a product or service that you're interested in the mass amount of people knowing about, or even you're particular niche like self-help. If you want your self-help niche to know about it, then you target the self-help niche on the sites.

For business in self-help, I would look at the top 30 sites on Alexa.com that you feel your content would be good on. For instance, like at Flickr.com, I would go and I would post, like for you, I would take your book images, and I would title and tag them "Joe Vitale" or "mrfire.com" and put them in Flickr in a public viewed photo album. That way, if anybody does an image search for self-improvement, you're going to come up. There are all kinds of ways to get really credible back links and increase your traffic. This isn't just a quick increase. This is a long-term smart way to use these free sites to get a lot of traffic to your website or blog. Another social site…you never what?

Joe:
I've never even heard of Flickr before.

Alicia:
Yes. It is a great site. Absolutely great.

Joe:
Really?

Alicia:
Yes.

Joe:

Okay. That's another one to put on my list. Flickr.com. Alright. Go ahead.

Alicia:

Okay, for instance, like Flickr, it's an image site. For you, I would find all the author groups and all the self-help groups on Flickr, and I would go upload or have your VA upload pictures again of your books, and you, you with a picture of your book. That way, a group of 10,000 people have all of a sudden seen a picture of you and your book. It takes two minutes to do this. This is something that's very, very simple to do. This is not hard, to upload a photo. The key thing is, that rather than just searching for terms, people are searching for a lot more specific terms now. For instance, they'll search for a video on self-help, or they'll search for an image for self-help. If you're on video and in images and in text as well, you're going to be inundated on Google, which is a good thing for you.

Joe:

And this is all done on Flickr?

Alicia:

Well, Flickr is for the images. YouTube would be for the videos. Then, for your content, I would recommend Digg and StumbleUpon, Reddit, Mixx, Propeller. Those would be the ones that I would target.

Joe:

Alright. You just said a few more names that I don't know, so I'm sure the Hypnotic Gold members aren't going to know all of them. Mixx, and you said one other one...

Alicia:

Reddit.com. Mixx.com.

Joe:

What are those two?

Alicia:

They are both like Digg; they're just not as highly trafficked as Digg. Mixx.com is a lot, I would say, friendlier than Digg. If that makes sense? On Digg, there are a lot of tech users. They're very, very tech savvy. So, it's a harder crowd to market to. Mixx is more of a community of everybody, so it's a great place to put your content. Reddit, is kind of in between the two, if that makes sense?

Joe:

Okay. What about StumbleUpon? Pat turned me on to it, so I've had fun playing with StumbleUpon, but you might want to describe what it is and why it's useful.

Alicia:

StumbleUpon is incredible. It's one of my favorite sites. It is the one that gets you just an immense amount of long-term traffic. Digg will get you quick instant traffic with very low page time and not great conversion. StumbleUpon gets over two minutes of page time each and has great conversion. It's a site that 10 weeks from now, a bookmark that was made today will still be popular. It's an excellent resource for everybody to use.

Joe:

StumbleUpon, I'll just ad-lib my own definition of it from a user, consumer, and fun perspective. You go to StumbleUpon.com. I think you join it, tell it what your interests are, and then you just stumble upon websites. It will randomly bring up websites that supposedly are relevant to what you said your interests are, and you vote on whether it was actually useful to you by saying, 'I like it' or you say 'I don't like it.' StumbleUpon memorizes that in an artificial intelligence sort of way, and does its best to only allow the next websites to be more relevant to you. You keep stumbling upon them. From the consumer/playful/visitor/browser aspect, it's a very fun, insightful, even surprising tool to use. But, from the other side, from the marketing standpoint, you're saying that if a website is actually listed in there, you're being stumbled upon by all these visitors who may never have seen it before.

Alicia:

Exactly. The great part about it is, if you use all these tools in connection with each other, if you sit down and you make a social media plan, which I encourage everyone to do, then you build upon the efforts that you're making at each site. For instance, if you Digg something, then Stumble it, then it gets traffic and long-term visits. Then you can literally take a single post, like your Valentines post, I took it and I placed it on Digg first. Then I Stumbled it. Then I shared it on Facebook. It went to three places and lists it in five minutes, and it got you 20,000 new visitors to your site.

Joe:

I love it. When you say to create a social networking marketing plan, I think that was the phrase you used, is there any model for something like that? Is there a website that gives us like a step-by-step, or do you have one, or is there a book that kind of holds our hands? Is there a social networking marketing for dummies out there of some sort?

Alicia:

I can certainly make you a list. I don't think there's a definitive guidebook. I mean, there are certainly books on the different sites. There's a Facebook book, and there's a StumbleUpon book. You can of course get the dummies guides to all of those. They've got them. There's not a book that has all of them. I can certainly write a little .pdf for you on everything we've gone over today. You can share it with everybody if you'd like.

Joe:

Oh, my goodness. If you'd do that, that would be golden. Wow. I'll politely request that happen. That's wonderful. Thank you.

Alicia:

I will put all the links in there.

Joe:

You are fantastic. What a gem. Well, I've got to ask you a couple other questions. I have been cornered into joining Facebook and then Twitter. I did it reluctantly because this is again, me not understanding the value of Facebook, Myspace, and Twitter, and all these other ones. I go to Facebook.com. I join it, and there's like 40 people waiting for me. It's almost like they knew I was going to show up. I sign in, and there are 40 people who want to be my friends. Of course, I okay that, and more and more people are okaying being my friend, their friends, and this, that, and the other. I still don't get it. Why is Facebook so important and so valuable? You may have answered it by saying, you know, we don't trust the traditional advertising. We trust other people. Here's a way for people to socialize. I certainly don't understand Twitter, which is a way for people to find out what I'm doing, and me to find out what they're doing at any particular time. They kind of stalk me in a polite, agreed upon way. What am I missing here with Facebook and Twitter?

Alicia:

Well, there are definitely stalkers on both, so you want to avoid those. Like in any business, there are some crazies out there, and there are definitely some crazies on both sites. You want to be a little selective about who you choose as your friends. I think that's the best advice I can give you right up front. If you don't know them, or you don't have a significant number of mutual friends, you might just want to be a little careful.

Now, if somebody writes you a message, which I try to teach everybody to do, when they ask for you to add them as a friend, it's very important to jot them a little note and say, "Here's why I'd like to connect with you." Just simple business etiquette of like, "Hi. I see that you're in a similar niche, and I think that we could share ideas," something just simple like that. Then, people are very responsive to that, and they'll add you. It's a very simple way in a very short amount of time to get to know people all over the world. Since I've started Facebook, I have people that are friends in the U.N. I have friends in 30 plus countries. Where else in the world would you have an opportunity like that if you didn't have the Internet?

Joe:

That is true, the Internet has changed my life of course, and has for the last 20 some years. It keeps changing with things like Facebook. Facebook is a way for me to meet other people, and all these other people are creating relationships with me, and they have their own relationships, so my name, my work has spilled out through this domino effect, I guess. But, within it, there are a lot of plug-ins. One I'm curious about is Twitter. What's your take on Twitter? Is that a useful, valuable…should we be doing Twitter?

Alicia:

Oh yes. Now, I use Twitter for different things than probably you would. But, I use it to find out about blog posts that I could submit since I'm a heavy social media user. For instance, John Kawasaki and Seth Godin and yourself and Tech Crunch and a lot of the top 100 blogs, they all post on there as soon as they make a new post to their blog. Since I'm a social media user, it helps me find good content to post. For instance, if you post, then there are a lot of people out there like myself that are looking for content to submit to these sites daily. Yours will get picked up and posted.

Joe:

I'm going to make sure I understand. I'm on Twitter now. In fact, I think if people look at my blog, I now have a live Twitter feed on my left column of my blog that tells people what I'm doing based on the last thing I posted to Twitter. It may be something like, "Now I'm interviewing an expert on social media and social networking," and stuff like that for my Hypnotic Gold. I've seen people post things on Twitter that say, "I'm having a cup of coffee," or, "I'm going for a walk," or "Boy, I'm doing the dishes now." I mean, is that the right thing to post, or does it matter? I'm still trying to figure this out. Help me here, Alicia.

Alicia:

Well, okay, Twitter is microblogging, where as a blog post is usually full of relevant content for a particular subject. Twitter breaks it down, and there are people that get up and they literally microblog every aspect of their day. They don't do the next thing without Twittering it. I personally do not use it that way, and I don't know many that do. But, you will have some people that end up getting in your group or that you follow, or that might follow you, that do that kind of thing. If you watch the public Twitter blog, that is like a blog of everybody, it is amazing what people will post on Twitter.

I'll give you a brief example. The Academy Awards came on. It was like watching it with a hundred friends because everybody was Twittering about what they thought about the Academy Awards. So, it's a way that you can, again, let people find out about you. For instance, one of the things that I've seen Seth Godin do, he will Twitter, "I'm going to be speaking XXX." Well, then people may see that and be intrigued, go to his blog to find out, "Hey, what's he speaking on?" It's a free way to get the word out about you. I mean, if people keep seeing, especially with you, with your clever titles, if you do some really little clever Twitter posts, people will come to your blog to see what it's all about. It's a free way to get more traffic. So, yes, you should be using it, definitely.

Joe:

Okay. Well, it's fun to use, I have to admit that. I've done silly things like say, "I'm going to go in the hot tub now." I've also posted things like, "I'm working on an email to announce my new MSS service." I know when I did that, it was just kind of a test, but the next day, somebody had emailed me saying, "Hey, I'm interested in the MSS. When's it going to be released?" I thought, wow, that's interesting. People are paying attention to Twitter. Another day, I posted, "I'm about to go have lunch at Cedar Grove Steak House in Wimberley. If you're available, come and join me." Anything could have happened. I could have sat there and had 100 people show up. As it turned out, nobody showed up, and that would be partly because first of all, I only gave them an hour notice. Second of all, I had just been on Twitter, so there is not that many people following me. But, I can see from a marketing standpoint, doing it the way Seth Godin did, by saying, "Hey, I'm preparing to speak at such and such," or, "I just made flight arrangements because I'm doing a seminar on attract wealth in Atlanta." That would, for those who are following me on Twitter, get them curious, and may get them to go check out that website.

Alicia:

Exactly. I've seen people do things like, "Does your back hurt?" Simple things like that. They'll just put something to intrigue people, and if it's somebody that is intrigued by that comment, they'll click on the link and check it out. The thing I think people have to understand, even if you aren't or they aren't currently using these sites, is that there are millions of people that are. You should take advantage of it in every way you can because it's free.

Joe:

I love it. Well, this leads to a couple of questions here. I hope you don't mind that we keep going because you're just so fascinating. You've got so much information. It's just astonishing. I heard of something called DocStoc.com, I think it is. I have no idea what that is, but I understand that you feel it's a way to market business products and services. Can you explain that, and did I get the website right?

Alicia:

Yes, you did. It is a new site that was one of the Tech Crunch 40 finalists that I discovered through just being online. I absolutely love it. It is a place where you can upload your documents or a sample chapter of your e-book, or your press release, or whatever information you would like to share with anybody out there. They get over a million uniques a month even though they are a brand new site, so they have a vast amount of exposure to a vast amount of people. That is one thing. You can link your blog inside your profile, which I love.

For instance, when you create a free account at DocStoc. com, there's a profile there, and you fill it out with your name, and your website address. It's one of the few places I know where you can actually link with a picture, even of your blog inside there. So, when people go, if they search for instance, for self-help, your documents will show up in Google very high because of their page rank. Particularly if you're a new business, and your blog has no page rank, and it's not being found on the first page of Google, it's good to use a site like Docstoc or any of the ones we've talked about already to show up on the first page of Google. That's a simple way of putting it.

For keywords that would otherwise be typically hard for you to rank very well for, a site like Docstoc is a godsend. By simply going there, creating your free profile, uploading a press release or a few documents that you'd like to share with people, like a sample chapter of your book or you know a small article or something like that, you can get ranked on the first page of Google very high, like usually in the top five on the first page for those keywords. That's not something that's very easy to do for a new blog.

Joe:
I'm stunned. I've never heard of this. Is it free, too? Is this…

Alicia:

It's free. Guess what else is great? If you have limited bandwidth with your hosting, and I don't mean to get too technical here, but I know that sometimes you have to pay for your bandwidth especially on digital downloads that can get quite expensive. It's free, if your document is stored at Docstoc, you can even mark it private, so that it's only available via a link that you send out. For instance, not just anybody in the public can go there and find it. If it's a special link that you only want to share with your list, you mark it private, but Docstoc will handle all the bandwidth and let you download it to your list for free. So, it saves you money, too.

Joe:

That's worth the entire call, all of this. You've given so much information with that one alone, I'm just jaw-drop impressed. As soon as I'm off this, I'm going to be going to Docstoc.com, filling out my profile, and doing all of this. Listen, I've got to ask you a question. How do you keep up with all of this? I mean, do you have an Internet connection just right in your vein or something? I've got Blackberries. I've got laptops. I've got computers, but gee, I have to go get sunlight sooner or later, and hot tub, and workout, and eat, and have a life. How do you keep up with all of this?

Alicia:

Well, you know it's really the same techniques that you use now. For instance, I'm sure in your marketing efforts you know how newspaper works for you, how radio works for you, how TV ads work for you. It's the same thing, except it's websites. Does that make sense?

Joe:

Yes.

Alicia:

So, what I do, it does take coming up with a system, which I think everyone must do. You have to come up with a system, and you have to make this so you spend the least amount of time with these efforts as possible. If you spend hours doing it, it's not productive, and it's not cost effective.

Joe:

Exactly.

Alicia:

You do your research up front. You come up with a social media plan, and you follow it and stick to it. I literally have gotten it down to where a business or even myself can use all of the sites that I've mentioned effectively in less than two hours a day.

Joe:

Wow. And they can even hire somebody to do that if they didn't want to do it themselves.

Alicia:

I recommend you hire somebody to do it. I mean, you can get a VA now, which is a virtual assistant, for $900 a month and they'll work for you 40 hours a week, for $900 a month.

Joe:

Where do you find that kind of VA? Do you have a recommendation?

Alicia:

I have a whole list. I'll include that in the list of links for you.

Joe:

You are amazing. Thank you for doing all of this. I'm not going to let you go just yet. I've got a few more questions for you. Are there like the top five sites that I, or anybody listening should get a presence on? I know you'll make a list, but is there a top two, three, four, five, something we should be really jumping on besides Docstoc.com?

Alicia:

Yes. Facebook. Facebook and LinkedIn. For business

professionals, you cannot have too great a resource right now. What I would do is if you're not on those, sit down and create a profile. Just like you would if you were going to create a press release, create a profile on a piece of paper for you or your virtual assistant, whoever's going to be doing it. Then go to these sites that I'm about to give you and use the information from that one sheet you just created, and put it on all of them, in the profile area. It's very simple if you just sit down and just do it. You can do it in 30 minutes, all five of these.

Facebook.com would be the first one. Linkedin.com would be the second one. I would create a profile on Digg. I would create a profile on Flickr. Then, I would create a profile on StumbleUpon. If you had to narrow me down to five, those would be the five that I would use. Then of course, Docstoc.

Joe:

Then Docstoc. Okay. Well, five and a bonus. That's pretty good right there. I love it. Well, I guess there are so many other things I could be talking to you about. When it comes to filling out a profile, are there any hints on doing that? I know when I opened Facebook, I just answered some basic questions here. But, there were some other things like my interests, what books I read, my favorite movies. Are those, this might be a dumb question, but were those opportunities for me to answer in a way that might have brought more traffic to my listing on Facebook? Are there some secrets to filling out a profile, I guess is what I'm asking?

Alicia:

Yes, there are. For instance, in every effort that you make online, if you are just very strategic like you are in any marketing effort, think of it as just that, a marketing effort. When you go to your profile, you have to fill it out for the group that you're trying to reach. So, for instance, in "interests" you should tag it with the appropriate tags, meaning put the words there, like self-help, law of attraction, attractor factor, hypnotic marketing, any words that people use now to find you on your other website, you should put in there as your interests so that if people search on Facebook by those terms, they find you.

Joe:

Got it. That's a major tip in itself. You know, a lot of people with Hypnotic Gold are actually authors. I wanted to see if you could give us a couple, two, three minutes of advice on doing, using some of these sites in social media to market a book. Do you have a couple of quick tips on that besides just getting listed on Amazon?

Alicia:

Sure. Let's say you were coming out with a new book tomorrow, or a month from now. What I would tell you to do is get the image and your Amazon affiliate link, of course. Have the image and the Amazon affiliate link handy. I would go to Facebook, and I would utilize some of the applications there such as Visual Bookshelf or Good Reads. Facebook has applications within it that you can use to help make your profile more appropriate for whom you want to share it with. For instance, if you're an author, you can have a bookshelf in there from Good Reads, or from Shelfari, you know, some of the popular book sites where people share their favorite book interests. You can also have an Amazon link, which I love, in there as well. It's a direct link to the book that you're about to promote. The great part is, is that they make it very easy, just literally a click of a button by like, there's a button called Share on Facebook that I'll include in this list how to find that button. You click on that button, Share on Facebook, and it immediately posts it to your profile so that everybody that comes to your profile sees that you now have this book posted there. Guess what's even better? This is what really excites me. Then, it goes into the news feed on Facebook, and everybody sees it, all your friends, everybody.

Joe:

That's a good tip right there. I can't wait. I have my book Inspired Marketing which I did with Craig Perrine, that comes out on Tuesday. People will know about it by the time they listen to this particular audio, but I want to go use this as one of my marketing steps here. That's a big one. I know Good Reads…

Alicia:

Can I say one more thing about that? What I typically do, for instance, if you were going to be promoting a book, I would do five things. I would immediately share it on Facebook. Then, I would Stumble it. You know, I would Stumble the actual Amazon page with your book on it, or your blog, whichever one you want to drive traffic to. I usually do both, the blog and the Amazon page. Even if it only gets like three other people that Stumble it, it's still getting book- marked in one more place on Google. That's just one more place that it shows up. You can never show up on Google in too many places. It's just impossible.

Another thing, if you share that image on Flickr, and some of the user, all of these groups that I've been telling you about today, Facebook and StumbleUpon, and Digg, they all have groups within them. There are author groups, and there are marketing groups, and there are web 2.0 groups. Go and share with the community, your ideas, or have your virtual assistant go post your books and so forth in these groups. If you join the groups that have 10,000 people in them, that's 10,000 more people that just heard you've got a book coming out.

Joe:

I love it. You said there are five things you'd do if you had a book coming out. The first was being listed on Facebook, the second, StumbleUpon, the third Flickr. What are the next two?

Alicia:

The next two would be to load up a sample chapter to Docstoc and any other site like Docstoc. You can load up a sample chapter like AuthorsDen. That's an incredible old site, looks awful, but it has great traffic. You can load your content chapter up there; it's a consistent top ranked link for you on Google, which is long-term traffic.

The thing I would do, and I would hate to throw another site in here at the last minute, but for authors in particular, this is a great site to use: Squidoo.com. It's the site that Seth Godin created. I would create a Squidoo lens about your book.

Joe:

That is a fantastic list of things, too. I'm starting to get it, and I'm starting to get more excited here. I still feel a little bit overwhelmed, so it's going to be very helpful to have that list that you are going to create for the Hypnotic Gold folks. If you wanted to, you know, people are going to want to try to reach you. Do you want to be reached? Do you want to put out a website or just say you're on Facebook, or do you just want to remain anonymous?

Alicia:

No, I mean it's fine if they want some help, they can reach me through Facebook. How about that?

Joe:

Okay. Alright.

Alicia:

It's Alicia Wright on Facebook. You can find me through Joe. I'm listed as one of his friends. Just befriend me, and I will help you whenever I can. I'm also on LinkedIn. I'm on any of the sites that we talked about.

Joe:

I would imagine you are. That is so amazing.

Alicia:

I'm on StumbleUpon. I'm on Digg.

Joe:

Well, Alicia, you have been just amazing. You are just a fountain of information. I could just keep talking and talking to you. Are there a couple other things that you want people to remember? I mean, Hypnotic Gold members are online entrepreneurs for the most part. So, I imagine they either have a website up, or they are about to have a website up. In many ways, they are overwhelmed. They've heard about putting content on their website, maybe they have a blog because they've been listening to me talk about how it's finally helped me. They might be selling digital information. Of course, you've covered a lot of material. I'm just giving you the opportunity to say one, two, or three things about, "Be sure to do this. Above all else, be sure to do this, or be sure to go to this website." I'm just giving you an open-ended question.

Alicia:

Okay. I think the one thing that I would say is, realize that there really is a new trend. This is not a fad. This is not something that is going to go away. It's here, and it's here to stay. It's getting even better. Any businesses right now that jump on this and participate in this web 2.0 social media world are going to benefit immensely from it. Social web is all about conversations with people, and you can have no better advocate than your customers. I just think if they get involved in the process, and there are some books that I would like to recommend.

Joe:

Oh, good. I love books. Tell me.

Alicia:

There are two of my absolute favorites. One of them is called, actually I'll give out the website. It's wordofmouthbook. com. It's Andy Sernovitz. It's *Word of Mouth Marketing: How Smart Companies Get People Talking.* I just absolutely believe in his five T's of word of mouth marketing, his principle. It is absolutely fabulous. If you have never read that book, that is one that you should absolutely get.

Joe:

Wordofmouthbook.com.

Alicia:

Yes.

Joe:

Okay. And what's the other book?

Alicia:

And I'll include that link as well. Another one that I like is *The Wisdom of Crowds*.

Joe:

Yes. That's a brilliant book.

Alicia:

I love that book. That is a great one. Those two right there, I think, give you a lot of good principles that you should follow when you're going to start participating in social media. Honestly, I think if people just remember that happy customers are your best advertising, I mean, you can't go wrong.

Joe:

Right. Keep everybody happy. They'll talk about you. It causes word of mouth marketing to take place. It's a crowd, wisdom of the crowds. Let me ask you…

Alicia:

Even that Joe, let me show you something about negative publicity. If somebody says something negative, you can turn that into an opportunity by listening and learning from what people are saying, and it makes you as a company and you as a marketer, even better. I don't think there's a downside to, you know, communicating.

Joe:

Yes. Even if there was something negative, you would turn it into a positive, you would write about it, you would correct it, you'd find some way to share it, so that people would start talking about how you turned it around. Is that what you're saying?

Alicia:

Exactly.

Joe:

I also forgot to say in the intro, for you Alicia, that you have been a top social media user on sites such as Digg, StumbleUpon, Reddit, Mixx, Facebook, and others, but your past clients have included Planet Hollywood, E! Entertainment, Coca Cola, the government of Argentina, ABC News, and other various businesses and Fortune 500 sites including mine. You are the guru of all of this, and I'm so astonished and so grateful that you've shared so much so openly and generously with me and all my Hypnotic Gold members. You're just a delight. Thank you.

Alicia:

Thank you, Joe. I've gotten a lot of your books over the years, and you're one of my absolute favorite sites on the Internet.

Joe:

Are you talking about my blog or Mr. Fire, or something else?

Alicia:

All of them. Mr. Fire, in general, the blog, the site, everything. I love it. I love your books. Trust me, I'm the first one to buy your books when they are released.

Joe:

Well, you don't have to do that anymore. Give me your address by email, and I'll send them to you. I'll autograph them and send them to you. I'm just really grateful. Let me ask you something that I'm curious about, and I think Hypnotic Gold members would be curious to hear an answer to. When it comes to my blog, what can I do right now to improve it? My personal blog.

Alicia:

Okay. You want to make it easy for people to find. Have it bookmarked all over the place; it's easy through these steps that I'll share with you more in the future and that I've shared with you today. But, mainly make it where people can find it. Number two, try to make it where, just like you do with any marketing effort, it catches their attention right away. That's very, very important. A headline and good relevant content that's updated daily. Yours is of course, but a lot of people, that's the biggest mistake they make. They have infrequent posts to their blog or to their website. They don't change the content. People aren't going to come back if it's not fresh and updated often. I'd say update it often. You want to make it full of ads. So, you want real subtle ads, like you do. I like your text ads. I think that's a great approach. You've got a great blog, you really do. I think once people find your blog, they end up staying.

Joe:

I'm going to relisten to this entire interview, take notes, then when you send me your little cheat sheet list, which I'll share with all the Hypnotic Gold members, I'm going to follow through and act on all of that. Then I'm going to get one of my assistants to help me. I'm going to do all of this because you have thoroughly convinced me and shown me the way to how to use the social media to profit online. I, for one, am very grateful.

Alicia, thank you very much for spending all of this time with me. I just can't say how grateful I am. Thank you.

Alicia:

Well, thank you. I have enjoyed it. I've enjoyed talking with you.

Joe:

Well, that's another episode of Hypnotic Gold for everybody. This is Joe Vitale over and out. Godspeed to all of you. I'll see you on the next month with another remarkable interview in the Hypnotic Gold series.

BONUS SECTION

How to Create a Hypnotic Viral Marketing Campaign

"There's GOT to be a better way!"

My girlfriend was freaking out. She put up her own website and was feeling overwhelmed by all the marketing she needed to do to get people to it. Since she lives with me (you know, the so-called marketing guru), I easily supplied her with ideas, tips, steps, sites, articles, reports and more. I even narrowed it all down and advised her to read just one or two handpicked books on marketing online.

In short, I didn't help her any.

"Can't you just give me three easy things to do?" she pleaded. "Isn't there a fast, cheap way to get promotion for my site and get me some business NOW?"

Her intensity shook me. I took her out to eat and we discussed her site and what we could do to promote it. We had just returned from a Vegas marketing seminar, where Jay Conrad Levinson and Mark Joyner gave us at least another 100 ways to promote ourselves online and off.

Again, it was just overwhelming.

But also in Vegas, the day before the seminar, we had drinks with Paul Lemberg, an author and executive coach. My girlfriend told him about her website, and he suggested she create a "pass along" image that could promote her site. It was a good idea. It planted a seed.

But nothing clicked for her, or me, just then. Finally, over our dinner, I had an insight.

"I remember something I did way back in 1995 to promote one of my books," I began. "The book was *Cyber Writing* and this may help you."

"Tell me, tell me."

"I met a comedy writer for Jay Leno at one of my seminars in Houston," I began. "We hit it off. I spontaneously had the wild idea to ask if he could generate some humor which could have my book as the butt of the joke. In other words, I knew that if he could write something funny, the Internet would spread it for me. The humor would promote my book online. After all, jokes get passed around easily. I figured this could work."

"What happened?"

"He wrote something called 'The Top 10 Reasons to Read *Cyber Writing*' and we sent it out to everyone I know by e-mail!"

"Yes? Yes? What happened?"

"That simple bit of humor got spread around the Internet within 24 hours. Virtually overnight my book became well known and began to climb the bestseller list at Amazon."

And your point?

"Well, if you can create something so good that people will pass it along, you will get them to act as your agents," I explained. "There's even a website called http://passiton.

com/ where you can see samples of what I mean. It's what Paul Lemberg was advising you to do in Vegas. What you are creating is a meme."

"A what?"

"A meme," I replied. "A meme is a symbol or phrase that represents a complicated idea. Jay Conrad Levinson's new book, called Guerrilla Creativity is devoted entirely to the subject of memes. He gives examples of memes, such as 'Ho! Ho! Ho!' for Jolly Green Giant and 'How do you spell relief?' for Rolaids. They are hypnotic, in a way."

"So you're saying I need a picture that people can pass around?"

"Something like that. Maybe you can create a picture of a critter and make it so good that people will *want* to pass it around. You can put your website on it in small letters so every time someone sees your picture, they also see your website."

"What could I do?"

"Beats me," I said. "I'm just planting the seed. You water it."

"I could use SOME suggestions!"

"Oh. Well, it needs to be funny, or patriotic, or bizarre," I began, not really knowing what to tell her. "The more unusual, the better. The more it touches the heart, the better. The more unique, the more hypnotic."

Dinner was over. The very next day she received a photo of my sister's cat, Snickers. It was a truly lousy picture. Half the cat was covered up by a blanket. The kitty's eyes were bright red from the flash. Good luck making anything out of THIS picture, I thought.

But my girlfriend is smart. She's a former Hollywood film editor. Her credentials on major movies, from *Ace Ventura 2* to *Evening Star*, are staggering. Besides, her website is all about taking regular pet pictures and turning them into art. That's why her site is called MakeYourPetaStar.com.

So I stood back and let her work.

To my honest amazement, a few hours later she had created a picture so good that it took my breath away. I immediately decided to send it out to my own list of 3,400 people. I sent it to my webmaster. He took one look and decided to send it to his list as well. In short, my girlfriend had created an authentic "pass along." She created Hypnotic Marketing.

Here's the e-mail I sent out to my list:

Subject line: Vote for this Spokescritter

My sister sent Nerissa a terrible photo of Snickers, her cat. A sheet covered half the kitty and her eyes were devil red from the flash of the camera. Yet, Nerissa took that lousy picture and made this original one. I think it's so good, and so inspiring, that I thought I would pass it along. If you feel like it, you are welcome to pass it along to your friends, too. This land is for all of us – our critters, too. Snickers gets my vote as spokescritter.

See www.mrfire.com/Rhotogallery/snickers.iRg

(2015 Update: this image is no longer available).

Joe

Within one hour (one hour!) I had 15 personal replies, all thanking me for the picture. One fellow with his own newsletter and subscriber list said he would feature the image in his next newsletter! Many people said they were already forwarding the image to their family and friends. On top of that, Nerissa's website began to see traffic for the first time ever, and she also began to receive e-mails from people about the picture, her site, and her service.

Not bad for a quickly made hypnotic meme!

In fact, only *one* person complained. He said the idea was "weird." As it turns out, he's not a pet owner and probably not a pet lover.

Oh well, you can't please everybody – particularly on the Internet!

The moral: Consider creating a joke, phrase, or image – some sort of meme or "positive thought virus" – that just happens to promote your site. Then e-mail it to your family and friends, peers and clients. If you've created a truly hypnotic meme, stand back! Traffic will be a coming. If you haven't, no worry. Just create something else.

Hey, this is the Internet. ANYTHING goes and testing is FREE!

The 10 Most Dangerous Marketing Books of All Time

I own one of the largest marketing libraries in the world. Many of these books are good. Some are outstanding. A select few are so powerful they should be banned.

In the last category, many of these truly awesome books are lost, locked away, privately printed, or only shared underground. Today, I'm going to tell you what the top 10 most dangerous marketing books of all time are.

With these books at your side, your marketing powers can become scary. I'm giving this list to everyone who buys my *Hypnotic Marketing* book as a bonus to help you develop the persuasive power of the gods.

Dangerous Selling by Elmer Wheeler. This is the least known book by the "sell the sizzle, not the steak" author of such classic books as T*ested Sentences That Sell* and *Sizzlemanship*. Wheeler was the Zig Zigler of his time. *Dangerous Selling* is his rare book on how to be more forceful with prospects to close more sales.

The Magic Power of Emotional Appeal by Roy Garn. If you've read most of my other books, you know I love this book. It reveals how to appeal to people's emotions so they will hand you money.

How to Covert White Space into Advertising that Sells by Clyde Bedell. This oversized collector's item by a famous ad man teaches you a tested method for creating ads that pull orders. The before and after ads are mind blowing.

How to Write a Good Advertisement by Victor Schwab. This 1962 work is actually "A short course in copywriting." Worth gold. Memorize it.

The Robert Collier Letter Book by Robert Collier. This one is a legend. It actually changed my life as a copywriter. Before it, I was an OK writer; after it, I was a hypnotic writer. Find it.

Advertising Copy by George Hotchkiss. This is the book that helped John Caples, the famous copywriter, learn how to write ad copy that sells. Caples wrote his famous 1925 ad, "They laughed when I sat down" after reading THIS book. Though first published in1924, it's still relevant and powerful today.

Motivation in Advertising by Pierre Martineau. This 1957 classic reveals the hidden motives that make people buy. A psychological masterpiece.

Profitable Showmanship by Kenneth Goode and Zen Kaufman. This 1939 gem explained how to make any business a "show business" by using circus and theatre techniques to grab consumers by the eyes, ears and nose.

Theory of Advertising by Walter Dill Scott. I'm a disciple of Scott. This 1903 book by him was probably the first work EVER published to explain how to use psychology for persuading people to shell out money. His later book, *The Psychology of Advertising*, is also fantastic.

Psyching the Ads by Carroll Rheinstrom. This 1929 goldmine took 180 ads and analyzed them. The insights are startling and priceless. Note: Do not get the reprinted edition, as the ad reproductions are lousy.

There are far more good books in my library on marketing. Anything by John Caples, Bob Bly, Joe Sugarman, Claude Hopkins, and David Ogilvy are all worth having. But the above ten books are the most powerful rare ones I know of.

How to Create Your Own Hypnotic Business Cards

Business cards are so important that I just spent hundreds of dollars, two months of my time, and a lot of sleepless nights creating a new one for myself – and *I* live in the Texas Hill Country, hardly see anyone any more, and have enough books and tapes circulating out there to act as "cards" for me.

In short, I don't even *need* business cards. Why did I go through all the trouble?

I remember seeing P.T. Barnum's card when I was researching him for my book, *There's a Customer Born Every Minute*. It simply listed his name and where he was from. It was a simple calling card.

The thing is, he was one of the wealthiest and most famous men in the entire world – and yet he needed business cards, too!

You and I are the same. We need cards to leave behind and, with luck, intrigue people to call us. I had cards, of course, and I thought they were pretty good. But then my girlfriend, Nerissa, started a new online business and created new cards for herself. Her cards were the most impressive, original, colorful, and direct ones I had probably EVER seen.

In short, she shamed me into wanting new cards for myself – especially since I am a so-called marketing guru.

Below are the seven steps I took to create a new card. It may be a process you can follow for your own needs. If nothing else, it will show you the importance of this often overlooked marketing tool.

- I thought about my message. What do I do? What did I want people to know? With little space to write on, a business card forces you to condense your business into one strong line. I went to my e-mail list a few months ago and asked for help. More than a dozen people offered suggestions. I finally settled on calling myself *"The World's First Hypnotic Marketer,"* which seems to be my strongest claim to fame, particularly since one of my e-books, *Hypnotic Writing*, continues to be a global bestseller, and my most recent e-book is titled *Hypnotic Marketing*.

- I then read Dr. Lynella Grant's definitive 500 page guide, *The Business Card Book: What Your Business Card REVEALS about You...and How to Fix It*. Talk about a humbling as well as overwhelming experience. Grant's book is packed with samples, ideas, advice, tips, and more. Since the author is also on my e-mail list, I wrote her and got some personal advice. I probably spent three weeks on this step alone.

- I then had a phone session with Ann Taylor Harcus to help me remove any limiting beliefs I may have had regarding success. I didn't want to sabotage my own plans. One hour with her and I was clear about my business cards, myself, and my goals. She also helped me "charge" my new business cards with an energy designed to attract the kind of clients I wanted. This is very Spiritual Marketing, and will make sense if you read that book.

- Once I had a feel for what I wanted to say on my card, I decided to add a new photo of myself to it. Friends who saw me in New York City on a recent trip said I didn't look at all like my old pictures. Today I'm called a "hipster" and "magical looking." Well, whatever. So I had Nerissa bring out her mini DV video camera and shoot some video of me. She then used a nonlinear editing system to grab frames from the video. Out of those shots, we found one we loved. But to be sure it was "the one," I sent several pictures to several friends and clients and asked for their vote. After all that, I chose one picture.

- Now I needed a graphic designer. I didn't want a card that looked like it was done by me, or with a software program I bought at a discount store. I wanted a unique design and new image. So I went to elance.com, where freelancers bid on jobs posted by people like you and me. I posted a description of my job. Within 24 hours I had 17 bids from graphic designers, freelance artists, and even full blown ad agencies. I settled on one, an ad agency out of Florida, and hired them to create my new business card using the elements I gave them.

- The agency stayed in contact with me, brainstormed ideas for me, and showed me mock ups of their ideas. This was fun. I had never worked with an ad agency before – though some had been my clients over the years – so this was a first for me. I was very impressed that one artist at the agency stayed in very close contact, e-mailing ideas, making changes, being sure I was happy.

- Finally, I needed a printer. While printers are a dime a dozen and can be found by the bag in any major city, I wanted one to do justice to my card and my new design. I asked around, asked for samples of their work, and finally settled on one my ad agency suggested.

I now have new business cards – ones that are striking, professional, and even hypnotic. I'm proud of them. The whole thing cost me less than $250 total. But what a process to get to this end-result!

In short, business cards are worth the time and trouble. If I think having impressive business cards is so important — and P.T. Barnum thought it was important — shouldn't YOU, too?

REFERENCES & RESOURCES:

Nerissa's new business is described at www.makeyourpetastar. com redirects to: http://www.nebelungs.blogspot.com/

Ann Taylor Harcus' website is at www.innerhealing.com

Hypnotic Writing is available at www.hypnoticwriting.com

Post your request for artists or designers at www.elance.com

Dangerous Selling - A New Way to Increase Your Profits

One day, a woman walked into an arts and crafts business and asked about a serving tray she had seen in the window of the store. The owner looked up at her and said, "Give me your name and address and I'll send it to your house tomorrow morning."

The woman stood there, stunned.

I was watching the whole scene and was truly hypnotized.

"Well, I'm just curious about it," she said.

"I'll send it to your house tomorrow and you can take a good look at it," the owner said, politely but firmly.

I waited, thinking the woman was going to blow her lid, read the riot act to the store owner, or just walk out in a cold huff. Instead, the woman gave her name and address to the owner.

"You are very brave," I said, after the woman left.

"I am?" the shop owner replied, smiling. "Not really."

"But that woman was just looking," I persisted. "She wasn't interested in buying and you put a gun to her head, so to speak."

"She would not have asked about the serving tray if she were not interested in it," the owner explained.

''I'll send it to her house tomorrow with food on it, and a bottle of wine. She'll buy it."

"How do you know?" I asked.

"Think about it. She is already interested in the tray and said so herself. And she gave me her address. That right there is solid proof she really wants it. When I send it to her, she'll feel obligated to me to consider buying it. When she sees food and wine with the tray, with my compliments, she'll be nearly shamed into buying it. She'd have to be a royal witch to not buy at that point, and no royal witch would have submitted to my request for her name and address."

"Lord, man, that is dangerous selling," I said, impressed.

"Just how much do you believe in your product is the real question," he explained to me. "If you know you have something valuable, and you meet someone clearly interested in it, why not be assertive and put it into their hands?"

I paused and considered what he said. I could see his point. I had to admit that I wasn't always as bold with my own selling. It made me consider that if I really believe in what I do, why not be politely forceful about it?

You can apply this method to online sales as well as offline businesses. It's a matter of showing your confidence in your goods by guaranteeing your work, being willing to send out product for examination first, and so forth.

And don't think some daring – or should I say confident – businesses aren't already doing this. One day I ordered an expensive magic trick from a website. They were new and didn't take credit cards. Yet they sent the trick to me without payment up front. Another time a company selling safe home products over-nighted a product to me so I could try it before I bought it.

"What did you come in here for today, anyway?" the shop keeper asked me.

"Oh, I was interested in those wooden book boxes over there on the shelf," I said, swallowing nervously. "Give me your address and I'll send over a few for you to see," he said.

Did I give him my address?

Just take a look at these magnificent hand carved book boxes.

What Bernice Taught Me About Advertising

Bernice Fitz-Gibbon revolutionized department store advertising back in the 1940s and 1950s. She invented the famous slogan "Nobody but nobody undersells Gimbels" for Gimbels department store. She also created the slogan "It's Smart to Be Thrifty" for Macy's. Her ideas and copywriting helped both stores skyrocket sales. She was a genius.

Bernice is long gone, but she wrote a wonderful book back in 1951, revealing her story and her ideas. It was titled "Macy's, Gimbels, and Me." Bernice lives and breathes in that book. I call her "Bernice" right now because I feel I know her. All I really know is what she told me in her book. I thought I would pay homage to her and revisit some of her ideas.

Here goes:

- **"A good headline should create a disturbance."** Bernice wasn't afraid to scare people to get their attention. She once wrote an ad for children's shoes that scared the hell out of parents. The ad said that wearing the wrong shoes deformed children's feet. Shoes sold.
- **"Use short simple blunt words."** Bernice told me, "Stylists should learn that 'begin' is better than

'commence' and that 'happen' is better than 'transpire' and that 'sleep' is better than 'slumber' and that 'bloody' is better than 'sanguinary.'" How true.

- **"Food interests all women."** Bernice was writing in the 1950s, and was heavily focused on women as the housekeeper. She learned that women could never get enough food recipes. You could get attention for any product by tying it to food. Today she would see that men AND women are equally interested in recipes. She once wrote an ad that said a new pie "trembled as it was placed on the table." People packed the restaurant, asking to see "the pie that trembles."

- **"You don't have to be brilliant to write a good ad."** Bernice said a little research can pay off in gold. She discovered that the human body has 210 bones. She wrote an ad for curved corsets that read: "There are 210 bones in the human body and ALL of them are curved." Sales soared.

- **"There are four rules for a good slogan."** Here they are:
  - It should contain five to seven words.
  - It should have a swinging rhythm.
  - It should have the name of something that will identify the product.
  - It should promote a universal truth and not just be self-serving.

- **"There are four ways to make ads more enticing."** Here they are:

a. Get urgency into your message.

b. Be specific – don't generalize.

c. Be easy, relaxed, informal.

d. Be FRIENDLY.

- **"Sometimes the smartest thing you can do is the opposite."** Once the department store was selling dolls that could walk, talk, burp and do everything but scrub the sink. Bernice advised the company to go against the trend, and to create an old fashioned doll. She wrote in her ad: "… this is not the latest mechanical jerk in the doll business. She is simply ... meant to be loved." They sold hundreds of this "new" doll.

Women aren't always appreciated for their contributions to any field, let alone marketing. Yet I've read of many, and met many, who are as brilliant as the more famous men in the same profession. Bernice Fitz Gibbon is one of the greatest. She belongs in the same category as John Caples and David Ogilvy. I miss her.

How to Create Sales after Creating Relationships

I just received an e-mail today that I want to share with you.

The subject line was, "Get publicity for your business using these tips ... in 48 hours or less" Here's the actual letter:

Dear Friend:

Sorry, this letter is late. I hope everyone's holiday was spectacular. Anyway, this letter is going to be quick and dirty and power-packed with tips you can use beginning next week. Let's get started.

First, get a copy of your local newspaper for the last 7 days and read the front page and second page of each section. Find a story that is similar, remotely close, or something that you have knowledge about. Once you do that contact the reporter via phone, e-mail, or fax and ask if they are planning a follow-up story. NOTE! Stories on the first two pages of its section are breaking stories, hot stories, or very important, hence that's why they are on the front page.

Let them know that you can enhance their story by informing their readers that you (fill in the blank). Here's what's going to happen. Either they will interview you on the spot or they will take your name and company information for future publicity. It's great!

Whenever a story comes up they will have your name and number ready to go. Your competitors won't have a chance. I recently did this with our local paper, which has 80,000 readers and I got free publicity for my company. Plus family and friends called and said "We read about you."

That brings me to my second million dollar tip. Which is the celebrity quotient. When famous celebrities get in trouble with the law, who do they call? They call Johnnie Cochran, yet there are plenty of attorneys with more experience, talent, higher fees, lower fees, expertise, etc.

But Johnnie uses the CQ (celebrity quotient) to a 'T.' Once you get known, you can charge higher fees because people expect you to be more expensive; after all you are a celebrity.

You don't need to be as famous as Johnnie. All you need to do is be well-known in your city or community. After contacting your newspaper reporters and getting publicity, you should contact every radio station and send them the same information.

If you ever listen to the radio and you hear "We have open lines in the next hour," this is your opportunity of a lifetime. It means that their booked guest has canceled or couldn't make it and they don't have a backup guest.

You will have a FULL HOUR of free promotion all to yourself. The radio stations will love you because they won't be put on the spot and they have to do something for that hour.

After customers, prospects, and employees hear you on the radio and read about you in the paper, you will have instant CQ. They will think that you are really big time and will brag to friends about you.

Don't let it go to your head. What you are doing is building your business and what I have just told you can be done immediately. So, go ahead and get the past few issues of your local paper, turn on your radio and television and get some major publicity.

The media needs you more than you need them. Believe me, I know. If you are nervous, I have a special deal just for you. I will let you "test" drive what it's like to get free publicity to sell your products and/or services. That's right! It's Christmas time and I am in a giving mood.

You can participate in the name-your-own budget PR campaign. You tell me how much you can spend over 3 months and I'll tell you how much publicity you can reasonably expect to get. One story is worth hundreds or thousands in free advertising.

How big do you want your company to be? There are so many media outlets i.e. CNN, CBS, Fox, NBC, ABC, MSNBC, *The Wall St. Journal*, *USA Today*, *Time*, *Newsweek*, and so on. We can even send press releases

to every newspaper, radio and television station in your
state.

What would that do to your bank account? I'll tell
you. You'd have to hire more employees, expand, and
get a bigger building.

One promotion I sent out only 21 announcements
to the media and I got interviewed by the USA Radio
networks, which has 1,400 affiliate stations, so millions
of people got my name and address and business
information.

Please use these tips because they will work for
anyone who wants free publicity. Your competitors are
too busy trying to make a sale instead of using strategies
that work better and faster.

Warmly,

Robert Smith

815-963-1497

Well, what did you think?

If that isn't a hypnotic letter, I don't know what is!

Not only does the author give you solid information in
a friendly way, but he doesn't sell himself at all. Yet, note
how you feel at the end of the letter: You want to contact
him, hire him, or do whatever it takes to learn more about
his publicity wisdom!

That's hypnotic e-mail, my friend!

In fact, while I had never heard of Robert Smith before
his e-mail arrived in my box (I must have signed up for

his *PR Hot Tips* newsletter to get his e-mail, though), after reading it I wrote to him and asked his permission to use his letter. He quickly agreed.

Robert Smith runs a PR and publicity firm based in Rockford, Illinois. He helps small businesses, entrepreneurs, and self-employed professionals increase profits by getting free time and space on TV, radio, magazines, newspapers, trade journals, etc.

It looks to me like Robert is practicing "relationship marketing." He sends out friendly and informative e-mails which build his credibility. In the long run, he'll end up selling all of his readers *something*. *Why?* Because his readers will have learned to trust him.

That's a wise strategy in today's world.

So if you're looking for a safe, soft way to conduct Hypnotic Marketing online, look no further than Robert's letter.

It's friendly. It's informative. And it will lead to sales.

What more could you ask from simple e-mail?

The Three Real Secrets to Success Today

"What do you owe your shift to?"

We were at breakfast. My friend sat across from me. He knew me 10 years ago. He remembered how I struggled, suffered, and squirmed through life. He sat today, in awe of my successes, my luxury sports car, my beautiful country home, my happiness – and he wanted to know my secrets to attaining them.

The thing is, his question made me uncomfortable. I don't really regard myself as a success. I have bad days. I have failed projects. Truth is, I'm just like you. I've struggled and at times I still struggle. I may have more or less figured out where the escalator is to get through life, but my life isn't by any means fitting for an episode of "Lifestyles of the Rich and Famous." So I decided to dismiss my friend's question with a quick answer:

"It took me 25 years to become an overnight success," I replied.

We both laughed. But he wouldn't settle for my answer.

"What are your days like now?" he asked me.

"Well, at night I sit on the front porch and count the cars that drive by," I began. "Last night there were three cars."

"So sad," he said, smiling. He probably remembered when I lived in Houston and herds of cars roared by my house as loud airplanes soared overhead.

He probably also knew I was lying.

Many nights I sit and read books, or meditate, or do sessions with healers to help me continue clearing myself so I can continue to create dreams that impress people like him.

"During the day I float in my pool and work on my tan," I continued, trying to bring humor into the situation. "Cleaning the pool is a daily chore."

"What a life!" he exclaimed. "You aren't the same person you were 10 years ago! I can remember when you cried as you drove to the job you hated at the time. What do you owe your changes to? How did you get here?"

He wasn't the first to ask. Another old friend – one who knew me before my Nightingale Conant tape set was recorded, or any of my books were published – looked at me and asked, "How did you do all this?"

While I'm still moving and growing and working towards new successes, I don't always stop to reflect on my current ones. My friends have helped me realize I have achieved *something.* And their questions have prompted me to explore the reasons behind my accomplishments. After several weeks of contemplation, here's my reply to the (rephrased) question, "How did you achieve these miracles in your life?"

1. RUTHLESS HONESTY

Most of us settle for what we get in life. I was married for more than 20 years. I love my wife and still love her today as my ex. But I had to admit I wasn't happy. I could have settled, however. I could have stayed in that marriage until I died and never once admitted I wasn't getting all I desired. I was, as Thoreau said, "Leading a life of quiet desperation."

Ruthless honesty with myself led me to realize I wasn't fulfilled. A knock from within myself – a knock as you or anyone else might get but which most of us ignore – told me to look for more. This wasn't easy. Social taboos, family concerns, and my own brain made it hard for me to leave my long- term marriage. But I had to admit I couldn't settle for a "very good" relationship when I could have a "great," or even a "fantastic" one.

I had to realize that my goal was to be happy – but my goal also included *others* happiness. I wanted my wife to be happy, too. I love Jose Silva's philosophy: Set a goal that will help you and at least two other people. Yes! I wanted happiness and I wanted others to have it, too. As a result, my ex is happy with her new life as a single woman and we remain best friends. And I've met a wonderful woman who loves me as I love her. Life is good.

Ruthless honesty with my marriage began the process of my being ruthlessly honest in other areas of my life. It opened me up to consider miracles on all levels of being. It may not be easy to admit that you or I or anyone is unhappy, but facing reality as we see it is the first step to massive change.

2. COLOSSAL DREAMS

The day I saw a deep blue colored BMW Z3 2.8 Roadster was the day I found a colossal dream. Something in me awakened. I had been driving Saturns and loving them. I was the poster boy for those cars. They are reliable vehicles and I still endorse them. But I didn't want to settle on a good car when I could have a fantastic one.

My wanting that expensive luxury BMW sports car led to my creating something no one else had ever done before in history: I created expensive e-mail only e-classes. Within 5 months I raised $68,000. How? Having the colossal dream stretched me to think of new possibilities, new solutions, and new miracles. Most of us are afraid to have big dreams. My friend Bob Proctor once told me, "A dream should scare you a little and excite you a lot."

The energy that rushes through you when you have a big dream is the energy that will help you manifest it. It will lift you out of your world view and into a new way of being. In that new "being" you will create the ways to achieve your dreams. And if you're *really* ruthlessly honest with yourself (step one), you'll know what your dream is. (Come on. Admit it. You know what you REALLY want).

Confused? Good. That's the wonderful state of mind right before a breakthrough. My advice is to choose a big dream and let it take you for a thrilling ride. Then you'll understand!

3. MIRACULOUS MENTORS

I worked with Jonathan Jacobs, a healer out of Houston, for over ten years. He helped me dissolve limiting beliefs about myself and my world. Without him, I would probably still be stuck where I was, doing what I was doing, and never getting out of the rut.

Today I work with Ann Taylor Harcus, an energy healer. Ann once told me I am one of the few people in the world who consistently seeks out mentors to help me. It's true. I'd still be living in a $200 a month dump and driving a clunker if it weren't for my mentors. Mentors lead to miracles. Ann herself once told me she spent $100,000 on personal growth. She told me that her own development was worth more than any other investment. I agree. Without it, you more or less grow at a snail's pace.

In my book, *Spiritual Marketing*, I talk about my dog, Spot. When I first had him, I put him on a three foot chain. I felt it was too confining for him, so I put him on a six foot chain. Well, Spot only went three feet on the six foot chain. He didn't realize he had more room to move until I put my arm around him and walked him the other three feet. Instantly he made use of all six feet.

I'm like Spot. I need someone out of "my box" and off "my leash" to show me that I can have, do, or be anything I can imagine. Jonathan and Ann – and an entire roster of other people – have served me as mentors, and helped me create miracles. If you want to go for – and get – your dreams, get a mentor.

I'm sure there is more to my, or anyone's, becoming successful. I'm always reading books, listening to new tapes, meditating, avoiding the news, thinking positive, and trusting my inner guidance. All of that helps me stay on a path to continued success.

But the next time a friend from the past walks up to me and asks me how I got from where I was to where I am, I'll tell him what I just told you:

- I am honest about what I REALLY want.
- I go after dreams a little bigger than what I think possible.
- I work with mentors to help me create miracles.

Maybe these three keys to success aren't so much unusual as they are not *used.* If that's the case in your life, you've just been issued a friendly challenge. Apply them today and see where you go in a month or two. I assure you, the journey IS the reward.

APPENDIX

You Are Here (and How to Get over There)

Yesterday I drove into Austin and met with the staff who run my Miracles Coaching® program and my Executive Mentoring Program.

I had some exciting news to share with them, and some astonishing news arrived while I was there.

In the morning *The Today Show* called, wanting information on my forthcoming book, *Zero Limits*.

That's pretty big, but not as big as the news that came later.

At lunch I handed out the recently completed bibliography of my life's work so far – 45 pages of books, e-books, audios, videos, software, fitness formulas, and more – an entire listing of everything I've created up to now. The heft of the document alone impressed even me.

But that wasn't the biggest news of the day, either.

At lunch with the staff, I stood up and told them something that I felt inspired to share.

I put a dot on the whiteboard on the wall and circled it.

"You are here," I said.

I told them the whiteboard is like the map at the mall where all the stores are listed and a little box says "You are here" to give you your bearings.

"Where do you want to go from here?" I asked.

"Up," someone said.

"Off the whiteboard itself," someone else said.

"This is all good," I went on. "You all want to move up. You want more sales, more results, more wealth. Right?"

They all agreed.

I then put another dot on the board, way up at the top of it, and circled it.

"That represents where you want to go," I said.

I then asked the key question, "How do you go from where you are to where you want to be?"

They were quiet for a moment, but then began saying things like "Take a straight line," and "Do one thing at a time," and "Make more sales calls," and so on.

"That's all good," I said. "Those are all practical answers. But I want you to think in terms of the movie *The Secret* and my book *The Attractor Factor*."

I added, "I'm going to tell you what I think is the greatest secret to manifesting whatever you want."

They were quiet, not sure where I was going with all this.

"Does anyone want to know what the secret is?" I asked.

They all burst out laughing. They definitely wanted to know.

I pointed at the little "You are here" dot and said, "The secret to getting what you want is to totally appreciate this moment. When you are grateful for this moment, then whatever is next for you will bubble up out of this moment.

You'll be inspired to take action of some sort. That will lead you up. But the only way to get to the upper dot is to live in this dot with gratitude."

They've all heard this before, but I wanted them to truly get it.

I then told them about my Maui friend who says my favorite line these days: "I'm totally satisfied, I just want more."

That's the key to success, I explained.

It's wanting more without needing more.

I went on and on about being grateful, and how it leads to that upward climb. Most of us aren't happy right now, thinking we will be happy when we get to that other dot. But the great joke is that when you get to the other dot, you won't be happy. You'll be looking for another dot on the map. You'll use unhappiness to whip yourself forward. The thing is, it doesn't have to be that way.

Just be happy now.

Out of this now will come the miracles you seek.

The group got the message. They shook my hand. Smiled. Showed light in their eyes. Walked away with a spring in their step.

Now here's the really juicy part.

I got a phone call right after that meeting. It was Suzanne, my assistant. She almost never calls me, and she knew I was in a meeting. So I knew this call had to be important.

I took the call and to my delight I learned that Oprah's

people wanted my media kit.

And they wanted it by midnight.

Oprah's folks are considering me as a guest for a show. Oprah!

Now get this: I was happy in the moment. As I'm happy, the next moment brings it's own rewards. As I'm happy in that moment, it too gives birth to more joy.

You can do this, too. You may not have Oprah call you, but you will get what is right for you. I explain all of this in the book, *Zero Limits*. But the essence of the message is this:

All you have to do is embrace the dot that says "You are here" and do what it tells you to do.

And when the phone rings, answer it!

Ao Akua,

Joe

MrFire.com

PS – If you want more information on either of my coaching programs, see www.MiraclesCoaching.com and also joevitalecoach.com

The Secret to My Success

A reader watched my new DVD, *Humbug* (http://www.amazon.com/dp/B000OYNSOC/), and was apparently impressed with it.

He e-mailed me this question:

"Was there one point in your life that was the turnaround? I often ask people who've obviously hitched themselves to a Saturn 5 rocket the same question."

I get that question a lot.

I've been thinking about it long and hard.

I know that taking on the attitude that *anything is possible* is part of the answer; so is knowing the Law of Attraction and the idea that getting clear leads to preferred results; so is always saying yes to life; and so is the idea of being ruthlessly honest about your desires.

But those are mindsets I've developed over time.

They don't answer the question about the single event that changed my life.

The thing is, there's no "one point" where everything shifted for me. It was more a series of defining moments, some more memorable than others. For example:

Landing the book deal to write the *AMA Complete Guide to Small Business Advertising* for the American Marketing

Association back in 1993, was a marker for me. I wasn't paid much money (almost none) but it was my first book deal with a traditional publisher and the project made me feel accomplished and important. It also got me more clients and more speaking engagements. (I still love the book and use it myself, though sadly it's now out of print. Some of it ended up in my new book, *Hypnotic Writing*).

Recording my program, *The Power of Outrageous Marketing* for Nightingale-Conant in 1997, was another turning point for me, one I had longed to have for over ten years. People who knew that company and their wonderful products began to treat me like I was a deity in the marketing world. That also influenced my own sense of value. (That's also when I raised my fees). The program still sells like crazy today, and I'm still very proud of it. (One of my favorite sections is where I stage an interview with the great circus showman and master marketer, P.T. Barnum).

Certain people helped me step up to a new level, as well.

Paul Hartunian changed my life. This publicity genius who once sold the Brooklyn Bridge as a PR stunt and got on Johnny Carson for it, once spent three hours over dinner in Houston telling me how to change my business. I took notes. I acted. Paul's giving was a defining moment in my career. I'll never forget him. He's one of my heros.

Mandy Evans has been a "miracles coach" in my life for more than twenty years. This wonderful author of such books as *Travelling Free* has always been only a phone call away. Whenever I feel stuck and ready for the next level, I call her. I love her. She helps me get clear.

Bob Proctor – a living legend in the self-help movement – changed my life when he politely nudged me to publish the little book I was fearful about releasing, *Spiritual Marketing*. That book became an Amazon bestseller twice, got me into *The New York Times*, and led to my rewriting it and seeing J. Wiley publish it as the now long running classic, *The Attractor Factor*. And of course *The Attractor Factor* got me into the movie *The Secret*, which led to my being on *Larry King*, *eXtra TV*, *Time*, *Newsweek* and...well, you get the idea.

Obviously, there's no one event that transformed me.

If you want to know more, I've written about my journey through life in such books as *Adventures Within* and of course *The Attractor Factor*. They reveal other defining moments and the people who triggered them for me.

I really wish there was a simple answer to the question of what was my turning point moment, so we could both learn from it.

But what may be better is to assume every moment is your turnaround one, and act from that perspective.

Life would then take on a glow.

Backed into a corner, and forced to say *something* was the one thing that changed my career, I'd give credit to the Internet.

I began as an Internet skeptic in the early 1990s. I didn't believe all the hype about gold in cyberspace.

I was wrong.

I later wrote one of the first books about online marketing (*Cyber Writing*).

And later, when Mark Joyner urged me to let him release my first e-book (*Hypnotic Writing*), I began to taste fame and fortune.

So I have to give credit to being *active* online as a turning point in my career. (Note I said active online. I was and am busy creating and promoting products, not waiting for the world to come to my door).

The Internet let me take what I was doing locally and distribute it to the world.

But, as you can see, it was one of many defining moments.

Maybe the best way to wrap this up is with the following story:

I'm hearing from people from my past who saw the movie *The Secret* and then searched for me online. When they get to my main site, they write me and ask something like, "Are you the same Joe Vitale I worked with thirty years ago?"

One gent did that recently. Turns out we had worked at Exxon together long, long ago.

He saw me on Larry King and couldn't believe my level of success. He wrote to me saying, "I wish I had known what a gem I was hanging around back then."

I thought, what if each of us treated each other like we were gems already – just unrecognized and maybe unpolished.

Wouldn't that single change of perspective make every moment of our lives a turning point?

As Goethe wrote, "Treat people as if they were what they ought to be, and you help them become what they are capable of being."

Ao Akua,

Joe

www.MrFire.com

TIP: A way to get a turning point moment for yourself is through Miracles Coaching®. I believe that trained mentors can help you leap to the next level, and I still employ them for myself today. Expect miracles. And remember, every moment counts.

NOTE: If you want help in making it online, consider my Executive Mentoring Program. See joevitalecoach.com for details, endorsements, and more.

A "Crazy" New Way to Increase Sales - from Zero

In my new book, *Zero Limits*, I talk about the unusual therapist who helped heal an entire hospital ward of mentally ill criminals – without seeing any of them.

I've since learned his method for healing, which involves "cleaning" yourself of all negativity in order to see change in others.

It seems bizarre, but when you take care of your own issues, they disappear in other people.

The whole idea is to love the problems away. You do it by saying "I love you," and a few other statements, non-stop. I've been doing it for two years now and my life is astonishing. I live in an almost moment-by-moment state of bliss.

Once I learned this method, I started to use it on other things besides illness. Since I'm a practical metaphysician and an entrepreneur, I wanted to see if this wild method would work on sales and other bottom line results.

Whenever I would write an article – much like this one – I would send love into it.

Whenever I would write another book – like my new one, *Zero Limits* – I would keep saying "I love you" in my mind.

What I noticed is my e-mails and articles would get read and distributed to *millions* of people.

And my book, *Zero Limits*, became an Amazon bestseller – six months *before* it was published.

But I didn't stop there in my testing.

Because I want to be sure this method works for others and not just me, I taught it to my close friends.

Bill Hibbler, coauthor with me of the book *Meet and Grow Rich*, was skeptical. But he borrowed a pre-publication copy of my book, *Zero Limits*, read it, and started loving his products and his list of subscribers. Here's what he said:

> *"Sales for Jan 1-4 were 41.39% higher than Dec 1-4. During the four day period in January, I didn't mail my list or launch any new promotion during that time. All I did was clean while reading your book and throughout the day."*

Bill went on to tell me he saw sales increase from sites like create-ultimate-ebooks.com – which he wasn't promoting *at all.* *(2015 Update: this website is no longer available).*

How is this possible?

How can "cleaning" yourself with a mantra like "I love you" make a difference in your sales?

It appears that there is nothing "out there." The entire world is a projection of what you feel inside.

So, if you feel love, you will attract love. Because love contains gratitude, you attract more things to be grateful for. This is the essence of my book, *The Attractor Factor*, and of course of the movie, *The Secret*.

You get what you feel. That's it.

At heart I think you (I) just want love. Well, so does everyone else. When you say "I love you" inside yourself, you cleanse yourself and you radiate an energy that others feel.

The result: more sales. Still skeptical?

Look at it this way:

Even if this whole method seems totally crazy to you, what harm can come from you saying "I love you" in your mind as you make calls, write e-mails, deliver pitches, and go about your day?

If nothing else, you'll have better feeling days.

Try it and see.

By the way, "I love you."

The Greatest Motivator Isn't What You Think
or, What I Learned from Drew Barrymore and Adam Sandler on Valentine's Day

It's Valentine's Day as I write this. Nerissa and I just returned from watching the new movie, *50 First Dates*, starring the beautiful Drew Barrymore and the funny Adam Sandler. Besides being a hilarious movie in a beautiful setting with a heartfelt message of true love, it also caused me to have an "a-ha" right in the middle of it.

Somewhere around half way through the movie, as Adam is again reminding short-term memory loss victim Drew that he loves her, I suddenly realized the power of the greatest motivator of all time.

But let me first set the stage.

Most psychologists, direct marketers, and anyone who persuades for a living will tell you there are only two basic motivators: Pain or Pleasure. You either go toward what you want or away from what you don't want.

The standard argument is that pain is more powerful. I've tended to agree, but also stated I would not focus on pain for idealistic reasons. I simply don't want to spread pain in the world. Focusing on it causes you to feel it. I don't want to contribute to the misery many feel. So my stance has been to focus on pleasure as a motivator in my sales letters and websites.

Most marketing experts agree that pain is the best trigger to focus on in any ad or sales campaign. They love to find a prospect's basic problem, and then rub their noses in it. They figure the pain would make the person buy or change.

The most common example they give is the insurance salesman who tries to sell you home coverage. If he focuses on pleasure, you will put off buying. If he tells you your house is on fire, you will buy. Pain causes immediate action.

So, like everyone else, I "knew" pain was the greater motivator. I simply focused on pleasure because it is a more noble route.

But then I saw Drew Barrymore and Adam Sandler in their new movie and suddenly I felt awakened, energized, and validated.

Here's the film's plot in a nutshell:

Adam is in love with a woman who can't remember anything from the day before, due to a head injury in an auto accident the year before. Every day is a new day. And every day Adam has to win her over again. Every date is new. Hence the title, *50 First Dates*.

At one point in it, as Adam was again wooing Drew, I suddenly realized what I was really seeing.

I saw pleasure was the greatest motivator of all.

Adam was pursuing Drew every day, despite the pain and the odds, because of his growing love for her. He was going after pleasure. The pleasure goal was so powerful it erased every pain he might experience.

In short, all the marketing experts who say pain is the greatest motivator have forgotten the power of our driving force in life: Love.

People will scale mountains with luggage on their backs, swim upstream in a hurricane, and battle armies and all odds in order to fulfill that hard-wired emotion in us to love and be loved. Love rules.

All the examples we were given were unfair. Someone trying to sell insurance and resorting to pain hasn't figured out the real pleasure button to make someone buy. They've been too lazy to search for the pleasure trigger. Focusing on pain was simply an easy cop-out, a handy approach.

It's the same with all the massive ad campaigns that fail. Trying to get someone to quit smoking or stop drugs because of the pain they depict in the ad is the wrong approach. If we suddenly focused on the pleasure someone would have when they stopped smoking or taking drugs, we'd be moving in the right direction.

This is so obvious to me after watching the movie. Our goal as marketing and business people isn't to tell people what's wrong with them or to remind them of their pain, but to help them imagine and then experience the pleasure they long to have.

It's noble, yes, *and* it works.

Love moves everyone.

Love is the great motivator.

316 DR JOE VITALE

Love is the great pleasure trigger.

According to my friend Kevin Hogan, author of *The Psychology of Persuasion*, love isn't an emotion but a mindset. And as a mindset, it is actually stronger than any emotion.

In short, you're dealing with the most powerful motivator of all time.

Reveal what there is to love about your product or service and you'll give people authentic reasons to do business with you. Call it Love-Based Marketing. You won't sell everyone with it. You'll sell only those who are a match for your offer. That, in the end, is all you want. Then you're happy and so are your customers.

Just like Drew Barrymore and Adam Sandler, you'll find a match to write home about.

And you might make a little money along the way, to boot.

Your "Secret Barrier" to Wealth

I just read Dan Kennedy's September No B.S. Marketing Letter and was thrilled to see him talk about mindsets and language.

In one section he explained that talking about negative things makes your clients and customers feel bad, which in turn makes them less inclined to buy from you.

People want to feel good. I talked about this in my book, *Life's Missing Instruction Manual.* Even Kennedy, who can be a grump, realizes that focusing on doom and gloom will simply make people tighten their hold on their wallets or purses.

Instead, focus on the good, talk about the positive, and help people feel better.

Dan's back page essay – always my favorite part of his No B.S. newsletter – is all about how your own thinking leads to the reality you create.

Dan begins his article by saying the other day he deposited $802,486.00 in the bank.

Not bad for a day's work. (It was for more than a day's work, but you get the idea).

Dan goes on to brilliantly explain that most of us – even him, even me – have a "secret barrier" within us that keeps us from bringing in a larger income.

Whatever income you have right now is there because you are comfortable with it.

You probably made far less money decades ago. As you grew more comfortable, as you raised your secret barrier, you could allow more money into your life.

In short, you are earning what you are expecting.

The way to sell more and raise your income is to help people feel good and to work on your inner secret barrier.

How do you change your secret barrier to wealth?

You read this blog. You read Dan Kennedy. You read books about the wealthy. You subscribe to magazines for the affluent. You read my book, *The Attractor Factor*. You watch the movie *The Secret*. You get into or create a mastermind group of wealthy people. You surround yourself with wealth and prosperity so you can begin to accept it, feel it, own it, and expect it.

In short, you get comfortable with the idea of wealth.

Two tips:

1. Subscribe to Dan's newsletter. He's a genius and a living legend. You can get a two month trial subscription, to try it out, at www.gkic.com

2. Get the *Milagro Manifestation Method* CDs and put them in your iPod or on your PC or Mac, or in your car or wherever you can soak up their music and messages. See http://www.milagromethod.com

These CDs are so powerful that last night at dinner, Bill Hibbler said when he puts one of the CDs on, he instantly becomes a powerhouse copywriter.

I think the CDs are so potent that I asked Pat O'Bryan at dinner last night to bring me another set, so I can send them to a company I know they may want to promote them.

Get your own set at www.milagromethod.com

Bottomline: You get what you expect.

Or, as Dan says in his newsletter, "You'll only get to bank what your internal system permits you to accept."

Ao Akua,

Joe

www.MrFire.com

PS – One of the ways I lift my own secret barrier to wealth is by dreaming about attracting new luxury items, like the Panoz sports car, the Panoz Esperante GTLM. I've yet to even see that beauty, let alone ride in it or drive it, but thinking about buying it (it costs about $120,000.00) stretches my mind to get comfortable with even greater amounts of wealth. After all, I already have two BMWs. Getting a third luxury sports car would be a stretch for me. But I want to lift my secret barrier. You can do this, too. Go to http://www.miraclescoaching.com for some help.

Willie Crawford's SEM Discovery
(Not for Everyone)

Willie Crawford just wrote me the following...

"Two weeks ago, a friend showed me how he had achieved a 'better than #1 position' on both Google and Yahoo, overnight, for an extremely competitive and highly searched term. He also showed me how anyone could, with a little work, do the same thing."

I asked to see the report.

Willie sent it to me. I was surprised to see how brief it is – under 30 pages – but stunned to see how brilliant it is.

It reveals the actual formula the author used to go higher (yes, higher) than #1 on Google and Yahoo with the most sought after words in history at that time – and he did it in under 24 hours.

I found it fascinating.

I read and re-read the report.

The formula in it isn't known by most SEO (Search Engine Optimization) professionals and certainly not by the average Jane or Joe – including me.

It's actually more along the lines of SEM – or Search Engine Marketing.

The system is a twist on one of the steps in my Hypnotic

Marketing $50,000 3-step formula.

The simple method revealed in his system takes a little work – work you should be doing anyway – but it's clearly the real thing.

It will work, if you will work it.

And get this:

The author added an addendum to his report, written while in the hospital, that is almost more of a breakthrough than the system he invented.

As an author and as a marketer, I found it a stroke of genius.

When you read it, you'll know what I mean.

Finally, Willie told me...

"I've wrestled the exclusive rights to introduce the world to this report and am looking for just a few JV partners who can send a mailing to their lists fairly quickly. The reason that the mailing needs to go out fairly quickly is that we've decided to ONLY market the report until the end of December. The reason is that we actually don't want everyone to know about and dilute the strength of the technique."

I jumped to be one of the few to offer this to you.

The report is a little pricey (depending on where your head is with prosperity), but the system is priceless.

And I wish the report was longer, but it's long enough to explain the system.

This is a serious technique. If you want to be one of the few to actually learn it, you must go here now: http://

williecrawford.com/blog. Go for it.

What Is the Secret to Getting Rich Today?

It's Saturday morning as I write this article. I'm headed out to the lake today. A friend bought a boat and wants to take Nerissa and me out for a ride. Since I haven't had a day off in months, I'm ready for the clean air, the sun on my face, and the fast ride with good company.

Still, I'm nervous.

I'm afraid he's going to ask me about last weekend's seminar. People paid $5,000 each and came from across the planet to attend my private intensive event on Hypnotic Writing skills. I allowed only 10 people in the room. And I screened everyone who attended. I was about to reveal the most advanced strategies known to humanity for persuading with words, and I didn't want any riff raff.

I'm not kidding. I even had a guest speaker reveal the chilling little known secrets of persuasion. He had been raised in a cult. Later, he was an undercover agent. He once had a shotgun held to his head for 40 minutes. He used words to escape with his life. It was all, well, hypnotic.

This is the kind of forbidden knowledge I revealed in my weekend intensive.

My friend knows this. Like a lot of people, he's curious. He heard that I revealed the three secrets to writing copy that I've never told anyone before.

He heard that I explained my own private formula for writing sales letters – a formula I've never revealed anywhere, ever before.

He also knows that I explained my private checklists for reviewing copy. And – I almost regret this – I gave away some of my original tricks for making all writing more engaging, almost irresistible to read.

I also revealed my ideas about Hypnotic Graphics, the "intimacy factor," the wisdom in comic books, a lesson from hypnosis, the power of optical illusions in words, the need to strive for the impossible, how to direct the mind, and more. I even explained how people think, and unveiled why I call myself the "Michelangelo of Words."

On top of all that, I gave the 10 people in my event a copy of my new volume, *The Hypnotic Writing Training Manual*, the definitive, ultimate work I will never sell or give away because it is so powerful. (There's one graphic in the manual so gripping that the man who bound the books for me looked at it and said, "Trippy!").

My friend wants to know what I revealed. He also wants that manual. Yes, he's a friend. But he's also in business.

He knows that if he learns and uses these proven methods, his business will double, maybe even triple.

People who attended the event said the experience was a "20" on a scale of 1-10, with 10 being fantastic. My friend is drooling.

What am I going to do?

Go to the lake, take the boat ride, and prepare myself to be grilled by my friend, or stay here and work on something important?

The truth is, the question is for you to answer.

That's right.

You.

Do you want to spend the day on the lake – or whatever the equivalent of that is to you – or to do you want to knuckle down and make some real money in your own business?

The question concerns choice, life direction, and your own personal power.

Most people get bounced around by the circumstances of life. As I say in my forthcoming new book, *The Attractor Factor*, you are the primary creative force in your life.

You can choose where you want to go, or you can let the winds blow you around like a mindless feather.

This morning my friend invited me to the lake. Will I go or will I stay here and work?

The answer is obvious. He's waiting for me right now.

But here I am, writing this article for you. This comes first. This is more important. This is crucial.

But what's your answer?

When you're torn between learning how to make a good living online, and a distraction, what do you choose?

Anyone serious about making money or even getting rich on the Internet, or anywhere else, needs to come from a position of mental strength.

After all, many people say they want to get rich. But how many of them are investing in their own success? How many invest in books, courses, seminars, and trainings? And of those who do invest in their own desire to get rich, how many actually use what they learn? How many choose to "go to the lake" rather than implement what they learn?

My question to you today is this:

Who is making your choices?

Your answer is the key to your success.

As for me, will I go to the lake today?

Maybe. Balance is good. Play is good. But I first have to finish this article for you. It contains a message for all of us. It's the top priority. It can help you, and others, discover the secret for getting rich.

Am I worried about my friend probing, wanting to get the confidential secrets of my $5,000 weekend?

Not anymore. I've set my mind to close that door. Anyone who wants my secrets knows how to get them. We filmed and recorded the entire weekend. I'll announce how to get them on October 5th.

The lesson here is this:

Who's in charge of you?

Will you read this article and make a decision to do what's right for your goal to be rich, or will you go turn on the TV?

The choice is yours.

Your future depends on your answer.

Your wealth depends on your answer.

Choose wisely.

That said, I'm now headed to the lake.

Sign up for Dr. Joe Vitale's Oct 5. webcast at http://www.HypnoticWritingWebcast.com

Joe Vitale's Unspoken Marketing Secrets

I showed the below list to two marketing consultants. They both asked me not to publish it. I then showed it to a non-marketing person. He said he was going to print the list and tape it to his computer, so he could refer to it every day. Apparently there is real dynamite here. It scares some people. It inspires others.

After writing eleven books on marketing, reading several hundred other books on persuasion and psychology published over the last century and a half, and spending more than twenty years creating advertising and publicity to convince people to do what my clients wanted, I sat down and compiled this list.

You could probably build an entire marketing campaign or improve an existing one with any one of the below insights into human nature. To purchase *Unspoken Marketing Secrets* in Adobe PDF format which includes full commentary for each of the below secrets…

For now, here's the list:

People can be persuaded to your side with a good story.

People only do things for the good feelings they get.

People will pay any amount of money to have their inner states changed.

People only buy from people they know, like, and trust.

People make snap decisions about you and your business based on little things you usually overlook, even the paper stock of your business card.

People pick up on your energy, more than on what you say or do, and decide to work with you or not based on what they sense.

People know when you are lying, though some may mistrust their own instinct.

People want you to do what you say you will do when you say you will do it; they will reward you if you go one step further and deliver more than what they expect sooner than when they expect it.

People only act for self-serving reasons, no matter what they say or you think.

People will never change their human emotions or basic desires, only their dress and their tools will change.

People never question their own beliefs, so don't try to change them.

People cannot tell you why they buy anything or predict if they will buy something.

People always respond to free offers of something interesting to them.

People will believe a wild claim if it is just this side of unbelievable.

People will spend their last dime to be entertained.

People respond to flattery.

People want to be happy. Period.

People want low prices while still wanting the best deal.

People can tell if you don't believe in your product or service.

People respond to enthusiasm.

People will follow commands that make them feel superior.

People buy for emotional reasons and justify their decisions with whatever logic they can find or create, no matter how ridiculous.

People idolize the past, complain about the present, and fear the future.

People will never argue with you if you never make them wrong.

People are deeply affected by what others think.

People always act for positive reasons, even if the behavior is negative.

People will read any length of sales copy as long as it is interesting to them.

People become information junkies when they are interested in buying.

People will respond to you if you get out of your ego and into theirs.

People want to be recognized.

People want to be loved.

People are interested in other people.

People are interested in the new, the off-beat, the

unusual.

People are always interested in women, babies, and pets.

People love food and will read a recipe stuck in a sales letter.

People universally feel deprived.

People do not care about you or your business until you show them how you can help them.

People will mentally fill in holes to complete a story or sales pitch.

People will deny that advertising works while responding to ads.

People will read an ad if it doesn't look like an ad.

People will believe a news story over an advertisement hands down.

People are collectors of something, whether of books or thimbles or recipes, though they may deny it.

People will continue with a bad habit until it hurts.

People will do whatever you want as long as they don't have a counter-thought to your request. Handle the objection and they will comply.

People unconsciously respond to your unconscious intentions.

People feel that something or someone else is in control and desperately seek ways to have power again.

People think about sex far more than they will ever admit.

People will deny that this list is entirely true.

My Top 15 Books of 2005

Matt Gill, co-owner of Nitro Marketing and the man who runs my Hypnotic Gold membership program, just asked me for a list of my top ten books for 2005.

I found it tough to create. I buy so many books, and even read enough of them, that creating a list of only ten seems impossible. But I did come up with a list of fifteen books. Here they are (in no particular order):

The Next Millionaires by Paul Zane Pilzer. I loved this one. Talk about a relentless optimist. I ended up interviewing Pilzer for my Hypnotic Gold program and found the man sharp and fascinating. He told me he's not an optimist but a scientist. He sees a profitable future for you and me. Get this book.

Fantastic! The Life of Arnold Schwarzenegger by Laurence Leamer. Arnold is simply fascinating. He'll be back.

The Irresistible Offer by Mark Joyner. The best book on marketing in 50 years. It's causing me to rethink all my sales letters and offers.

177 Mental Toughness Secrets of the World Class by Steve Siebold. A masterpiece. You can't read this in one sitting. Take a bite a day, chew on it, and change your life. Genius.

Empowerment by Gene Landrum. Gene's research

proves that you don't need good genes to excel in business or sports. You need the right mindset for success. I interviewed him for my Hypnotic Gold program and found him a sheer delight. Brilliant and inspiring.

The Autobiography of Dan Kennedy. I love Dan but think he's a gloomy, grumpy guy. His life story is riveting, though I left the end of it feeling down. His outlook on life is not sunny, and mine is. (He needs to read the Pilzer book mentioned above).

Extreme Muscle Enhancement: BodyBuilding's Most Powerful Techniques by Carlton Colker. I'm overwhelmed by the amount of information out there on muscle building. This one seems to speak to me. Since I've lost 80 pounds and transformed my life through fitness and mental toughness, I love hard hitting, clear books like this. It's muscular.

500 Ways to Change the World edited by Nick Temple. Inspiring. These ideas are from people just like you and me. I'm refreshed and renewed when I see the cleverness of the human mind.

No Such Thing as Over-Exposure: Inside the Life and Celebrity of Donald Trump by Robert Slater. Trump is a publicity machine and this book gives you a peek inside his window.

The New Handbook of Cognitive Therapy Techniques by Rian McMullin. I'm fascinated with how beliefs create reality. This intense but freeing book reveals ways to help yourself see through and change your own mental programming.

Devil at My Heels: A World War II Hero's Epic Saga of Torment, Survival and Forgiveness by Louis Zamperini. Whew! What a read! As hypnotic as any novel, yet it's all true. Read it.

The Power of Impossible Thinking by Yoram Wind and Colin Crook. A mind-expanding book about how your view of the world creates your world.

The Mind and the Brain: Neuroplasticity and the Power of Mental Force by Jeffrey Schwartz. Sounds tough but it's easy to read. The message, as I remember it, is that your own decision can over-ride any mental problems. Again, intention rules the earth.

How Consciousness Commands Matter: The New Scientific Revolution and the Evidence that Anything Is Possible by Dr. Larry Farwell. Just read it.

Motigraphics: The Analysis and Measurement of Human Motivation in Marketing by Richard Maddock. A noble attempt to graph human emotions so we can control them. I read and re-read this one and I'm not sure I get it, but I love the attempt. Well worth wrestling with.

I'm probably going to think of 15 other books that should be on this list, but for now the above will do.

Wait! I just remembered another hypnotic read from this year:

The Spiritual Journey of Joseph l. Greenstein by Ed Spielman. The life story of this old time strongman was, well, hypnotic. It would make a great movie. It was written by the creator of the Kung Fu TV series.

Happy Reading.

Ao Akua,

joe

www.mrfire.com

PS – You may have to get Pilzer's new book from PaulzanePilzer.com, but I'm pretty sure the other books are available at www.Amazon.com or from your favorite bookseller. While book shopping, be sure to pick up a few copies of my books. (I've written several, you know). They make great gifts. And they slide into Christmas stockings just fine.

Thresholds: Is It Serving or Selling?

Most people complain that they don't have enough money.

They look at their bills, they look at their wants and needs, they look at their checkbook, and then they look terrified.

How will they pay their bills?

How will they feed their family?

How will they attract more money?

I'm sure you know the feeling. We've all been there. You may be there right now.

Now what's really curious to me is this:

The movie, *The Secret*, and many of the teachers in it offer proven ways to attract money and other material things. This obviously works, given the thousands of testimonials from people who now have money when previously they couldn't find it in a bank with the vault door open.

But some people are complaining that the focus of the movie is only on money or material things. They say it's self-serving. They say it's egotistic.

Do you hear the cultural programming at work?

"Money is bad."

"Taking care of yourself is bad."

"Material things are not spiritual."

Please note the discrepancy: when you want money and at the same time say focusing on it is bad or selfish, you are pushing it away.

Even the fans of the movie are doing this.

Some of the very people who use the Law of Attraction to get out of debt or attract a new car, at a later point only attract so much money before they begin to think they are being selfish. At that point they unconsciously turn off the flow and wonder what happened. They then begin to criticize the movie, too.

It's a strange thing to see.

First, people scramble to find money and worry and fret about it.

Then, they actually learn how to attract it, get some, and begin to complain that money isn't spiritual.

Wait a minute.

Weren't these the same people who wanted money in the first place?

Why was money good when they didn't have it and bad when they finally got it?

All of this is because of people's beliefs.

They hit their threshold of deservingness.

My father plays the lottery. But when the lotto gets to a hundred million dollars, he quits playing. He says that amount is "too much" and "that much money will ruin you."

Winning ninety-nine million is OK but one hundred million isn't?

Again, we're dealing with beliefs.

We're dealing with thresholds of deservingness.

I was at an event once when a fellow called his wife and handed me the phone. He wanted a star of *The Secret* to surprise her.

I took the call, said my name, and heard her scream.

She was talking to a celebrity. She was giddy with excitement.

But then she started asking me what I was doing to save the world.

This woman had gone from being a fan of *The Secret* and using what she learned to manifest a few things, to hitting her comfort zone and now not wanting anything else.

What happened?

Another example is this: many of the teachers in the movie *The Secret* create products and services to help you achieve your goals. When your mindset is open, you thank them for their services. When your mindset is closed, you say they are just "selling."

Well, are they selling or serving?

It's both and it's neither. It depends on your beliefs.

It depends on your threshold of deservingness.

If you think they are taking advantage of you, you call it selling (because you think selling is bad).

If you think they are helping you, you call it serving (because you know serving is good).

Again, it's all about beliefs, and particularly your belief

about what you feel you deserve.

That belief creates a threshold that you won't get past without some work.

It reminds me of a question a therapist used to ask patients:

"How good can you stand it?"

Most of us can't stand it really good.

"What will the neighbors think?"

"What will my family think?"

"If it's too good, surely something bad will happen."

"I don't deserve it too good."

"If it's too good, it won't last and I'll be miserable again."

"If I'm happy, I won't do anything to save the planet."

Those are all limiting beliefs.

Your life can be fantastic. Truly amazing. But very often we hit a comfort level and won't go past it. Why? Because of our self-imposed limits.

Because of our threshold of deservingness.

You can deceive yourself with rationalizations and criticisms about *The Secret*, me, others, the world, etc; but the end result is, you limit your own good.

I keep reminding people that once you get clear, there's not much you can't have, do, or be.

Your goal should always be happiness, what I call spiritual awakening, but the only limits along the way are your own.

How good can you stand it, anyway?

Ao Akua,

Joe

www.MrFire.com

PS – In the spirit of serving, here's some news you may like: I gave two talks on "The Missing Secret" last February. Apparently these presentations awakened a lot of people. You can see a two-minute video excerpt and read more over at www.MissingSecret.info I think these talks (now available on two DVDs) represent the best work I've done yet. They also include material from my forthcoming books, *The Key* and *Zero Limits*. I explain counter-intentions and beliefs in such a way, with a simple illustration you'll never forget, that these may become the most transformative DVDs of your life. Go watch the preview. Hey, it's free. You deserve that, don't you?

The Third Ghost or, Why I Offered $1,500 for a Book

I've been haunted by three ghosts in my life. The third one just appeared last month. I never know why they pick me, but the relationship usually leads to a brief glimpse of fame and fortune. Maybe this time won't be any different.

The first ghost came to me in 1989. I was reading the famous *Robert Collier Letter Book* and came across the name Bruce Barton. I'm sure thousands have read the same book, saw the same name, but did not have the same experience I had.

I got chills. Something awakened inside me. I began a two year quest to learn all I could about this now forgotten advertising genius and bestselling author.

The result was my book, *The Seven Lost Secrets of Success*. It's been through 11 printings. One person bought 19,500 copies of it. The ghost of Barton led me to write the book. It has touched lives around the world, and continues to do so.

But he was only the first.

The second ghost was P. T. Barnum. The famous showman and circus promoter came to me while I was reading his autobiography. That led to my quest to learn his business secrets. A year later, I wrote the book, *There's a Customer Born Every Minute*. It also led to my audioprogram with Nightingale- Conant, *The Power of Outrageous Marketing*. The program has been a bestseller for over 5 years now.

The third ghost came to me last month.

I have been a fan of Neville, the mystical writer of several books, for a decade or more. I even mention him and quote him in my latest book, *The Attractor Factor*. I even called one of the steps in the book, on manifesting with feeling, "Nevillize." You Nevillize a goal when you feel as if you already have it. But apparently that wasn't enough for Neville.

A few weeks ago I noticed an article about him in a major magazine. That reawakened my interest in the Barbados mystic. I searched and found some of his audios. These are actual recorded talks from speeches he gave in the 1950s and 1960s. I found a man who owned all known recordings of Neville. I bought all 106 of them. I felt as if Neville was speaking to me as I listened to them.

Then I found five lessons Neville taught in 1948. These are very rare. They are about practical metaphysics and how to manifest your heart's desires. Pure gold. I relished the fact that I was somehow led to the lessons. But something shocking happened as I read them.

Neville was talking about needing to take a ship back to his home country. He said the boat's name was "Nerissa." That is the second time I've heard that name. It's the name of my beloved partner, who I've been with for six years now. Too weird.

But the ghostly events didn't stop there.

In the very same week that I found the rare lessons, someone posted five books by Neville on eBay. All were first editions, perfect condition, and autographed. Neville showing up on eBay is odd enough. For five signed books to appear was even stranger. I, of course, bought them all.

The adventure didn't stop there.

A few days later eBay notified me that another Neville item was just put online for bidding. I looked and couldn't believe what I saw. It was the original published lesson plan from the 1948 lectures I had discovered – and the manual was autographed.

Then, a few days after that, yet another Neville item went on eBay. This turned out to be a truly rare book from 1939 called *At Your Command*.

I had never heard of it before. Apparently neither had other Neville fans, who had been quiet until now, as the bidding grew hot. In only one day people were bidding $500 for this little gem. I, of course, wasn't going to let this one slip by. I bid $1,500 for it and won it for $515.

Is the book worth it? I used it to attract a new car: a BMW 645Ci is being built for me right now in Germany. So if having ghosts in my life isn't weird enough, I paid $515 for a little book that is sharpening my powers to manifest what I desire, which is today a $90,000 luxury sports car.

This is getting too strange. The events were reminding

me of my experiences with Bruce Barton and P.T. Barnum. I have no idea if the ghosts of these great men were actually contacting me or not, but you have to admit that the synchronicity of events leading me to write my books has been uncanny. No wonder I've been a fan of Rod Serling, who I met when I was a teenager. I *live* The Twilight Zone.

I'm not sure why Neville is contacting me. Maybe it's just to dust off his message and present it to a new audience (meaning you). Meanwhile he'll notify me tonight, or tomorrow. I know he would like his ideas made available, so I put some of them online at AttractANewCar.com.

But there's a greater lesson here.

The joy in life is in following joy. What I mean is, whether paying attention to these "coincidences" leads to a new book or not isn't as important as the thrill of acting on them. The adventure is in the journey, not in the destination. The destination is simply a pause before the next journey.

Are you acting on the nudges you get, even when you have no idea where they will lead?

If so, you will find life exhilarating.

And you might even meet a ghost or two.

The Story of the Hypnotic Writing Monkey

The world's first Hypnotic Writer Author of *Hypnotic Writing* and *Advanced Hypnotic Writing*.

A monkey could use *The Hypnotic Swipe File*, a brand new e-book by Larry Dotson and myself, to write a riveting sales letter, ad, or e-mail message. The only condition is the monkey needs to be able to read.

I'll prove it to you.

Right now I have no idea how to write this article. So, in this case, I'm the monkey.

Now follow my path....

I grab this new e-book and flip through it – which is what I'm doing right now – and I spot a phrase...

"You don't realize it, but in the next few minutes you're going to learn..."

I add to that phrase something my monkey mind gives me, "...how to get people to do your bidding by using this amazing collection of hypnotic materials."

I now have this: "You don't realize it, but in the next few minutes you're going to learn how to get people to do your bidding by using this amazing collection of hypnotic materials."

There, I just wrote a good line. Any monkey could do

it, as long as said monkey can type.

If you're like me, you'll probably want another example. Stop! Did you notice that "If you're like me..." is a hypnotic line? It is. It's in this book. My monkey mind found it and used it.

And "Stop!" is from this book, too. I saw it and tossed it into the above paragraph. Made you look, didn't it? Here's a fact for you: Any man, woman, child or monkey can flip through the pages of this new e-book and find words, phrases, and complete sentences to help them lead and control the minds of their readers.

Hey! Did you catch what I did? The phrase "Here's a fact for you..." is also from this collection. It's a way to assume logic without having any. It works. And did you notice that "Hey!" grabbed your mind? It, too, is from this collection. It's a powerful, yet simple tool for practically yelling out your reader's name in a crowded room. It GRABS attention.

Are you beginning to see how you can use this material? Think about making use of this collection of hypnotic material and you'll begin to feel real power.

And did you notice that "Think about making use of..." is yet another golden nugget from this incredible e-book? Yes, a monkey with typing and reading skills just might be able to write a good letter with this amazing collection of tried and true hypnotic words and phrases. But more importantly, since YOU are smarter than any monkey, by the time you finish reading this material, you will be able to take these words and phrases and weave them into hypnotic letters and ads that get people to act on your commands and suggestions.

Stop! Note "by the time you finish reading..." is ALSO from this priceless new bag of tricks!

Can you see why I'm so excited?

As you get and then study every word of this book you will become amazed at how easy it will be for you to start writing your own hypnotic material.

(I can't resist. "As you study every word of this book you will become..." is also swiped from this collection. This is becoming way too easy).

But let me confess something: (Yes. "Let me confess..." is a hypnotic phrase).

When Larry Dotson, the primary author of this new e-book, wrote to me and said he compiled this material, I was angry. ("I was angry..." is from this collection, too).

I wanted to be the author of these gems. I even offered to help add more gems to the package if Larry would let me be co-author. He agreed, but I could barely think of anything to add! Larry already did most of the work – and did it very well! The further you read into his collection, the more you will realize why professional copywriters always have "swipe files." They use them for inspiration. In this case, Larry has done ALL the leg work for you.

("The further you read into this..." is from his swipe file).

Remember when you were in high school, and you

cheated to get a passing grade? Admit it. You did, at least once. Well, this collection is your cheat-sheet.

("Remember when you were in high school..." is swiped from this book, too. Do you see how easy it is to write with this collection at hand? It's so easy I feel silly accepting money for writing material like this for clients. But not THAT silly).

Have you noticed yet that I began with no idea of how to write this article and now, with the help of Larry's collection, have written a very interesting and maybe even hypnotic piece?

("Have you noticed yet that..." is from this fantastic swipe file, too).

So here you are. You're holding dynamite. Do you light it and throw it in a field to watch the dirt blow up, or do you light it and throw it where you know lay hidden gold?

FACT: The choice is yours.

See a hypnotic sales letter for the "Hypnotic Swipe File" e-book at http://www.HypnoticWritingSwipeFile.com

("FACT" is swiped, too).

Go forth and profit.

The Shoe That Thinks

I suffer from heel spurs. These are calcium deposits on the bones that make running painful. I created them years ago, when I was an obese jogger. All that pounding on the pavement with all that weight caused the bones to make heel spurs.

Mine are large and painful. I went to the doctor and she said they were the biggest she had ever seen. I had to stop jogging. I had to wear shoe inserts. It was no fun.

Because I have the core belief that anything can be healed, I kept searching for a cure. One day I saw an ad for a new running shoe that seemed promising.

The shoe has a computer chip in it that analyzes where you are running and adjusts the shoe's heel to give you the best cushion. I know this sounds sci-fi but I was desperate. Plus I love cool gadgets. So I ordered a pair.

They arrived in a large box, protected by foam inserts. There were batteries and an instruction manual. I felt like I had ordered an odd new laptop.

But the shoes.

Ah, the shoes.

They looked like they were designed for Flash, the famous DC Comics character who could zip around the world in seconds.

I put the shoes on, turned them on, and grabbed the dog. We went for a run. I was amazed at how easy and smooth it was to jog again. I was running faster than the dog. I felt like I could run forever.

I felt like *The Flash*.

But the real deciding factor would be the next day. If there was going to be any pain, I'd feel it in the morning. In the past, if I did too much on my feet, I'd wake up with an aching heel. And I'd limp all day.

Well, the next morning came and there wasn't any pain at all. None.

In fact, I just moments ago went for yet another run in my new shoes. I got the idea to write this article for you while jogging down the road.

Now notice something:

Are you curious about the shoes I bought? Has this story made you interested in them? Do you want to know the name of them?

When I was in a meeting the other day, I told everyone about the magic shoes that think. My excitement was contagious. I saw people writing down the name of the shoes. Even though I wasn't "selling" the shoes, they wanted to know more and would probably even go buy the shoes.

Are you feeling the same way?

If you've ever suffered from heel or knee pain, you are probably reading this and yelling "TELL ME THE NAME

OF THE SHOES, JOE!"

My point is this: A good story, told with passion, that promises a benefit, will always be hypnotic. It will always compel people to want to know more.

In short, hypnotic marketing is nothing more than sharing your sincere passion with the people who most want to hear it. I'll say that again:

In short, hypnotic marketing is nothing more than sharing your sincere passion with the people who most want to hear it.

And now for your relief: The shoes are called Adidas 1. Wear them and fly.

The Shocking Truth about E-Books

Last August the *New York Times* announced that e-books were not selling. A reporter wrote, "The main advantage of electronic books appears to be that they gather no dust. Almost no one is buying. Publishers and online bookstores say only the very few bestselling electronic editions have sold more than a thousand copies, and most sell far fewer."

Is that true? I've learned to weigh everything the media tells us with more than a grain of salt. As the author of numerous traditionally published books, as well as the author of several popular e-books, I'm here to tell you that e-books are selling and selling far better, in many cases, than most traditional books. Here's just a little proof:

- Corey Rudl made $400,000 from his e-works,
- Stephan Mahaney made $800,000,
- Michael Campbell made $10,000,
- David Garfinkel made $35,000,
- Larry Dotson made $5,000 in less than a month,
- Allen Says made $15,000 on a Sunday,
- Bob Gatchel made $30,000 in one weekend.

My own "Hypnotic" series of e-books, all published by Aesop Marketing, have broken sales records and left my printed books in the dust: *Hypnotic Writing* has sold in the tens of thousands – at $29.95 each – for more than two years now; My follow-up book *Advanced Hypnotic Writing*, has sold well into the thousands; and the recent work by myself and Larry Dotson, *The Hypnotic Writing Swipe File*, came out of the gate with a bang – selling at the whopping price of $197 a copy.

And keep in mind that these e-books have no printing or shipping costs associated with them. They are "invisible" books. You don't have to warehouse them, either. When they sell for $29.95 or $197, that's virtually all profit. (A very nice feeling).

I don't blame you if you are skeptical. I was, too, at first. Mark Joyner, CEO of Aesop Marketing, begged me for two years – years! – to give him a work of mine that he could release as an e-book. I'm a book lover and never thought anyone would EVER buy an e-book. (So much for me being a futurist).

But apparently there is an entire world out there – or online – that don't care for printed books or big bookstores, but instead love instant information delivered with a click. My *Hypnotic Writing* sold hundreds of copies within 24 hours. I'm now a believer in e-books. They've enabled me to live in the Texas Hill Country, drive a BMW Z3 hot-rod, own a pool, and travel as I please.

My friend David Garfinkel grew up in the traditional publishing world and, in fact, worked for McGraw-Hill, the world's largest publisher of business information. He didn't give e-books much thought either until he published a couple of them himself. His most recent one is titled, *Advertising Headlines That Make You Rich*. David told me, "I'm astonished by the results. I can honestly say my life has undergone quantum changes for the better in many ways since my first e-book hit the Internet a year and a half ago."

So what's with the *New York Times*? My hunch is that they are asking traditional publishers about their e-books sales. Well, traditional publishers don't know beans about marketing. Never have. They can't sell their printed books, so how can you expect them to sell their e-books?

To give you an example, one of my recent books is *There's A Customer Born Every Minute: P.T. Barnum's Secrets to Business Success*. AMACOM, a division of the American Management Association, published it. I got national radio, print and TV coverage for that book. A&E Biography created a new special on the life of Barnum and at the end of it, the host held up one book – and only one book – and basically urged people to get it to understand Barnum as a businessman.

That was MY book. Sales skyrocketed. My book became an overnight bestseller at amazon. Yet what did my publisher do? They let the book go out of print. I bought their leftover inventory. The books are in my garage. I never received one single royalty check. You can now only get the printed book through me – though, ironically, the e-book version of it remains for sale online.

There's more. My most recent book is titled *Spiritual*

Marketing. I released it as an e-book through www.1stbooks. com, as well as in paperback and hardcover formats through www.amazon.com. Which sells the best? The e-book version! (Paper is second and hardcover last).

Again, what is the media trying to tell us when they forecast gloom for e-books? Remember that the media focuses on the negative. Good news isn't generally considered newsworthy, to them.

Finally, here's the moral of this story: Don't let the media talk you out of releasing your own e-book. As long as you have solid information that a specific group of people would enjoy, you can write an e-book and let that target group know about it. Even if you only sold a few hundred copies, you would receive PURE PASSIVE INCOME – which no traditional publisher – including the *New York Times* – can promise or deliver.

The Secret of the Hypnotic Buying Trance

What you write to get someone to do something will influence what they actually do. Your words will create the perception that leads to their action. Wrong perception will lead to the wrong action.

What you want to do is create a Hypnotic Buying Trance, the mindset where people are prepped to buy. But not everyone knows how to do this, including me. This brief story will explain what I mean:

Pat O'Bryan just released his long awaited CD and DVD set called, *Your Portable Empire*. I wanted to drive traffic to his website and see the sales roll in. Because I loved his site, and particularly the graphic at the top of the site, I wrote the following e-mail and sent it to my list:

• • •

Subject: What may be the greatest website of all time?

Pat O'Bryan just sent me a link to look at his new website. I wasn't interested. I was tired, just on a teleseminar, and didn't want to go look. But it was for Pat, so I did. And it fried me. The graphic at the very top not only made me smile, but the words on it have to be the greatest summary of an irresistible offer I've ever seen online. I don't care if you're busy, or tired, or what. You simply have to go

look. It won't take but a sec. It's at – http://snipurl.com/
unseminar or – http://www.marketerschoice.com *(2015
Update: these websites are no longer available).*

Go see.

Joe

PS – If you want to create your own Portable Empire,
which is what Pat is known for, then get your rear to http://
snipurl.com/unseminar *(2015 Update: this website is no
longer available).*

• • •

What do you think?

Is that a good e-mail?

I sent the e-mail and waited.

And waited.

Sales receipts did not burst into my e-mail box. While
my e-mail created traffic to Pat's site, there were no sales. I
found this very perplexing.

As it happened, Internet marketer Mark Joyner sent
me an e-mail to say "hi." Mark is the author of *The Great
Formula* and *The Irresistible Offer*. He's a genius at online
marketing.

I told Mark about my e-mail and the lack of results.
He surprised me by pointing out that my "framing" was
all wrong. He said by driving people to look at the site to
study a graphic, I sent people to the site with the wrong
end in mind. They need to be going with an urge to buy,
not with a desire to look.

I know this. But I needed a reminder. With Mark's

lesson in mind, I wrote this follow-up e-mail and sent it to my list:

• • •

Subject: I goofed – and you can learn from my mistake

I sent out an e-mail yesterday urging you to see one of the best websites I've seen in a long time at http://snipurl. com/unseminar *(2015 Update: this website is no longer available).*

Many of you went, but not all of you bought. When I mentioned it to Mark Joyner, he said my positioning was all wrong.

He explained that by having you go to look at the site, you didn't go to look at the benefits of the product.

In other words, I violated one of my own principles of how to lead someone to buy.

Mark said I should have focused on all you get, such as – you learn how to set up your own online business in 30 days or less – you learn about hypnotic writing, hypnotic marketing, hypnotic publicity, and much more – you learn the quick-start secrets for building a money-making business.

You get the idea. By sending you to the site to look at the hypnotic graphic, you went there with a mindset to learn about hypnotic graphics.

Nothing wrong with that, except I also wanted you to go BUY.

This is the lesson: Whenever you want to get someone to do something, how you lead them there will determine what they do.

I led you to look. But I needed to lead you to buy. So let me try again.

Please go review Pat's site because the product he offers can put you into business – and making money – with your own "portable empire" in about 30 days.

If Pat – a once struggling musician with several CDs out but always broke – can do it, then so can you.

See http://snipurl.com/unseminar *(2015 Update: this website is no longer available)*. In one of my next mailings, I'll send you the e-mail you should have gotten in the first place. But don't let that stop you from reviewing his site.

Go for it.

Joe

PS – This very e-mail ought to prove that nobody knows it all (except maybe Mark Joyner). If I can still learn something new, then so can you. Get Pat's package and get to the head of the class. Go see http://snipurl.com/unseminar *(2015 Update: this website is no longer available)*.

• • •

What do you think of that e-mail?

Is it good?

This new e-mail brought in sales. I learned my lesson: How I direct people somewhere determines what they do when they get there.

The bottom line is this: Think of what you want your readers to do after reading your writing. What you say will influence their next actions. People only buy when they're in the right state of mind. What you write helps mold that buying mindset, which I call the Hypnotic Buying Trance.

Mind Gaps: or, How Wrod Illsuinos Can Imrpvoe Yuor Slaes

I'm teaching an intensive seminar on Hypnotic Copywriting techniques in September. One of the principles you'll learn there is the idea that the mind is easily tricked by optical as well as literary illusions.

You're probably familiar with optical illusions.

There are numerous books and sites showing pictures that can be seen in a variety of ways. One famous image looks like an old woman – until you stare a little longer and suddenly see the profile of a young woman in the same image.

Something similar can happen with words. After all, words are images, too. They are subject to the blind spots in our brains. For proof, read the following.

Aoccdrnig to a rsceearcehr at Cmabrigde Uinervtisy, it deosn't mttaer in waht oredr the ltteers in a wrod are, the olny iprmoetnt tihng is taht the frist and lsat ltteer be at the rghit pclae. The rset can be a total mses and you can sitll raed it wouthit a porbelm.

Tihs is bcuseae the huamn mnid deos not raed ervey lteter by istlef, but the wrod as a wlohe.

Fascinating, isn't it?

I'm *not* advocating mis-spelling words or intentionally misleading people. I'm demonstrating a principle. Your mind is vulnerable. It can see things that aren't there and miss things that are there. This is important information. It's what allows magicians the ability to fool us.

So, how does this fact help you with your sales letters, ads, e-mails, websites and any other writing you do?

Here's how: You can consciously weave your words in such a way that people fill in the blanks. In other words, you can help them imagine buying your product or service without asking them to get it.

This is the sport of hypnotic writing. Here's an elementary example:

"Imagine driving this sleek car down a country road."

What did you see in your mind?

Most likely you imagined a sports car.

But why a sports car?

The word "sleek" led your mind to create a visual.

That image came from your mind, not mine. I gave you a prompt and your mind leaped to a conclusion.

Minds are like that.

Also, in the paragraph before that example, I planted the word "sport" in your mind.

Did you notice it?

It's where I wrote, "This is the sport of hypnotic writing."

The word "sport" was already in your consciousness, and was easy to bring up when I asked you to imagine a "sleek car."

Here's another example: Go back to the opening paragraph of this article. Look at the second line. It says: "One of the principles you'll learn there is the idea that the mind is easily tricked by optical as well as literary illusions."

Notice anything unusual?

You shouldn't have. But your mind interpreted the sentence that YOU will attend my event in September. I could have said "One of the principles *people will learn at my event* is the idea that the mind is easily tricked by optical as well as literary illusions." But by writing it so YOU would be in the sentence, I am leading your mind to imagine signing up for the actual event.

I was talking with my hero Kevin Hogan (author of *The Psychology of Persuasion* and everything else about influence...) and he says that if you can actually get your customer to see themselves doing or using whatever it is your product does, you win big. The trick is, they have to imagine *themselves* with your product.

Showing how another person is going to experience something or has experienced something isn't enough to push the "yes" button in most people.

In other words, "Yeah, John felt the same way, then he tried this and found it worked" is a weak persuasion tool.

Kevin explains it this way:

*"Joe, what you want your participants to do is see *themselves* writing ad copy and then have them see *themselves* getting the incredible results of Hypnotic*

Writing. Specifically. The orders racing into *their* e-mail box. Not yours or mine."

My earlier sentence – "One of the principles you'll learn there is the idea that the mind is easily tricked by optical as well as literary illusions" – is a psychological switch to get you imaging yourself at my event.

That example may be difficult to grasp at first.

It's actually an embedded hypnotic assumption, or presupposition. It's explained in my e-books and will be demonstrated in my seminar in September. So let's take a final quick example:

I went to the MSN home page and saw a headline that read, "See a Ferrari laptop." I like sports cars, so I clicked. Imagine my surprise when I saw a picture of a laptop computer, not a convertible. My mind highlighted the word Ferrari and let me slide past the next word.

I could go on and on. For example, sometimes I end a letter with "Stop buy and see us." Few note I used the word "buy" instead of "by." The mind sees it as "stop and buy."

I learned that subtle method when a friend of mine out of town ended an e-mail with the words, "Take Car." He meant to say, "Take Care."

He slipped and wrote "Take Car" as a way to speak to my mind and urge me to drive and see him.

In short, these "mind gaps" can be cause for confusion, or for communication. I can't explain all the ins and outs of this rarely looked at subject here (that's what my seminar is for), but let this article be a stimulus for your own thinking – without the mind gaps.

Hypnotic Selling—or, Where's the Magic?

I love magic. I know many magicians and often attend magic conventions and shows. I haunt the dealer room, where magic tricks are sold. I'm looking for the tricks that make people gasp in surprise and delight.

Unfortunately, most magic is on the level of a prank or kid's joke. That's not for me, so most magic that I see disappoints me.

But one day I met a magic dealer at a convention who was very friendly. He took his time with me, listened to my needs, and then responded with some truly hypnotic stories. For example:

"I went into one of those big discount stores," Mr. Williams, the dealer, began. "The woman behind the counter seemed bored so I decided to do a little magic to liven up her day.

"I asked her to pretend I had a deck of cards in my hand. I then let her shuffle the make believe cards, cut them, deal them out, and pick any card she wanted.

"Remember, all of this was done in her head," William explained.

"After I let her choose her card, I asked if she wanted to change her selection. She said no. I then announced that her card was the seven of spades."

Mr. Williams paused before telling me this next statement:

"Well, you could hear this woman's scream all throughout the store.

"But the story doesn't end there," he continued.

"There was a man and his son who heard the scream and went over to see what happened. The woman who saw the trick pointed at me and said, 'He just fried me by reading my mind!' They were all as white as ghosts after that."

As this magic dealer told the story, I could see it all happening in my mind. The details were rich enough to help me picture it in my head. And when he said the woman screamed, I felt that rush of excitement that said, "Get that trick, Joe."

And yes, I bought that trick.

This same dealer told me two more stories, about magic tricks he did for people and their reactions to them. In every case I was there, mentally, and I ended up buying the tricks.

If you haven't caught on yet, this is Hypnotic Selling at work.

I'm sure the magic dealer has no idea what Hypnotic Selling is. He does it naturally. So let's review some key points:

1. He listened to me.

He couldn't offer any suggestions or stories to me until he first knew what I wanted. So he probed to discover I wanted magic that made people gasp. That clued him to what he should offer me. Had I said I wanted magic for kids, I'm sure he would have told me a story about performing magic for kids. He tailored his story to me. By doing so, he met me in my existing trance.

2. **He told true stories.**

He didn't make up his stories. He told me exactly what happened when he used these tricks in the real world. That subliminally communicated to me that he was honest, and that these tricks would work for me, too. People are always making conclusions based on the little information you tell them. Always be honest, so trust is there when it's time for the order.

3. **He used lots of details.**

He told me what store he went to, the name of the woman he performed the trick for (I left them out here, though), and all the details of her reaction. This brought the story to life in my mind and made it easy for me to see myself performing and receiving the applause. People will generally "live out" the story you tell them in their head. The more specifics you can offer, the easier it will be for them to relate to your story.

You get the idea. Hypnotic Selling is all about delivering a message to people that fits what they are looking for, and is delivered in a vivid way.

Do this and you'll see real magic. People will marvel at your storytelling skills – and they'll pay you real money, too.

And that's the best trick of all.

Note: The magic dealer was Emory Williams, Jr. (WilliamsMagic.com).

Case Study: Does Hypnotic Writing Really Work?

If you've ever wondered if the words on a website were very important, then keep reading.

Brad Yates is a master at EFT, or Emotional Freedom Techniques. EFT is a method for tapping away psychological issues so you are free to have, do, or be what you want.

Some people call it "psychological acupuncture." You use a finger or two to "tap" on certain areas of your body, which releases stuck energy so you can move forward without any internal blocks.

Snicker if you like. EFT has been used for well over ten years and is now practiced by tens of thousands of people. They can't all be faking problems and then faking resolutions. EFT works.

Brad Yates was one of my guests when I did my *Attract a New Car* teleseminar a while back. I liked him and told him about an idea I had for a series on *Money Beyond Belief.* It would be a course to help people remove their barriers to having money. Brad would teach people EFT so they could remove their blocks to receiving money.

Brad loved the idea, we conducted the seminars, and then quickly put up a website to sell the audios. Now,

Brad knows EFT but he doesn't know marketing, so the site wasn't the strongest in the copy area. The words left something to be desired. I offered some advice but didn't have the time to rewrite the site. So we left it alone and opened it for business. You can see it at http://www.bradyates.net/page45.html

Take a moment and look at the site.

What do you think of it?

Is the copy strong?

Is it hypnotic?

What's missing?

And here's the million dollar question:

Does the copy make you want to buy the product?

Brad and I told our lists about our product. We stood back and waited for orders.

And waited.

And waited.

Orders trickled in.

Weeks later, we still didn't have enough orders to make either of us very happy. We ended up using EFT on our disappointment.

While I wanted to rewrite the site, I just couldn't get to it with my books, projects, media appearances, travels and more. Thank goodness a young copywriter by the name of Sam Rosen came to Brad and offered to help. Sam had studied all of my Hypnotic Writing materials and was game to prove his skills.

Sam completely rewrote our site. You can see the new

copy at http://www.MoneyBeyondBelief.com

Take a moment and look it over.

Now here are the same questions as before:

What do you think of it?

Is the copy strong?

Is it hypnotic?

What's missing?

And here's the million dollar question:

Does the copy make you want to buy the product?

Here are the results:

The first website, which we'll call exhibit A, bombed. It barely made 100 sales in 100 days.

The second website, exhibit B, blew down all the doors and made $8,500 in sales in only one day.

So, does copy make a difference in selling?

Consider:

• The product was the same.
• The price was the same.
• The audience we promoted it to was the same.

The only change was the writing.

Please note: *The only* change was the copy.

The next time you scratch your head and wonder if hypnotic writing will help your sales, re-read this article.

And then expect money beyond belief.

Member BBB Online 2005
http://mrfire.com/article-archives/new-articles/hypnotic-case-study.
html

How to Write an E-book Faster than It Takes to Read This Article

How fast can you write an e-book?

Though Jim Edwards and I wrote a #1 bestselling e-book titled *How to Write and Publish Your Own – OUTRAGEOUSLY Profitable – e-book in as little as 7 days*, you can do it even quicker than 7 days.

How?

Here are at least three ways:

1. Don't write it.

   That is, speak your book and then transcribe it using a service such as www.idictate.com. Or use one of the voice recognition software out there, such as Dragon Naturally Speaking. Either way, if you're more comfortable speaking rather than writing, speak your book first.

2. Coauthor it.

   You can make yourself almost instantly famous by associating yourself with someone who is already famous. Jim Edwards came to me over two years ago and asked to coauthor a book with me. He said he would do most of the work. I agreed. The result was the e-book I mentioned above, which continues to be a bestseller. Since then, Jim is now a recognized authority in his own right and has written several other e-books.

3. Make soup.
   This is the "Chicken Soup for the Soul" approach to creating a book. You don't write a word. You simply ask people for contributions. Joe Kumar did this with his popular e-book "30 Days to Internet Marketing Success." Joe is a teenager in Singapore, totally unknown until he compiled his e-book and made himself an online celebrity. Jo Han Mok and I just did this with our new book, *The E-Code*. We simply wrote people and asked for their contribution. It's amazingly easy to do. You can be unknown, and famous people will give you contributions.

Again, writing e-books doesn't have to be hard or take a lot of time. The trick is in delivering something people want. Do that and no one will care if you wrote your baby in an hour, a day, or a week.

But once it's written, you can make passive money from it for a long, long time.

Go for it!

Evil Marketing? What a Buffalo Rancher Taught Me about Selling

Yesterday I met a rancher who raises buffalo and sells bison products. He clearly loves his job. He gushed facts. For example:

I didn't know buffalo never get cancer. Or that buffalo meat is leaner, healthier and better for you than any other red meat. I also didn't know that buffalo contains less calories than even chicken.

"Most people just don't know how to cook it," the rancher explained. "Since the meat is lean, it needs to be slowly cooked on a really low flame."

He went on to add:

"People on the Paleo Diet, sometimes called the caveman diet, really love it. It helps them lose weight and get trim naturally," he said. "I eat one to two pounds of bison every day, some veggies, and I'm fit and strong."

Since I'm into wellness and just lost over 70 pounds, I was eager to hear all this. I was so taken by this new information that I placed a large order on the spot.

But the rancher also had some opinions that made me curious.

"I'm just a rancher," he told me. "I run my ranch by

myself and I work night and day, yet at the end of it all, I have to go out and market this stuff. I almost hate it."

"You hate marketing?" I asked.

"I just saw the actor Billy Bob Thornton on television and he said, 'Marketing is evil.'"

"That's interesting," I countered. "The reason Thornton is on television is he is marketing the latest movie he's in."

"Well, I don't like marketing," the rancher told me. "Maybe it's because I don't know how to do it."

At this point, Nerissa came out and met the rancher, too. He offered her a sample of the buffalo jerky he made. He held it out in front of her as he said:

"You'll eat this and you won't want anything else the rest of the day. This is the most filling and satisfying food you'll ever have," he said. "There are no preservatives and it's all natural."

Of course, at that point I wanted some jerky, too.

When the rancher went to write up our order, he pulled a beautiful notebook out of his truck. He started to place it on the hood of my BMW Z3 sports car when I stopped him.

"I don't want it scratched," I said.

"Look at this," he said, rubbing the leather on the notebook. "Go ahead and touch it and see how smooth it is."

I did. The leather was melted butter soft.

The rancher then asked me something hypnotic:

"Can you imagine walking into a meeting with one of

these under your arm?"

Of course, that natural question activated the visual part of my brain and engaged my ego. I instantly wanted the unusual product.

"How can I get one of those?" I asked.

"I can have one made for you, if you want."

I ordered one of the buffalo notebooks, too.

I then paid the rancher, shook his hand, and he got in his truck, still muttering that he didn't like marketing. He said he was so behind in learning marketing that he was prehistoric in his practices.

"Guess you're doing Paleo Marketing," I offered.

He laughed and drove off.

He didn't seem to notice that his "non-marketing" made a lot of sales that day. I bought meat, jerky, and a notebook. I also bought a case of honcy, which I forgot to mention. None of it was cheap, either.

I've said it before and I'll say it again: Marketing is simply engagingly informing the people most likely to be interested in your product or service that it's available.

This is what I teach people in my Executive Mentoring Program. I'll repeat it:

"Marketing is simply engagingly informing the people most likely to be interested in your product or service that it's available."

It's not about manipulation.

It's about information.

The more passionately and sincerely you convey your

information, the more hypnotic your marketing will be.

But if you try to market your business to someone who has no interest in it, you may be considered evil.

That rancher was marketing, though he'd never admit it. His love for his product was apparent. He eats buffalo, wears buffalo, raises buffalo, and talks buffalo. He doesn't talk bull, he talks buffalo. And when he talks, if the people listening are at all interested in bison, they buy.

Marketing is only "evil" when you lie or mislead people to make a sale, or when your message isn't appropriate for the audience you reached. No one should ever do that sort of misguided marketing. Ever. There's no excuse for it.

If you're offering a product or service you believe in, then share your excitement for it to the right audience. (If you don't believe in your product or service, what are you doing trying to sell it)?

Said another way, if you have something that would truly benefit a certain group of people, and you don't tell them, aren't you doing them a dis-service?

Again, marketing is basically sharing your love. Your passion. Your belief. When you share it with someone who welcomes it, more often than not it leads to a sale. Naturally. Easily. Effortlessly.

And that's no BS.

Member BBB Online 2005
http://mrfire.com/article-archives/new-articles/no-bs.html

Dangerous Hypnosis?

Someone wrote me a nice letter recently, thanking me for my books, but also taking the time to tell me she was "put off" by my use of hypnosis in marketing. She said it removed choice from people. She thought it was evil.

Since you may be thinking the same thing, let me point out a few things:

1. **Hypnosis never removes choice.**
   You can't be made to do something under hypnosis that you didn't already want to do while fully awake. For proof, just ask yourself if you buy everything I offer. Probably not. Yet I'm the father of Hypnotic Writing. Obviously, you used your power of choice to buy or not, despite any "hypnosis" in my marketing.

2. **Hypnosis is not evil.**
   It is used by dentists, doctors, and psychologists to help people get more of what they want out of life. It's been sanctioned by the American Medical Association since the 1950s. Anyone still thinking hypnosis is evil is caught up in a cultural myth, which is a kind of trance all by itself.

So what is hypnosis?

My definition of hypnosis is anything that holds your attention. A good movie, or book, is a type of hypnosis. So is a good sales letter, or sales pitch, or infomercial. I'm not talking about manipulating minds, I'm talking about entertaining them.

- **Britney Spears is pretty hypnotic.**
  But not everyone buys her music. (I don't).

- **Dan Brown, author of "The Da Vinci Code," is pretty hypnotic.**
  But not everyone buys his books. (I don't).

- **Harry Potter has much of the world in a trance.**
  But not everyone buys the books. (I don't).

Bottom line: Hypnosis is just another tool. It does not control people and it does not give God-like powers to anyone. In marketing, it gives you an edge, but if you use it to try to sell a lousy product, it won't help you at all.

Kevin Hogan, hypnosis trainer and author of several books, including, *The Psychology of Persuasion*, says, "Hypnosis makes life better in most every way. It gives a salesperson or marketer a decided advantage over the competition but not over the client."

You want to learn hypnotic writing and hypnotic marketing because it helps you get and hold attention. It also makes you a much better communicator.

After all, if you aren't getting attention, and you aren't holding it, you aren't doing any selling, are you?

For more info, join my exclusive membership program at HypnoticGold.com.

http://mrfire.com/article-archives/new-articles/dangerous-hypnosis.
html

The Cure for Despair

During dinner the other night, one of the people in our group looked at me and asked the question I didn't want to hear –

"How did you become homeless?"

By now most people have heard my story of being on the streets of Dallas in the late 1970s and struggling in poverty in Houston for many years after that. Some of it is explained in my new audioprogram, *The Awakening Course*: http://www.theawakeningcourse.com/

But I had never explained exactly how I ended up in such dire circumstances.

When I answered the question at dinner, everyone at the table stared at me.

The woman who asked the question sat there with her mouth open and eyes un-blinking.

She asked, "Why have you never said this before?"

My friend Mark Ryan was sitting there, also staring, and said, "As long as I've known you, you've never told this story before. It's riveting. This changes everything."

Changes everything?

Riveting?

They all said I had to tell the story now.

"Given the current financial crisis and with people losing their homes and their jobs, this story needs to be told more than ever before," Mark said.

I heard them and realized I agreed.

So here's the story...

I knew I wanted to be an author when I was a teenager. I wanted to write books and plays that made people happy. Everywhere I looked I saw unhappy people. I believed I could help them with humor and stories.

During that time of the mid-1970s, I watched sports. I don't today but back then the Dallas Cowboys were the rage. Roger Staubach and Tom Landry were heroes. I got caught up in the excitement and felt the place for me to make my name was in Dallas, Texas.

I lived in Ohio at the time. Born and raised there. I worked on the railroad as a trackman, doing heavy labor all day long, working weekends and summers since the age of five.

I saved my money, packed up my bag, and took a bus to Dallas. It took three days to get there.

I was lost in the big city, of course. Being born in a small town in Ohio didn't prep me for the hustle and bustle of a city the size of Dallas.

Before long, I wanted out.

But I still wanted to be an author.

At that time major companies were building oil and gas pipelines in Alaska and the Middle East, and offering to pay big bucks if you were willing to go to either place.

I wasn't keen on going to a foreign country and doing more labor, but I saw a chance to make money, save it, and then go on a sabbatical where I could write for a few months or even a year.

It seemed like a brilliant strategy.

I answered one of the newspaper ads that promised to get me pipeline work at an extraordinary hourly wage. I went in their office, met an upbeat sales person, and ended up giving him all of my money – my entire savings, about a thousand dollars at the time – based on his promise that I'd have overseas pipeline work in a week or two.

You might guess part of what happened next – but you won't guess all of it.

Within a week or so, the company that took all of my money went out of business.

Their doors were closed, no one answered the phone, and no forwarding addresses could be found.

Shortly after that, the company went bankrupt.

And not long after that, the owner of the company committed suicide.

There was no one left to try to get my money back.

I was alone.

I was broke.

I was in Dallas, far from home.

I confess that my ego got in the way here. My family back in Ohio would have taken me back in and welcomed me back home. But I was head strong and determined to somehow survive.

Well, I did survive – by sleeping in church pews, on the steps of a post office, in a bus station.

It wasn't an easy time, as you can imagine, and I never used to talk about it. It was too embarrassing.

When I told this story at dinner, everyone agreed I had to share it with you.

They said that people are finding themselves in the same situation – they trusted a government, or a corporation, or a person, or a bank, and now they are losing their homes and their jobs.

Hearing that I went through the same thing three decades ago and not only survived but prospered to a level that the Joe Vitale of thirty years ago could hardly imagine, ought to be inspiring to you, too.

I got off the streets and out of poverty by constantly working on myself – reading self-help books, taking action, scrambling at times by taking whatever work I could find, but always always always focusing on my vision: to one day be an author of books that helped people be happy and stay inspired.

If you're in a place right now that doesn't feel so good or seem too safe, I urge you to remind yourself that this is only temporary.

This is the cure for despair.

As I say in my book, *The Attractor Factor*, this is simply current reality, and current reality can change.

You can help it along by doing what you know and need to do.

But remember, the sun will shine again.

It always does.

Your job right now is to focus on what you want and keep it in sight.

Yes, keep taking action.

Yes, stay positive and surround yourself with positive people.

Yes, be of support to others.

But remember, if I or anyone else can survive homelessness, poverty, job loss, or any other hard time, then you can survive it, too.

Please hang in there.

One last thing:

I admit that there were times I wanted to throw in the towel and get myself out of this life.

Thank God I stuck around. Had I left early, I would have missed a life of magic and wonder, success and fame I never dreamed of before, priceless relationships and experiences, and more.

I have no idea what wonderful good is headed your way – and neither do you.

What you have to do is stay the course and follow your heart.

And remember – Expect Miracles.

Ao Akua,

Dr. Joe Vitale

Founder of the movement to end homelessness

www.operationyes.com

Confessions of an Internet Whore—or, How Often Should You E-mail Your List?

Last month someone on my e-mail list wrote me a long e-mail calling me an "Internet whore." He went on to say he was unsubscribing from my newsletter. He added that I was "slocking *****" and that I had "lost my ethics."

I thought about the anonymous writer and reflected on what he said. It made me wonder how often any of us doing business online should send out our e-mail. Weekly? Monthly? Hourly?

Are there any rules at all?

Let's explore this together...

Personally, I only endorse products I use and believe in. Because of my perceived status in the world these days as a bestselling author and marketing guru, I'm contacted by dozens of people *per day*, all asking me to sell their latest what-have-you. I do not endorse or sell 99% of them. That saves me from mailing my list too often.

Usually, as in the case of helping Kevin Hogan's book hit #2 at Amazon and Peggy McColl sell $30,000 worth of books in one day using the strategy I taught her, I don't make a dime for my efforts. I'm not complaining, either. I wanted to help them, and did. But I did not profit in any way. I felt telling my list about their offers was a gift to my list. So I mailed them.

Often I will discover something that sets my soul aflame. That's what happened when I discovered *The Millionaire's Mindset* book from Slovenia. I felt it was a great gift to the world and am honored to share it with people. I'm profiting from that, and gladly so. It's an astonishing book. I didn't mind sending out three e-mails about it to my list. My list didn't seem to mind, either, as hundreds of them ordered almost instantly. My friend, Rok, over in Slovenia said –

> *"Your list actually outperforms lists that are up to 8 times bigger ... and it outperforms them by about 85%. Your last mailing (which was the third mailing you did for the same book) generated 85% more responses than any other affiliate mailing in the pack."*

I continue to create new products, too. Obviously, I want the people on my list to know about these. And just as obviously, I believe these products will help them – or I would not be offering them. They are not ***** or in any way fluff. They are all useful and inspiring. Even when I release three e-books in one week, I think my list should be the first to know about them.

So back to the question we are wrestling with:

When is it too much? When are you e-mailing your list too often?

Now, what I'm about to tell you may shock you. But it's the key point of this article.

I think if you have something of importance for your list, you should tell them as fast as possible. If that means you mail twice in one day – again, assuming you just got news your list would want to hear – then you mail them twice in one day.

I did that once. I sent an e-mail to my list in the morning. A few hours later I received an e-mail with such thrilling news in it that I couldn't resist sending out a follow-up e-mail. I did. I knew I might be flamed, but felt it was worth the risk. As a result, 12 people thanked me. No one unsubscribed.

Look. If you are doing business online and have news of value to your followers, why *aren't* you telling them?

I think the only reason you wouldn't tell them is – fear of being flamed, which means fear of receiving hate e-mail.

If you are afraid of being flamed, then you probably know you don't have anything of value for your list.

Think about it.

I'll repeat my statement: If you are afraid of being flamed, then you probably know you don't have anything of value for your list.

Let me explain:

If I'm on your list because I want to hear of your new products or services, and you have a new product or service and don't tell me, I have every right to be upset. I should have been given first shot at the offer.

For example, I'm a member of the Kenny Wayne Shepherd fan club. He's a hard rocking blues guitarist in the tradition of Stevie Ray Vaughan. Well, I signed up for Kenny's e-mail list to be notified of his new releases and concert appearances. You might imagine my surprise – and disappointment – one day when I saw a new CD by him in a music store, one I never heard about by any e-mail from him. While I was glad to discover the new music, I was upset that no one notified me. After all, that's why I signed on to get his e-mails in the first place. I unsubscribed.

Here's another example:

Another friend of mine is a professional entertainer. I sat in the audience at one of his shows and heard him tell people, "If you sign on to my e-mail list, I'll send you occasional updates about my appearances." He added, "I won't abuse your e-mail and send you too much e-mail."

Well, he blew it. Anyone who signs up for his e-mail *wants* to hear from him, not just whenever he has an appearance, but whenever he has news of interest to them. In my opinion, the entertainer was thinking of himself, not his audience. He was coming from pure fear.

I also know an executive coach who mails his list once a quarter or so. I keep wondering, "Doesn't he have a life? Doesn't he have any news? Doesn't he ever come across anything he's excited about and can't wait to tell his list?" Apparently not. To me, he looks lazy, inept, or just plain scared. I would never hire him as a coach.

According to *Newsweek* magazine, 90% of all spam is sent from a group of under 150 people. You're probably not one of them. Neither am I. But if you were considering doing bulk e-mails to strangers (known as spamming), you should also know that one spammer admitted she got only 25 responses – after sending out 1,000,000 e-mails. And naturally, even the 25 responses weren't what she was looking for. Never, ever, spam. Ever. It doesn't work.

BUT if you have a list of people who have *asked* to receive relevant information and offers from you, then not sending them e-mail when you have news for them is a big mistake.

Are you with me here?

I'm *not* advocating e-mailing your list mindlessly, just because *you* think you have something to say.

I *am* advocating e-mailing your list whenever you have news *they* will deem important. If that means every day for a week, then so be it.

Finally, what about the person who wrote me the flaming e-mail and called me an Internet Whore?

I have no idea who he is. He may not know who he is, either. I showed the e-mail to a peer and he said, "That guy needs a therapist." I don't know if he does or not, but the great gift in his e-mail is that he prompted me to again think about how often we E-mail Marketers should e-mail, and it resulted in this article.

I hope it has been thought provoking.

Now, I have another important mailing to get out to my list...

P.O. Box 2924
Wimberley TX 78676
Member BBB Online 2005
http://mrfire.com/article-archives/recent-articles/how-often-to-email.html

How to Control the "Command Center" in Your Prospect's Mind

Here's a million-dollar secret I've never shared with anyone before. When you use it, you will get inside your prospects' heads and manipulate their thinking to get them to do what you want — including sending you money right now for your product or service. Sound hard to believe? Keep reading and I'll prove my point to you.

Right now, as you read these words, you are practicing the very thing I'm going to describe. Centuries ago people read books by moving their lips. Over time — and probably due to complaints from the family — people learned to close their mouths. But virtually all people still read the letters you send them by saying the words in their head, almost as if they were speaking them out loud, but in reality speaking only to themselves. You're probably doing it right now.

You are, aren't you? It doesn't reflect anything about your intelligence. It's how most of us read. I read more than most people and I still read the same way you do, "mouthing" the words in my head. It's how most of us humans accept the written word. Relax. You're normal.

Why is this important?

Because this is a way for you to plant hypnotic

commands right into the skulls of people. This is staggering power. When people read your sales letter, you are, in essence, right INSIDE the head of the very person you want to persuade. They are speaking your words – your commands, if you do this right – to themselves. You are in their "command center."

Think of the power you have!

Unless you've taken a speed reading course – which teaches you to scan pages and avoid seeing single words – you are like everyone else: Hearing what I want you to hear right now, in your own mind. In reality, I'm in your head! What am I going to make you do?! Buy my books? Hire me to write copy for you? Make you go out with me and do my bidding? Hmmmmmm.

You can imagine the kind of power this gives me, and can give you once you learn how to do it, too. And that's what I am going to give you a quick-start lesson in: How to control your prospect's mind.

First: You need to accept that people are reading your sales letters (or ads, memos, e-mail, web copy, etc.) by pronouncing your words in their heads. This means you are in the "forbidden zone" and ready to re-wire their brains.

Second: Keep in mind that as people read, they think. You are doing it right now and you have been doing it throughout this article. You are talking to yourself as you read. You are thinking.

People read your words and also ask questions, as if you were there to answer them. Your job as a Hypnotic Writer is to anticipate those questions and answer them. Do so and people will follow your commands.

Are you with me? As I mentioned earlier, I've never discussed this concept before because I felt it was too damn powerful to release. But when Mark Joyner asked me to expand on the material in my bestselling "Hypnotic Writing" series of books, I figured I owed the man my ace in the hole.

Here it is!

And here's how it works:

You write your sales letter with all the hypnotic writing skills you learned from my books. You use every trick you've learned to grab and hold attention, build desire, and lead to a strong close, because you know that's how you create truly hypnotic writing.

And AS you write, you are also asking yourself, "What is my reader thinking right now?" This is much like trying to handle objections in a traditional sales call. The difference is, you are doing this in writing. Your customer isn't standing in front of you. He or she may be thousands of miles away.

But that person is reading your words – voicing those words of yours in their head – and that person is asking him or herself questions. Anticipate them and answer them and you will up the odds in creating a sales letter that easily persuades.

Let me explain this another way: Hypnotists know that you will obey their commands as long as you don't already have a counter-suggestion in you to the contrary. They can tell you to "Go open the window," and you will do just that UNLESS you have a counter-thought, such as, "But it's cold outside" or "I don't have a good reason to open the window."

This same dynamic goes on inside your readers. You can tell them to "Send me money now for my new gizmo," and they will do exactly that UNLESS they have counter-thoughts (read objections) in them. As you probably know, most of your readers will have counter-thoughts. Your job is to anticipate them and answer them and THEN give your command.

I use this little known hypnotic skill in all my sales letters.

I work hard to create a headline that relays a benefit in a curious way. I sweat to write an opening that yanks attention from wherever it was, to my words. And then I use this "hypnotic dialogue process" to write the letter.

In other words, I write my letter while pretending to talk to one person about my product or service. In a real way, I'm talking to myself. As I "talk" on the page, I imagine what my prospect will ask next. It's a dialogue in my mind. But the truth is, that same dialogue will end up in my prospect's mind if I do this right. You've been doing it throughout this article. You've been reading my words and asking yourself questions. Right?

Throughout the writing of this article, I kept asking myself, "What will he ask?" By anticipating your questions,

I could handle them in a persuasive way. I could, in short, lead you to my way of thinking and to doing what I want.

For example, right after my opening paragraph, I wrote, "Sound hard to believe?" I placed the question there because that's probably exactly where you ASKED the question in your own mind. You read my opening lines – about my big promise to show you how to get people to send you money – and inside yourself you said something like, "That's pretty hard to believe. Prove it."

And right there, right on cue, comes my question. I anticipated your thoughts and answered them by using the dialogue process. And what did I install in your mind while you were reading?

Go back through this article and see if you can find this "dialogue process" at work. And then notice what you do next, because that action will reflect the command I secretly embedded in you. And now that your objections are handled, you have little choice but to act on it, or not.

"Cider House Writing"

In my e-book, *Hypnotic Selling Stories*, I tried to explain how the messages you send out have a double meaning. There's the meaning you intend, and then there's the meaning your readers conclude. There's often a major difference. This is hard to explain, but let's try, anyway.

Nerissa and I watched a wonderful movie a few days ago called *Cider House Rules*. It stars Michael Caine and Toby MacGuire. It takes place in Maine, in the 1940s, in and around a home for orphans. The film is beautiful to watch, slow and moving, like a great colorful painting come to life.

The essence of the story is this: Toby is an orphan who learned to deliver babies from his mentor, the doctor played by Caine. While Caine would perform abortions as needed, Toby would never do them, saying they were illegal. They were against the rules.

As the story moves on, Toby decided to leave the orphanage and see the world. He does, at least the world of Maine. While working as an apple picker, he befriends the fellow workers. One of them gets pregnant by her own father, and needs an abortion. Toby, backed into a corner and realizing the necessity of the situation, performs it.

Now the rules don't matter.

I've over simplified the movie's story to make my point obvious. So let's see if my plan worked.

Okay. On the first level of communication, the movie is about people growing up in the 40s and dealing with their personal problems, with a focus on orphans in Maine. The characters are deep and the plot is engaging. You can watch it and say, "I enjoyed that one."

But on another level, there are messages in the movie designed to sink into your mind without doing so with a hammer.

For example, what does the title – "Cider House Rules" – mean?

In the house Toby and the apple pickers lived in, there was a set of rules posted inside. No one could read them because no one could read. When Toby appeared, he read the rules. The first was no smoking.

Well, the pickers laughed, as they were smoking as they heard about the rule. So, "Cider House Rules" referred to the rules posted in the house where the apple pickers lived.

But what does it mean on a deeper level?

The movie was about abortion. It showed that rules made by people who don't live in the situation the rules affect, were rules worth nothing. That when reality set in, the rules would be ignored. When push came to shove, so to speak, a person would get an abortion if their situation called for it.

But the movie never came out and said that!

And that's the point. Hypnotic Writing is often subtle. It sneaks in a message under your mental radar. It tells you a story that entertains you, while the message slides into your consciousness. The next time you think of abortion, you'll unconsciously remember the lessons from "Cider House Rules."

You may even make a different decision because of it, and you may never even know it.

Hypnotic Writing is more than clever phrases and a knowledge of language. It's also remembering that people make unconscious conclusions about your messages. Be careful what you say, yes. But also be careful to what people may conclude.

Take this brief article. On an apparent level I am telling you to be aware of your communication. But on a secondary level, I am communicating my own knowledge of hypnotic language. Somewhere in you is the thought, "Wow, Joe sure knows a lot about Hypnotic Writing."

This may even get you to sign up for my upcoming private seminar on hypnotic writing.

You might also note that I plugged one of my e-books in the first paragraph of this article, which seeded the idea that you should go buy it right now. This whole article, in a way, is a hypnotic story designed to sell you on my work.

Again, there are at least two messages in every communication – the obvious and the concluded.

Take a look at your own writing. What are you trying to communicate – and what are people concluding? You may be surprised by what you find.

Why Didn't My Pool Guy Show up? Or, What's Better than Your Current Goal?

I hired a pool repair person one day who told me he would be at my estate promptly at 9 am the next morning. That was three months ago. I still haven't heard from him.

Why didn't he follow through?

This isn't uncommon among self-employed people. Nerissa hired a web designer who promised to help her with a subscription box on her site. But the designer never did the work. Never apologized, either.

Why is that?

When Nerissa and I went to Ohio recently to visit my parents, we had lunch with a friend of ours. Over the meal he confessed that he had a problem.

"I find myself only doing enough work each day to survive for that day," he explained. "If I make enough money right away in the morning, I stop work for that day. If I make enough money for the week, I don't work any more that week."

Why is that?

A few days later I overheard a well-known marketing professional confess that the most money he ever made was a sudden $50,000 in one month. The thing is, he took the money and quit working for the next four months.

Why is that?

There are at least two psychological principles going on here:

1. People often sabotage their own efforts to succeed. Why? For a variety of reasons, everything from not feeling they deserve the wealth, to having limiting beliefs about money, how they use it, how comfortable they are with it, etc.

2. People often don't have big enough goals. Wanting to just pay the bills keeps you on the survival level. Having goals to make a difference in the world, or to get yourself or loved ones luxurious things, will stretch your acceptance levels and push past your limitations.

Personally, I think having a bigger goal solves most issues. But the goal has to be something that affects more people than just you. If the desire only benefits you, you may still sabotage your own efforts to succeed. But if the goal helps you and other people, you're on the way to massive success.

Here's an example of what I mean:

I have a new book coming out soon. It's the revised, expanded, and greatly enriched new version of my *Spiritual Marketing* book. It will have a new title, too: *The Attractor Factor*. I'm very excited about it. One reviewer said, "This book has the potential to change humanity."

Now, a goal I have is to sell 100,000 copies of the book

the first week it comes out. That's an okay goal. It certainly helps me, and the publisher, and since the book changes lives, it will help others.

But what would be an even bigger goal?

Well, selling one million books the first year it is out is better. And that would also influence at least one million people. Now THAT's a goal worth getting up early to pursue.

But what would be better than even that?

Now my mind is buzzing with possibilities. I'm thinking beyond my book, myself, and even the immediate customers who get the book right away. I'm stretching my mind to go for what others might call impossible.

This is what everyone has to do who wants to succeed in life. The people who just want to get by are just going to get by. The people who just want to pay their bills are just going to barely do that. But the people who shoot for the stars are going to hit the moon, go into space, and break records.

Where are you?

Do you just want to make enough money to pay the bills?

If so, you'll struggle to do so. When I first met Pat O'Bryan, he said he just wanted to make enough money to pay his rent. Now that we've coauthored several books and he's making thousands every month, his goals have changed. Now he wants a new truck.

Do you want to pay off all your bills, pay off someone

else's bills, and maybe buy yourself something big? If so, you'll surpass all the people who just want to pay their bills. Jose Silva once said a goal should benefit you and at least two other people. When you state a goal that helps many people, you are moving beyond your ego and your limitations.

Do you want to be financially free and make a difference in the world in some giant, unforgettable way? If so, you'll soar through life with an energy others will envy. You may or may not achieve your wildest dreams, but you'll certainly make more progress and break more records than the person who just wants to get by.

My new goal is to establish an Intentional Meditation Foundation with hubs around the world, all using my book, and the meditation I teach in it, to lower crime and increase wealth globally. Now THAT is more than a goal, it's a mission.

No one knows what is achievable, or impossible, so any giant goal – or mission – you can imagine is fair game.

What's yours?

http://mrfire.com/article-archives/new-articles/better-goal.html

Attract $175,000 Today

In 1931 Vash Young inherited a fortune. This was during the Great Depression in the USA when much of the country lost jobs, savings, hopes, dreams, and more. Young was so grateful for his inherited fortune that he spent his entire life sharing it.

Last week I inherited his fortune.

It was strange, unexpected, and yet incredible.

I didn't know Young before last week, though I had heard of his fortune.

I never imagined he would pass it on to me.

I'm grateful for it, of course.

Who wouldn't be?

And I'm now going to share that fortune with you.

Let me explain.

A friend of mine in the Miracles Coaching® program told me about an old book he found that he thought I might like. But he couldn't recall the title or author. He was obviously moved by the book. I'm a bookaholic, so I was interested, even without all the details. I asked him to send me the book's info when he came across it. I didn't think any more about it.

But last week my friend sent me a package. Inside was

the mysterious book. The title is *A Fortune to Share*. The author was Vash Young. I had never heard of the book or the author. Since I was busy with projects, such as scheduling the launch of my new audio program (*The Abundance Paradigm*), and already had fifteen books to read either on my ipad or my desk, I just put the book aside. It would have to wait.

But the book wouldn't wait.

Something about it called me to it. Maybe because the book was from 1931 and looked like a lost gem in self-help and self-improvement; maybe because I love success literature and this title seemed like it was from that category; maybe because I hoped the author had been a friend of a man I wrote about from that era, Bruce Barton, in my book *The Seven Lost Secrets of Success*; maybe because the author put a spell on the book. I don't know. But before I knew it, everything else got pushed aside and I started reading *A Fortune to Share*.

Within minutes, I was captivated.

The book is written in the first person, with the author talking to me about his fortune and how it changed his life. The old Young of poverty and reckless living was gone; the new Young was now so rich that even the Great Depression couldn't touch him.

His mission became the lifelong quest to share his fortune with others.

I was riveted.

Young explained that you own a factory. Most of the

time you make junk in that factory. As a result, no one buys from you. No wonder you were broke and struggling. No wonder life looked bleak. Your factory wasn't producing what anyone wanted.

He went on to explain that the same factory could make gold.

Gold?

How?

In your mind.

In your mind!

As it turns out, the fortune Young inherited was the gold inside himself: his ability to control his thoughts, beliefs, moods, and attitude. He could let the factory of his mind create a life that was miserable, or he could take charge of that factory and get it producing new thoughts, beliefs, moods and attitude that he and others would want.

He inherited a *mental* fortune.

As long as Young accepted his fortune and shared it, everything he wanted would come his way, and without trying to make it happen.

Young literally did attract a financial fortune (he sold over $80,000,000 in life insurance) due to his discovery and his sharing. He went from a life of go-*getting* to a life of go-*giving*. (He later wrote a book titled *The Go-Giver*). The more he gave, the more he attracted. His mission truly became one of sharing the mental fortune inside himself to awaken your own understanding that you have a mental fortune *inside you*, too.

While it's easy to wish that Young's fortune was all cash and he shared it by writing checks (which he often did, just not to you or me), what he actually gave us is something far more valuable: he pointed out you have a cash-making machine in your head.

In short, we attract "junk" when we think from selfishness and fear; we attract "gold" when we think and act with love.

A Fortune to Share contains much more information, and many wonderful stories. It's a hypnotic read. Breezy. Easy. Fast. It also delivers some unforgettable wisdom, such as:

"Any experience can be transformed into something of value."

"Prosperity can not be built on fear!"

For a long time, Young would hold "Trouble Day" every Saturday. He would let anyone walk into his office, dump their troubles on him, and then Young would do his best to help the troubled soul with his philosophy, and often with money.

In talking to an unemployed man one day, Young tells him, "You haven't been unemployed all these months, you have been working for the wrong boss. You have been working for failure, discouragement, fear and worry and the sad part of it is that there has been no salary for your labors. You seem to be destitute, but I am going to tell you how to become rich overnight. I want you to deposit the following thoughts in your mental bank tonight: 'I am not afraid – I am a success, not a failure – I have an inexhaustible supply of *courage, energy, confidence and perseverance.*'"

Young helps the man out with a suit of clothes and a little money, and reminds him to draw on his new mental bank account when he needs it.

Within a week, the man has a job he loves.

Young's first book was so sincere, helpful and timely that it became a national bestseller. He followed it with several others (which I have yet to read but eagerly await), including *The Go-Giver*, *Be Kind to Yourself*, and *Let's Start Over Again*. All were bestsellers. All were booster rockets for a weary country suffering during The Great Depression of the 1930s. When Young was in his seventies in 1959, he wrote a final book summing up his philosophy of life, called *Fortunes for All*.

I found *Fortunes for All* and read it. Loved it, too. On the cover the publisher says, "Let Vash Young show you that your mind is worth $175,000 or more!"

How can your mind bring you $175,000?

Here's the secret:

Young explains that instead of asking, "How can we have more?" we should ask, "How can we be more?"

He then invites you to try an experiment:

"Go off by yourself with a pad and pencil and write out your own ticket for a happy and successful life. By that I mean put down all of the things you would like to have or be."

He adds, "After imagining every wish has been granted,

then go one step further. Start in being the ideal person you think you would be if you had everything your way."

Young's philosophy of fortune basically said that once you began to be that happy, successful person now, then you would naturally attract all you wanted from the being.

Sounds a whole lot like step four in my book, *The Attractor Factor*, and step five in my book *Attract Money Now*: http://attractmoneynow.com/ where I suggest you "Nevillize" a goal to help bring it into reality.

In other words, feel what it would be like to already have the thing you want or be the person you long to be. Feel it now.

But Young is also wanting you to be something greater than a satisfied person. He wants you to embody the traits of – dare I say it – God.

Decades ago, in Houston, I gave a talk where I encouraged people to think like God. I said God wouldn't think in terms of lack and limitation. Why should you?

But Young wants you to act like God, meaning live love, compassion, forgiveness and all the other positive, enlightened states that a God would have.

Be God.

Young was a great believer in taking action, too.

A chapter on selling in *Fortunes for All* proves that he sold such a staggering amount of life insurance by focusing on giving, thinking of others over himself, and following his being principle. But he also took non-stop action. Even when Young was on jury duty for three weeks, he still held the sales record for the month. How? He kept taking action.

All of this is so inspiring and powerful that I wish Vash Young was still alive so I could thank him in person. But I've inherited his fortune. And I'm sharing it with you. I'm hoping you will now share it with others, too.

Take control of your mind and you can live a life of magic and miracles – a life of good fortune.

It's Vash Young's inheritance.

It's my inheritance.

And now it's yours.

What do you *think*, anyway?

What is your factory producing?

Who's the boss of your own mind?

Who are you *being*?

Enjoy your new fortune.

Ao Akua,

Joe

PS – Be sure to pass your fortune along to others by telling them about Vash Young, his books, and this blog post's message. Together we can share the wealth, and make a difference in the world. Thank you.

A Secret about Money

Pat was beginning to learn how to act when an opportunity popped up.

"I'll do it," he said.

We met in the parking lot after the group meeting.

He asked, "Would you go ahead and write a letter asking people making money online if they would contribute an article to our book? We just want to know what a typical day for them is like. I bet they don't sit around doing nothing."

Suddenly I was the coauthor in this project. Well, I see opportunities and jump on them, too. I agreed.

I went home, went to my computer, and drafted a letter. It was simple. I asked people online if they would tell us what a day was like in their "passive" world. I sent the letter to Pat.

He approved it almost instantly.

I then sent it out to every list owner I knew. This all happened within maybe three hours.

Within 24 hours we had wonderful articles by David Garfinkel and Tom Antion. Later the same day I heard from Jim Edwards, Yanik Silver, Jo Han Mok, and other online giants, all agreeing to send articles for our book.

And we just released the e-book today. (See it at http://www.MythOfPassiveIncome.com).

Now note what happened here:

A spontaneous joke became a project. That project began to take form within three hours. And within one day the book was being written – and not by Pat OR me.

This process is how I created such money-making digital products as my online e-classes, several bestselling e-books, and even a few online promotional campaigns. I came up with the ideas and within minutes acted on them. The result: Success.

So what does money like?

Money likes speed.

That's the secret few know about money.

Money comes to those who act fast.

If you think, wonder, question, doubt, plan, meet, discuss, or in any other way drag your feet, money goes to the next person in line.

If you want to know how I've managed to write so many books and articles, it's because I act fast. This very article is an example.

Twenty minutes ago I got the idea to write something about "Money liking action." I thought I should write it some day. Then I thought, "Why not NOW?"

Well, here you go.

It's done.

And I'm now sending it out to the online world. It will tell people about me and my products, send some people to my site at www.MrFire.com and others to Pat's site at www.InstantChange.com and still others to http://www.MythOfPassiveIncome.com and we'll both make money now and later.

It happened because I know a secret about money.

You now know the secret, too.

So – What are YOU waiting to do?

A New Way to Easily Achieve Your Goals

I've learned at least two things about achieving goals: There is an easy way and a hard way.

The hard way is to work night and day, stay obsessed, rarely sleep, and never give up.

Since everyone talks about the hard way, I want to address the easy way. After all, why struggle if you don't have to?

I've used the easy way to create bestselling books, lose 70 pounds in 8 months, find my ideal mate, get healthy, increase my wealth, and much more.

Obviously, it works.

Here's the formula in brief:

1. Be grateful for what you already have.
2. Playfully declare what you would like to have with positive emotion, feeling as if it is already achieved.
3. Act on the nudges and opportunities that appear.

That's it. In my latest book, *The Attractor Factor*, I explain a 5-step formula for getting what you want. It's useful for those times when you don't feel grateful, or can't decide on what you want, or don't understand the concept of letting go while taking inspired action. It's also helpful when you have issues about money, or deserving, or feel in any way blocked from your goals.

But the bottom line for me is this: Declare what you would like with no attachment and plenty of good feeling, feel grateful for what you already have, and act on what appears. The result will be the manifestation of a happy life.

Let's explore this in depth.

1. Feel grateful now.

    It doesn't matter where you live or what you have. If you're reading this, you're most likely living like a king or queen compared to people in third world countries. You may even be living better than kings or queens from history, as they often lived in cold, violent, frightful times. You've got it made.

2. Choose what you want without attachment, feeling as if it is already achieved.

    There's magic in saying "I'd love to – (fill in the blank) but I won't die if I don't have it." Since the world is simply energy taking form, when you declare you want something, you begin to attract it. But when you say you need something, the need pushes it away. You want to select your desire, and feel the joy of already having it, without feeling any desperation. Need will push it away; desire will attract it. If you feel as if you *already* have it, then you *will* have it.

3. Act on your opportunities and intuitions.

    You may get offers, calls, or who knows what. Act

on them. You never know what will lead you to your goal. Your ego cannot see the big picture. Intuition and opportunities will come to you from the larger view, and your job is to act on them. As you do, you will be taken to your goal, even when it appears you are being blocked away. Trust is key.

Is that really all there is to it?

Again, the fuller procedure in *The Attractor Factor* will take care of any snags in the process, but the basic process is simple. Let's walk through it:

1. Look around your room. What are you grateful for? Make a list. Get into the authentic feeling of true gratitude. In other words, be happy now. You don't need a reason to be happy. But if you want one, find something, anything, to be grateful for right now. When you're grateful, you're in a mental place that will attract more to be grateful for.

2. Look around the playground of your mind. What would you like to have, do, or be? What would be fun? Write it down. As you do, feel what it would be like to already have it now. Pretend you won the lotto. What would you want for yourself or others? What would be fun? The key is playful non-attachment while experiencing its completion *now.*

3. Now pay attention. As you go about your life, listen to your hunches and act on them, and pay attention to the opportunities and act on them.

436

You never know what will take you in the direction of your goal. Your job is to take inspired action. You may have some work to do in this step, but the work will be from your heart, and will take you in the direction of getting your goal.

Why not go through the steps right now?

Write them down, experience them, and then check back in a few weeks and see how they are doing. You may surprise yourself by how easily and quickly your goals are achieved.

If you find yourself doubting the process, thinking negative, or in any way not enjoying the simplicity of the easy way to attain your goals, then consider learning the 5-step process in *The Attractor Factor*.

Above all, have fun. Keep smiling. Be playful. Stay grateful. These are all elements of the new secret to manifesting your goals.

Remember the words of a famous song that also perfectly summarizes this new way to achieve your goals: "Don't worry. Be happy."

How I Made $68,000 Teaching E-Classes
(or, What I Learned from Wanting a Z3)

One day I pulled up beside a truck delivering new cars. One of the cars on his flatbed made my heart leap and my blood dance. I had never had a piece of machinery turn me on before. This one did. I fell in love.

It was a BMW Z3. A Roadster. A hot-rod. One of the sexiest cars ever known to man and made by gods. Okay, maybe I'm overplaying it. But the point is, this car spoke to me. I wanted it. And wanted it bad.

I also knew BMW's are pricey. So the first thing I did was try to win one. I entered two contests where Z3's were the big prizes. I knew I would win. I was destined to have that car. But I didn't win. Alas. So much for the laws of chance. It was time to create my future.

So I decided I would just buy the car, and that I would pay cash for it. I had just completed a book on how to create miracles, called "Spiritual Marketing," and I figured I would prove to myself that I could create a Z3. So I used my own five-step method to get the sexiest car of my hottest dreams.

I began by setting an intention for getting that car. Oprah once said that "Intention rules the Earth." I know it. My car's license plate holder says, "I am the power of intention." Once you declare that something will be so, you send a signal into the universe that begins to move that something to you, and you to it. Call it Real Magic. I call it one of the most powerful steps in the Spiritual Marketing process. From that step alone, miracles can happen.

After I set my intention to have that car, I then acted on the hunches that bubbled up within me and the opportunities that came my way. To be more exact, here's what happened: One day it occurred to me to offer a seminar on the subject of my new book. I could rent a hotel. Write a sales letter. Invite everyone I knew on my online and off-line list to it. I could make a killing in a weekend. That's the ticket!

But then it occurred to me that I don't like to market seminars, that I didn't know if it would sell, that postage and printing to promote it would cost a fortune, and that I'm not such a big fan of speaking in public, anyway.

And here's where the shift occurred:

I began to play with the idea that I could hold the seminar online. I would simply announce the "Spiritual Marketing" e-class to my email list. It would cost me zip. If no one signed up, so what?

But---BUT!---if they *did* sign-up, I could teach the entire class by email. Every week I would send out a lesson. I would give assignments. They would complete them and email them back. I would then comment on their homework. It would all be nice and neat, easy and convenient. Sounded good to me.

I decided to teach five weeks of classes, mainly because there were five chapters in the "Spiritual Marketing" book. I would send out one chapter a week as a lesson. I would add assignments to each one to make it more of a legit course.

Then I wondered, "What do I charge?" I spent a lot of time on this question. Most people give away their e-classes, if they teach them at all. A few charge low fees. But I wanted a BMW Z3. They cost $30-$40,000 each. Yikes!

Well, I decided I wanted 15 people in my class. That was an arbitrary number. I just figured if 15 people actually did their homework over a 5 week period, I would have my hands full reviewing it. So, like everything else in the developing of this first e-class, I simply "made up" the class size.

I then divided 15 by how much I wanted to raise for my Z3. If 15 people paid me $2,000 each, I'd have enough to pay for the car in cash. But two grand a person seemed a bit high. So I settled for $1,500 a person.

I then issued a sales pitch/invitation to sign-up for the class to my email list. I have about 800 good names on my list. Sixteen of them immediately signed-up for the class.

Talk about easy money!

The class was easy to do, too. The students loved the lessons, my assignments, and my feedback. Only one person immediately asked to bow out, saying the class wasn't for him. So I ended up with 15 people after all. I made $22,500. I was happy.

But I didn't stop there. A few weeks later I announced another e-class. This one on how to write, publish and promote your own e-book. I just followed the same model that already worked: I issued an invite to my email list, I went after 15 people, I charged $1,500 per person for a 5-week class. I got 12 paying customers. I made $18,000. Boy, am I loving this!

At this point I had been thinking about writing a sequel to my best-selling e-book, "Hypnotic Writing." But I didn't want to write it and hope it would sell. I wanted *paid* to write it.

So I created yet another e-class. This one would be on "Advanced Hypnotic Writing." It would be three weeks long, rather than five, because I wanted to take it easy this time around. (I was getting lazy.) I still charged $1,500 and I still went after 15 people. I then announced the class to my email list.

Here's where something wild happened:

Almost 18 people immediately signed-up for the class. But when I asked them to pay the $1,500 fee, every single one of them said they thought the class was free! I was stunned. I re-read my invite. It clearly said there was a hefty fee. All I can figure is that people skimmed the letter, got excited, and just shot back emails to enroll in the class. Or maybe they read the word "fee" as "free." Go figure.

But that's not the only odd thing that happened with

this class: I had trouble filling it from my own elist. So I went and asked a person with a giant email list if he would promote my class to his people. He would---for fifty percent of the pie. Yowsa! That was a lot, but I wanted to get paid to write my sequel to "Hypnotic Writing," and I'd still end up with good money, anyway. So I agreed.

Well, twenty people signed up. And the really oddly wonderful thing is that no one---no one!---did their assignments. So I got their money (half of it, anyway: $15,000), I got paid to write my "Advanced Hypnotic Writing" ebook, and I had no homework to review or grade. What a cool business!

Most recently, I announced yet another e-class. I was about to buy a large country estate and wanted more money fast. This new class is on my new proprietary marketing formula, called "Guaranteed Outcome Marketing." I raised the price on this 5-week e-class to signal its value. I asked for $2,500 a person. Since I normally charge $25,000 to create a Guaranteed Outcome Marketing strategy for someone, asking for only $2,500 to teach someone how to do it seemed very fair.

I lowered the class size because I wanted to be sure to give each student personal attention. I promoted this class to only my own email list. I got five students. Which meant I raised $12,500. Not bad for a month's "work."

And yes, I bought the country estate. I'm writing this article from it. The moral here? There are several:

1. Intention rules: You can float with the

circumstances life brings you or you can create you own direction and your own circumstances. It begins with a decision. What do you want? Decide. Choose. Declare.

2. **Break the model**: Just because others are selling their services for a song doesn't mean you have to, as well. Respect yourself. What are you worth?

3. **Go for something other than money**: Wanting my Z3 caused my mind to stretch in new ways to raise the money needed to get the car. If I were just going after money for money's sake, I might not think so boldly in my ideas or my pricing. What do you REALLY want?

4. **You can do this, too.** Just look at what you know that others would pay you to learn. Then turn it into an e-class, complete with lessons and assignments. After the class is over, you might even compile the material into a book. Or a tapeset. Or--? Think big! What would you teach if you had no fears?

5. **The spiritual is not separate from the material.** Since I've focused on money in this article, it may be easy to declare my focus was only on the dollar. Not so. I used spiritual principles---as outlined in my new book---to create wealth. Once you realize that the spiritual and material are two sides of the same coin, you are free to have happiness as well as cash. As it says on the dollar bill in your pocket,

"In God we trust." Do you trust?

Finally, yes, I got my Z3. It's a 1999 Montreal Blue stunning piece of rolling beauty. I've never had so much fun in my life driving. In fact, I think I'll aim it up and down some Texas country roads right now...

EPILOGUE

THE HIDDEN SECRET TO GETTING RICH IN ONLY 79 DAYS

Congratulations on finishing this book!

You are to be applauded for taking the time to learn these ideas. You are one of the few in the world who truly realizes the importance of educating yourself in order to become successful.

And you are now armed with one of the most powerful marketing strategies ever created. The four steps you now own are explosive.

To review, here they are:

STEP 1: Create a practically outrageous event to drive people to your website. Be sure your news is NEWS. Be sure it contains an embedded command to get people to your site. Be sure you alert the media.

STEP 2: Create a website with such powerful copy on it that it closes sales, OR, create a website that is so information rich that people love it and return to it often, over time, buying lots of your products or services.

STEP 3: Create hypnotic e-mails and consistently and persistently send them to your prospects.

Develop an e-mail newsletter. Build it. Stay in contact with your list. Send them irresistible offers.

STEP 4: Create a following using all the tools as described in Hypnotic Social Media.

Remember: being active on Social Media is an excellent way to become interactive with your fans and customer base and lets the world know that you are still current.

That's it, my friend.

Those four steps can make you rich.

But remember, your own mindset is the hidden element in your success. If you doubt that these steps will work, they won't. If you believe they will work, they will.

It's that simple.

So if you don't believe this method will work, I suggest you look into your own thought processes.

Stand guard over your own thoughts. Think positive. Visualize success. Act with confidence. Read my book, *The Attractor Factor*. It will help you explore any negative or self-limiting beliefs in the way of your achieving success.

I also recommend *Attract Money Now* -- my proven 7-step formula to attract money FAST that will work for YOU – it's free!

And as a parting gift to you, let me share with you the famous "Optimist Creed" by Christian D. Larson.

This creed was written in 1912. It's from Larson's book, *Your Forces and How to Use Them*. A shortened version of it is used today by Optimist International, a worldwide group of people who are focused on making a positive difference in the world.

You might want to print out this creed and frame it. Refer to it daily. Let it help you promise yourself that you will use Hypnotic Marketing to get rich – in only 79 days!

Go forth and succeed!

Joe Vitale

PROMISE YOURSELF...

To be so strong that nothing can disturb your peace of mind.

To talk health, happiness and prosperity to every person you meet. To make all your friends feel that there is something in them.

To look at the sunny side of everything and make your optimism come true.

To think only of the best, to work only for the best, and to expect only the best.

To be just as enthusiastic about the success of others as you are about your own.

To forget the mistakes of the past and press on to the greater achievements of the future.

To wear a cheerful countenance at all times and give every living creature you meet a smile.

To give so much time to the improvement of yourself that you have no time to criticize others.

To be too large for worry, too noble for anger, too strong for fear; and too happy to permit the presence of trouble.

To think well of yourself and to proclaim this fact to the world, not in loud words but in great deeds.

To live in the faith that the whole world is on your side so long as you are true to the best that is in you.

ABOUT THE AUTHOR

Joe Vitale is the world's first Hypnotic Marketer. Joe's marketing methods have made people millionaires. He's been involved with every aspect of marketing, from traditional direct mail to publicity to infomercials. He created a home-study course called Hypnotic Selling Secrets -- and made $450,000 in 3 days selling it online.

He is the author of numerous books, including the bestselling ebooks *Hypnotic Writing* and *Advanced Hypnotic Writing*. He wrote the only book revealing the marketing methods of famed 1800s circus promoter P.T. Barnum in *There's A Customer Born Every Minute!*; known for his outrageous publicity stunts, Joe received local and national media attention from the likes of *The New York Post* for "The World's First Canine Concert" (http://www.canineconcert.com/) in order to promote his bestselling Barnum book. One of Joe's early books, *Cyber Writing*, pioneered Internet marketing.

Another book by Joe, titled *The Seven Lost Secrets of Success*, has been hailed as the greatest self-improvement book since *Think and Grow Rich!* He's also written many more books on marketing and business, such as *Buying Trances: A New Psychology of Sales and Marketing*.

He also wrote the bestseller, *The Attractor Factor: 5 Easy Steps for Creating Wealth (or anything else)* from the inside out. It became a #1 bestseller twice, even beating the latest Harry Potter book of its time.

Additionally, he wrote *Life's Missing Instruction Manual: The Guidebook You Should Have Been Given at Birth*. It, too, became a #1 bestseller and was picked up by WalMart.

One of his most popular titles, *Zero Limits: The Secret Hawaiian System for Wealth, Health, Peace, and More* reflects an ancient Hawaiian practice, known as Ho'oponopono. A fan favorite, Joe has hosted multiple live events on the subject, nation-wide, and he has created quite a following on this title alone. In January 2014, he released the sequel to *Zero Limits*, entitled *At Zero*.

His popular title, *Attract Money Now*, is taking the world by storm as he is giving it away for FREE! It includes his easy 7-step formula proven to manifest wealth. Stay tuned for his soon to be released book, *The Secret Prayer!*

Besides all of his books, Joe also recorded the #1 bestselling Nightingale-Conant audio program, *The Power of Outrageous Marketing*. Additionally, he's recorded the following audio programs for Nightingale-Conant, to name a few, *The Awakening Course, The Missing Secret, The Secret to Attracting Money, The Abundance Paradigm, The Ultimate Law of Attraction Library* and his latest, *The Zero Point*.

No stranger to self-improvement, he's being called "The Buddha of the Internet" and after his huge weight loss, "The Charles Atlas of the Internet."

Joe has also been in several movies, including the blockbuster *The Secret*. He's been on the following TV shows: Larry King Live, Donny Deutsch's "The Big Idea," CNN, CNBC, CBS, ABC, Fox News: Fox & Friends and Extra TV. He's also been featured in *The New York Times* and *Newsweek*.

In addition to *The Secret*, Joe has been featured in the following films: *Try it on Everything*, *The Opus*, *Leap!*, *The Meta Secret* and many more!

He is a sought out speaker who travels the world to such countries as Canada, Russia, Poland, Peru, Kuwait, etc. to spread his message on the law of attraction, "The Missing Secret," ho'oponopono and much more. He was also a Keynote Speaker at the prestigious National Speakers Association Convention in San Diego, CA in July, 2007 and for Hay House "I Can Do It!" Conference in Austin, TX (2013).

One of his most recent accomplishments includes being the world's first self-help singer-songwriter as seen in 2012's *Rolling Stone Magazine®*. To date, he has released 10 albums! Several of his songs were recognized and nominated for the Posi Award, regarded as "The Grammys of Positive Music."

He created a Miracles Coaching® program and helps people achieve their dreams by understanding the deeper aspects of the law of attraction and the law of right action. This man was once homeless but today is a bestselling author who believes in magic and miracles.

For more information on Joe Vitale, go to: www.mrfire.com.

37796650R00266

Made in the USA
San Bernardino, CA
03 June 2019